WAGNER AND NIETZSCHE

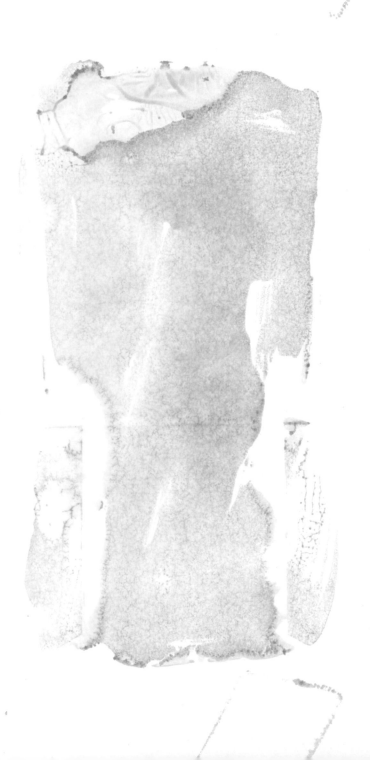

WAGNER
AND
NIETZSCHE

Dietrich Fischer-Dieskau

Translated from the German by

JOACHIM NEUGROSCHEL

A Continuum Book

THE SEABURY PRESS · NEW YORK

For Gerda and Hans Erich Riebensahm

The Seabury Press, Inc.
815 Second Avenue • New York, New York 10017

Published by arrangement with Deutsche Verlags-Anstalt. Originally
published as *Wagner und Nietzsche,* by Deutsche Verlags-Anstalt.
Copyright © 1974 by Deutsche Verlags-Anstalt GmbH, Stuttgart.

LIBRARY OF CONGRESS CATALOGING IN PUBLICATION DATA

Fischer-Dieskau, Dietrich, 1925–   Wagner and Nietzsche.
(A Continuum book)
Includes bibliographical references and index.
1.Wagner, Richard, 1813–1883. 2.Nietzsche, Friedrich Wilhelm, 1844–1900.
I. Title
ML410.W19F53   782.1'092'4   75-45489   ISBN 0-8164-9280-8

CONTENTS

PREFACE

This book is a new attempt at depicting the memorable relationship between two giants in our cultural history. Great emphasis must be placed on the constellation of these two men with each other and with their time, the late nineteenth century. As a result, less attention is paid to their work and its effects on intellectual life.

The author feels that Wagner's great appeal to, and influence on, Nietzsche are tightly interwoven with the philosopher's ambitions as a composer. This is a side of Nietzsche's creativity that his readers have barely noticed. The perception and appreciation of Nietzsche the musician must comprehend the reason why two polar individuals strove towards one another yet were destined to be close only briefly and then to have an "astral friendship."

This specific viewpoint and the author's intimate knowledge of the musical output of both masters may justify the fact that this time a musician has attempted to draw their double portrait.

Let me begin this book by thanking all the people who have helped me to write it. First of all I want to express my gratitude to earlier writers (and how could it be otherwise?) who investigated and described the lives and relations of Richard Wagner and Friedrich Nietzsche. My book leans on their labor. I would like to underscore a few of these: Martin Gregor-Dellin, *Wagner-Chronik* (Karl Hanser Verlag, 1972); Robert W. Gutmann, *Richard Wagner* (Verlag R. Piper and Co., 1970); Ivo Frenzel, *Friedrich Nietzsche*, translated by Joachim Neugroschel (Rowohlt Verlag, 1966); Friedrich Nietzsche, *Complete Works*, edited by Karl Schlechta (Karl Hanser Verlag, 1969).

I am grateful to all the people who made it possible for me to

PREFACE

work on this book between concerts, especially my secretary
Dieter Warneck, and Frau Margot Adrion, who wrote the manu-
script, as well as my brother, Joachim Fischer-Dieskau, and Heinz
Friedrich for critical advice.

Dietrich Fischer-Dieskau

1

THE TRISTAN OVERTURE

ᕦᘏᕤ

Socrates, while awaiting death in prison, was haunted by a dream that kept urging him: "Socrates, make music!" The old man felt he had always served art with his philosophizing. But now, spurred on by that mysterious voice, he turned fables into verse, indited a hymn to Apollo, and played the flute. In the face of death, philosophy and music briefly went hand in hand.

Intellectual history, however, shows that a lack of intimate knowledge and, most likely, of artistic instinct kept the philosophers away from music. But then, at bottom, both music and musicians were indifferent to what the thinkers had to say about their art and whether they saw in it "the idea of the world" or the "will" or a "reflection" of the world. It was only when the philosopher became enough of an artist, especially a musician, that he could voice ideas crucially influencing the fate of music.

Prior to Friedrich Nietzsche, intellectual speculation made almost every philosophical approach to music completely abstract. Theoretical studies never got beyond depicting the technique of such musicians as Carl Philipp Emanuel Bach or Leopold Mozart, who served the cause of practice by seeking to hand down the basis of their knowledge to posterity. Moreover, there flourished a poetic contemplation of music aimed at arousing a purely emotional rapport in the layman.

But with Nietzsche, the world obtained a thinker for whom music became the dominant experience in life. Artistic and cerebral creation were one and the same in his person. For it was as a musician that he began his career.

On October 15, 1844 (when Richard Wagner was putting the final touches to his orchestral sketch of *Tannhäuser* in nearby

Loschwitz), Friedrich Nietzsche came into the world in Röcken, near Lützen, in the province of Saxony. He was the first child of the vicar Karl Ludwig Nietzsche and his wife Franziska, née Oehler, likewise the child of a pastor.

In 1849, the father succumbed to "softening of the brain"— according to the diagnosis of the physician in charge. And in 1850, Friedrich's brother also died (of cramps while teething). The family moved in with Friedrich's widowed grandmother at Naumburg on the Saale River. There he attended the *Knaben-Bürgerschule*, the town school for boys, where he first became friendly with Wilhelm Pinder[1] and Gustav Krug.[2] In 1851, the three boys transferred to a private school in preparation for the Cathedral Gymnasium, which Nietzsche entered in 1854, starting in the fifth form (approximately the level of an American junior high school).

Nietzsche, as an alumnus, had good cause to be proud of his Gymnasium, Schulpforta near Naumburg. Honorable representatives of the "Nation of Poets and Thinkers" such as Klopstock, Fichte, Schlegel, and Ranke had spent their "golden rule" days there. But the somber classrooms, the severe faces of the teachers, the many older pupils who looked down on the "greenhorn" at first made him fearful and timid. It took him a while to come into his own.

Those days saw the burgeoning of certain interests, one of which, music, became fateful for him. Nietzsche's love of music actually started when he was eight. "Aroused by some special fluke," he had begun composing—"if one can call it that, those efforts of the excited child to commit harmonizing and consecutive notes to paper and sing out Biblical texts with a fanciful accompaniment on the piano."

His studies were constantly made difficult by headaches and eye pains, so that in summer 1856 he had to drop out temporarily. In October 1858, at fourteen, he received a full scholarship as a live-in student at the State School *(Landesschule)* at Pforta. The rigorous discipline constricted his intellectual mobility, which he always tried to regain during vacations.

In fall of 1860, Nietzsche, together with Pinder and Krug, started a small literary and musical club, the Germania. The statutes required each member to write a musical and literary composition every month and present it for mutual criticism. With their limited funds, they subscribed to the *Zeitschrift für Musik* (The Journal of Music), which exerted no small influence on their tastes. This periodical, edited by Brendel,[3] was probably the only one supporting Wagner and his works. It thus brought the composer to the attention of these young people. In late 1861, Gustav Krug spent the last pennies of the Germania treasury on a piano score of *Tristan and Isolde,* which he placed on the music stand in front of Nietzsche. The latter, oriented exclusively on Classical and Early Romantic works, was completely won over to Wagner. From then on, the sounds emerging from his keyboard fantasies had a suspiciously modernistic character.

Nietzsche's piano playing, his improvising and fantasizing, have been enthusiastically reported, not only by his sister but also by Deussen,[4] Gersdorff,[5] Kretzer,[6] Peter Gast,[7] and von Seydlitz.[8] According to Gast, Nietzsche's touch, extremely intense without being hard, was widely nuanced and orchestral in its effect, which would seem to indicate a style practiced on keyboard arrangements.

During the next few years, Nietzsche's headaches became worse and worse. The medical record of Pforta reads: "Nietzsche is a stocky man, full of vim and vigor, with a conspicuously hard gaze, short-sighted, and often tormented by erratic headaches. His father died prematurely of softening of the brain and was conceived at an advanced parental age; the son [was conceived] at a time when the father was already ill. No serious symptoms are as yet evident, but heed must be paid to the antecedents."

Nevertheless, in 1864, Nietzsche got through all his diploma examinations, with "Excellent" in the major subjects, but just barely passing in mathematics. His valedictory paper *De Theognide Megarensi* was an attempt at an overall delineation of Theognis of Megara,[9] and his poetic oeuvre. (He was so interested in this theme that he continued working on it at the university.) Thus, at the end of his schooldays, he distinguished himself with an outstanding contribution in classics.

Next came two unproductive semesters of classics at Bonn. The student circles there could hardly appeal to a young man describing himself as follows: "Earnest, easily going to extremes, one might say passionately earnest, in all manner of circumstances, in grief and joy, even at play."

Still, the Bonn winter of 1864–65 brought his first encounter with the art of Clara Schumann,[10] whose renderings of Mozart, Chopin, and Mendelssohn made a deep impression on him. Robert Schumann became a focal interest, as shown in his own compositions: eight lieder based on poems by Petöfi and Chamisso, as well as attempts at writing music for Byron's *Manfred.*[11] Nietzsche also sang in the chorus at the Rhenish Musical Festival, and his fellow students regarded him as an authority on music. Certain compositions had the following impact on Nietzsche, still a dyed-in-the-wool Romantic: "Utterly sublime rapturousness— Gloria in Beethoven's *Mass.* Floating sense of peace—Schumann's Evensong. Brilliant champagne intoxication—Beethoven's Phantasy. Crystalline ecstasy—the singing of the blissful boys in Schumann's Faust. Elan vital with scattered pages of memories—last part of Beethoven's Seventh Symphony (Bacchic-Orphic). Warm self-pity—'To thee, the untouchable woman,' Schumann's Faust. Such effects make a piece of music worthwhile and unforgettable for me."

At Easter 1863, Nietzsche even penned a two-part treatise on *The Demonic in Music.* Much later, in *Ecce Homo,* he reports: "The moment there was such a thing as a piano reduction of Tristan (my compliments, Herr von Bülow), I was a Wagnerite!"

Nietzsche always kept asking himself: What is musical Romanticism? Is it an end, an episode, a preparation, or a transition? And he devoted his life as a philosopher to seeking the answer, which, he conjectured, held the key to the future of music. He, a Romantic par excellence, ultimately refuted Romanticism when attempting to find a way out of negation to a liberating affirmation. He thus anticipated a theme occupying the first half of the twentieth century.

Nietzsche experienced the Romantic disease in his own being. He received crucial impressions from Jean Paul while at the Gymnasium, and he loved Schumann's music above everything else. But, characteristically, he disliked Weber's *Oberon* and *Freischütz* at the university. It was only Wagner who dampened his enthusiasm for Schumann.

At first, Nietzsche was fascinated by Romanticism's rejection of everyday life. His visionary daydreaming found a resonance here, all sobriety seemed banished. Instead of the worship of Reason, he encountered a cult of feeling. It was the German musicians in particular who, more successfully than any verbal artists, appeared to be building the new temple of Imagination and Metaphysical Yearning.

Yet at the same time, Nietzsche started having qualms about the Romantic maxim that the goal of music was to arouse emotions. Wasn't music meant simply to bring itself into effect? Wasn't this always a musical and biological task, ever in conflict with Romantic errors? Such doubts were crushed by the impact of music, which seemed to be a kind of incarnation of that incomprehensible something that touches man only through music. Now the Romantics emphasized this very quality of music. Never had the soul of the musician been so overwhelmingly revealed as in Romanticism, which signifies an ultimate superlative—if not of the feelings than of their sensitiveness. The logical upshot for Nietzsche was the question: Why is German music culminating in the age of German Romanticism?

The fugue and sonata had been brought to perfection by Bach and Beethoven. Now composers were looking for new means of expression. With Romanticism, poetry took over in music. The most fitting utterance for intimate spiritual stirrings was at first found in the small forms, the miniature. Schubert, as a middleman between the old era and the new, gained further dimensions for the lied and created the poetic piano composition. Opera, too, participated in the musical revolution. The inconceivable, the peculiar, the exotic aspects of stagecraft, its harmony of fancy and reality, simply challenged and elicited mystical surges and feelings as scenic visions.

And in turn, the love of the mysterious was transformed into Christian mysticism, and music apotheosized the Catholicism of feelings. Music could conjure up spirits, and, by rebelling against the rule of pure reason, Romanticism became a protest. The emphasis on emotion logically found its most decisive outlet in music. For all his reservations, Nietzsche had to admit that in Romanticism music had achieved its highest maturity and formal richness. To be sure, he presumed that the Romantic movement could only be fulfilled as music; in literature, it had merely remained a promise. If music testified to the living soul of nature, twilight, dichotomy, eternal longing, mystery, and dreams, it was a mouthpiece for Romantic ideals and was bound to evolve into something Nietzsche hated about it: "the most un-Greek of all forms of art."

Of course, he could scarcely resist its emotional voluptuousness and extravagance, as in the prelude to *Tristan*. In October 1868, he wrote to Erwin Rohde:[12] "I simply cannot bring myself to remain critically aloof from this music; every nerve in me is atwitch, and it has been a long time since I had such a lasting sense of ecstasy as with this overture."

The study of classics at Bonn was disrupted by the feuding between two teachers, Ritschl and Jahn. After near-scandalous incidents Ritschl decamped to Leipzig. It was only here that Nietzsche, following him in fall 1865, managed to get hold of himself again. He could now personally experience the total effect of the *Tristan* prelude—at a concert given by Leipzig's Euterpe Society. Previously, he had known only the piano version. The concert took place in fall 1868, a time when as yet few people were charmed by such an art of *dissoluto*. On the other hand, Nietzsche ultimately outgrew Wagner at a point when the general public was only just turning to his art.

A correct picture of what Nietzsche was discussing with friends is recorded in Wilhelm Pinder's lecture *Music, a Daughter of Poetry*. It contains the following sentences: "One cannot rail against a striving to unite the arts as fantastical, for even though the mind of a single individual were denied the possibility of engendering such a union, it could nevertheless come about, if one artist submits to another's work and delicately goes along with his accomplishments. A harmonic fusion of all that was previously asunder can never be attained, the artwork of the future is and shall remain an unattainable ideal."

Both Nietzsche and Krug protested vehemently. Krug chronicled his and Nietzsche's opinion: "I would like to ask why it can never be achieved? Hasn't Wagner, in *Tristan and Isolde* and in the *Nibelungen*, already demonstrated the practice of his theory? With poetry and music so intimately linked in these words, wouldn't it be possible, say, for the singer to be a true actor? Haven't such performers as Schröder-Devrient[13] and Johanna Wagner[14] proven that an excellent singer can also be an excellent actress?"

Pinder cites Brendel, the editor, who had written: "Hitherto, opera has always been caught in the predicament of laying claim to all the arts but not doing justice to its own particular nature. The artwork of the future shall resolve this contradiction. The solution will have to be realized with the assistance of the other arts."

2

THE ENCOUNTER

~~~W~~~

Both Wilhelm Pinder and Gustav Krug had fathers who hated Wagner's music, and so the friends played the piano score of *Tristan* during holidays at Nietzsche's mother's home. At times, she herself found this music dreadful. But Elisabeth heard her brother Fritz cry out: "Everybody has got to be enraptured by it."

"No, not by any means," declared Nietzsche's mother, "a lot of people have told me that this music is rejected by the finest connoisseurs. For instance, there is a musical circle that meets at Frau Frege's salon in Leipzig, and they won't listen to a single note of it. Now once, a visiting artist who didn't know about their dislike began playing some Wagner in the salon. Frau Frege had to be carried out in a dead faint, and the others felt perfectly wretched."

Laconically, Nietzsche admitted that it *was* difficult to understand Wagner's music. The Freges, whom Nietzsche's mother mentioned, had put up young Hans von Bülow in their home a few years earlier, and their musical prudishness had made life very hard for this "musician of the future."

Still, Nietzsche's enthusiasm was far from blind, as indicated in a letter to Gersdorff on October 11, 1866.

"I've done very little here in Kösen since I have no piano at my disposal. However, I was accompanied by R. W.'s *Valkyrie,* and my feelings about it are very mixed so that I cannot venture to express an opinion. The great beauties and virtues are counterbalanced by equally great eyesores and defects."

From the same letter we learn that Wagner was preoccupied with a Hohenstaufen opera in honor of the "gracious patron of his life," namely Ludwig II of Bavaria. Then comes the striking sentence: "It most likely wouldn't hurt if the king 'carried on' with Wagner ["carry on" in its most outré sense]. But naturally with a decent annuity." (The German word *Leibrente,* annuity, literally means a "body-pension.")

A few years earlier, when Ludwig II had ascended the Bavarian throne at eighteen, Wagner's fortunes took an upswing. A messenger of the Bavarian government reached him in Stuttgart on May 2, 1864, when he was about to flee his Viennese creditors. Like a fairytale hero, he was spirited away into regions with neither debts nor creditors.

And now the composer saw the possibility of living only for his artistic goals and surrounding himself with his proven paladins. But none of the people he summoned could deny to themselves that the abnormal relationship between the king and Wagner was not without its dangers for his circle, and they realized they had to stay on the alert. Even Hans von Bülow,[1] one of Wagner's closest friends, was fully aware of this.

Munich believed that its artistic situation was secure, and it admired Franz Lachner, the General Director of Music, who was well disposed toward Wagner. Thus the young ruler's excitement might strike many people as a royal whim. They knew little about Wagner's greatness—but a good deal about his arrogance and extravagance. They might have shrugged when the young king covered Wagner's debts and gave him a house. But when the architect Gottfried Semper[2] was entrusted with building a Festival Theater, not only were the philistines amazed and scandalized, but there was also some concern in the king's Exchequer.

Scarcely a month after Nietzsche's concert experience in Leipzig, Wagner left Munich incognito on a secret trip. Arriving in Leipzig, he stayed with his brother-in-law Professor Hermann Brockhaus and his wife Ottilie. Nietzsche had known the couple for some time, and had been frequenting their house. On November 9, 1868, he was in the best of spirits. That morning, he had visited Zarncke,[3] the editor-in-chief, to discuss the "province of criticism," which was given to Nietzsche as a free-lance writer on Zarncke's newspaper. He was to cover all Greek philosophy with the exception of Aristotle.

When Nietzsche came back to his room, he discovered a letter from Rohde, his friend from Hamburg. Rohde was only one year his junior, and the friendship was of great importance to Nietzsche. More than, say, his fleeting love for Hedwig Raabe, an actress who had played in Leipzig during the summer of 1866, and whose talents were hailed by all. Nietzsche, a timid young man, admired the lady from afar, and his infatuation moved him to compose a few songs, which he sent to her with a stilted inscription. This amorous experience was typical of Nietzsche's cramped, distant, and uninvolved relationships with women (except for Lou von Salomé).[4] With Rohde, a person had come into his life who didn't simply admire and acquiesce, but whom he saw as his peer in many ways. Like Nietzsche, Rohde had attended Bonn for the summer semester of 1865. From there, they had visited the Cologne Music Festival together. Rohde, like Nietzsche, followed Professor Ritschl to Leipzig, where their friendship first developed. Rohde, who shared Nietzsche's interest in classics, launched fiery debates in which his combative polemics offered Nietzsche a welcome counterpart to his own nature.

Rohde, in the letter that Nietzsche received on November 9, spoke of poor health and a bad mood. The news upset Nietzsche and he was glad he had something to do that evening. A philological student association had been founded by the friends, and the opening lecture was to take place during the semester. Nietzsche, seeking an opportunity for "boning up on academic weapons," went to speak there and found, to his delight, a "black mass" of forty spectators. Heinrich Romundt,[5] a fellow student, had been told to see what Nietzsche's lecture, voice, style, and disposition were like and what effect they had. With the aid of only a small note, Nietzsche spoke freely about Varronian's satires and Menippos the Cynic.[6] At the close of his lecture, Nietzsche felt: "This academic business will probably work out after all!"

At home, he found a note with the terse message: "If you want to meet Richard Wagner, come to the Café Theatro at a quarter of four. Windisch." Instantly, his triumph was forgotten, and his mind buzzed with excitement.

The next day, at the meeting place, he found his sturdy friend Windisch, who explained what was happening. This time, the press, which was usually and ubiquitously informed and chatty about Wagner's whereabouts, hadn't gotten wind of his coming. Wagner preferred to visit his relatives in Leipzig strictly on the sly. Absolute secrecy had been drummed into Brockhaus' servants, whom Nietzsche surreptitiously described as "graves in livery."

Wagner's sister, whom Nietzsche considered a "clever woman," had a friend named Sophie, the wife of Friedrich Ritschl, professor of classics from Bonn. The sister introduced her friend to the lionized prodigy, and bragged about Wagner and Sophie to one another. At Frau Ritschl's request, Wagner played a song composed by Nietzsche and expressed his pleasure and surprise. He then imperiously announced his desire to meet Nietzsche incognito, and recommended inviting him over the following Friday. Windisch stammered that the young man would be unable to comply because of his duties, functions, and obligations. So Wagner proposed Saturday.

Nietzsche, with Windisch, hurried over to Brockhaus' home punctually. There, they found the professor's family, but Wagner was missing. Wearing an enormous hat on his large head, he had gone out. With great courtesy, the "excellent family" asked Nietzsche back for the next evening. Nietzsche described his state of mind in those days as "unreal." The preparation for this meeting seemed almost like a fairytale, for he knew the eccentric composer was unapproachable. Assuming a larger group had been asked, he decided to dress up for the occasion, and was delighted that his tailor had promised to finish a tuxedo for him by that same Sunday.

On the appointed day, it was raining and snowing terribly. His nerves could therefore not be calmed by a stroll. Thus, Nietzsche was glad when a fellow student came by that afternoon to talk about his doctoral theme *The Development of the Notion of God Until Aristotle,* and to discuss the god in philosophy. Twilight was gathering, there was no sign of the tailor, and the visitor left. Nietzsche nervously went along, dropped in on his tailor, and found all the assistants hard at work on his suit. They promised to deliver the fine creation in three quarters of an hour.

In a somewhat better mood, Nietzsche sauntered over to a *kaffeehaus,* picked up the *Kladderadatsch,*[7] and read with gusto that Wagner was sojourning in Switzerland but that a lovely house was being constructed for him in Munich. Nietzsche knew better; he would be seeing the Master that evening. And he had heard that a letter from King Ludwig had arrived the day before, addressed "To the great German tone-poet Richard Wagner."

No tailor was to be seen when Nietzsche arrived home. But while reading a dissertation on Eudocia,[8] he sensed that someone was standing at the old-fashioned iron-barred gate below. Since both the gate and the house-door were locked, Friedrich shouted down across the garden, telling the figure where to meet him. The plashing of the rain made communication difficult. The house was in the throes of excitement when the door was finally opened and an old mannikin stepped into Friedrich's room with a package. Correct! The man had the suit! The clock showed half-past six, high time to get dressed. After making sure that the fit was right, the man presented the bill for immediate payment. Astonished, Nietzsche pointed out that it was the tailor and not one of his employees who would receive the money. The man was insistent and time was pressing. Nietzsche's attempt to put on the suit was met with violence. He was wrangling in his shirt. "At last, a display of dignity, a solemn threat, a curse on my tailor and his henchman, an oath of revenge. End of Act II: Myself brooding in a shirt on the sofa, wondering whether a black jacket is good enough for Richard. Outside, the rain is pouring. . . ." But then he charged into the night, with no tails but in high tension.

Together with Windisch, he entered the cozy salon of the Brockhauses. Only the immediate family and Richard Wagner were present. After introductions, the young newcomer with the black mane spoke a few admiring words. Wagner, whose interest in others usually focused on his own person, promptly inquired whether and to what extent Nietzsche was familiar with his music. Then he railed and ranted against all the productions of his operas, except for those in Munich, and ridiculed the conductors. He was cheerful and lively that evening; being within the immediate circle of the Brockhaus family put him in high spirits. In Saxon dialect, pure because it was "native," he parroted the run-of-the-mill conductors calling to their dozing orchestra: "Gentlemen, more passionate, don't you know! 'Pon my word, just a smidgen more passionate!" The student laughed along with the others; he found the celebrity amusing and human.

What had been the course of Wagner's life until this time? It has been depicted often enough with great precision, so that we can content ourselves with a few main points.

In the year of Hebbel's and Otto Ludwig's birth, just a few months before the great Battle of Nations, Richard Wagner first saw the light of day on May 22, 1813. He was born in the house of the "Red and White Lion" on the Brühl in Leipzig, the son of the high police official Friedrich Wagner.

That very November the father died, and the mother married a family friend, the actor Ludwig Geyer. With the family moving to Dresden, the boy (who, at six, lost his stepfather, a member of the court theater) came into contact with theater at an early age, particularly since his sister Rosalie and his brother Albert also went on the stage. His uncle Adolf was deeply involved in literature, and this encouraged the boy's artistic interests. In 1831, the year Hegel died, Wagner entered the University of Leipzig as a *studiosus musicae et philosophiae* for two years. He received his training in musical technique from the St. Thomas cantor Weinlig.[9] From early on, he devoted himself to attempts at writing poetry and music. At eleven, he composed a eulogy on the death of a fellow student. As an adolescent, he translated whole books of the *Odyssey* and scenes from Shakespeare's dramas. He also wrote a tragedy called *Leubald,* in which the word "Schurke" (knave) occurs no less than one hundred and four times. All the characters are murdered before the last act so that several have to return as ghosts. An Overture in D Minor by the nineteen-year-old was premiered in 1832, followed by performances of a Symphony in C Major at Leipzig's Gewandhaus, and a scene with an aria at the Leipzig Theater.

The career of the young musician began with years of wandering and conducting. In Würzburg, he worked as a chorus director; and in Magdeburg, Königsberg, and Riga, he wielded the baton. When these stages closed down, he was forced to wander anew. The twenty-one-year-old had his maiden stage-work *Die Feen* rejected by the Leipzig City Theater; and the twenty-three-year-old had to endure the failure of his second opera *Das Liebesverbot (The Prohibition of Love)* in Magdeburg after a single performance.

In Königsberg, he married Minna Planer, an actress two years his senior. Thus began a marriage marked by decades of conflict. A temporary residence in Paris offered no chance of settling permanently, but did bring to fruition a *Faust* overture.

At thirty, Wagner obtained a position as Royal Conductor in

Dresden, where three of his operas were mounted: *Rienzi, The Flying Dutchman* (which, after only four performances, vanished from the boards for twenty-two years), and *Tannhäuser*.

In 1848, the musician, swept up by the wave of politics, gave a speech at the Dresden Fatherland Association, which was striving for the Republic. The following year, after taking part in the Dresden Uprising, he was banished as "politically dangerous" and hunted by the police. He fled to Switzerland, then on to Paris, finally landing in Zurich, where he associated with Herwegh,[10] Wille,[11] and Gottfried Keller.[12]

Literary works filled the time between 1848 and 1851, the year *Lohengrin* was premiered in Weimar under the baton of Franz Liszt, who had also conducted *Tannhäuser* there in 1848.

At forty Wagner was busy with the words and music of the *Ring of the Nibelungen*. At forty-four, he moved into the villa that Otto Wesendonk had put at his disposal "for all time," on the Green Hill near Zurich. There he wrote the libretto of *Tristan* and began the score, which he finished two years later in Venice and Lucerne.

The years 1859 to 1866 brought his moving to Paris, his concerts there, and, at the order of Emperor Napoleon, the Grand Opera's French premiere of *Tannhäuser*, which was disrupted by a good deal of heckling.

In Vienna, during 1862, Wagner first heard his *Lohengrin*, and that same year he published the book of the *Meistersinger*. Despite 77 rehearsals, the production of *Tristan* did not come off in Vienna.

At fifty-one, Wagner was summoned to Munich by Ludwig II. The composer, free of the pressing burden of debts, was jubilant: "Now everything is won, my most daring hope surpassed."

The year that Wagner met Nietzsche, the *Meistersinger* was premiered in Munich, under Hans von Bülow. The new opera was still unknown in Leipzig, and so Wagner played the most characteristic passages for the Brockhauses, boisterously imitating all the voices.

"He is a marvelously lively and fiery man, who speaks very fast, is very witty, and makes such a highly private get-together quite cheerful. I've had a long talk with him since then about Schopenhauer. Ah, you can imagine how overjoyed I was to hear him speak about him with absolutely indescribable warmth, saying how much he owed him, he was the only philosopher to recognize the very essence of music! Then he inquired as to what the professors think about him, laughed at the philosophers' congress in Prague, and spoke of the 'philosophical vassals.' Next, he read us a passage from his autobiography, which he is writing now, an exceedingly delightful scene from his student days in Leipzig, and I have to laugh every time I think of it; his writing, incidentally, is extraordinarily skilful and witty." (Nietzsche to Erwin Rohde.)

Out in front of the house, as they were leaving, Wagner warmly shook hands with the young classics student and invited him to come by at some point and discuss music and philosophy. He also offered to show Nietzsche's music to his sister and relatives. The brilliantly gifted student, hardly a year older than the royal friend Ludwig of Bavaria, had made a deep impression on Wagner, who was about the same age as Nietzsche's father would have been.

The first consequence of the friendship was that Nietzsche enthusiastically perused Wagner's poetic and aesthetic writings. One thing that few people have noticed and that Nietzsche clearly realized was Wagner's admiration of Antiquity. In 1872, in a letter to Nietzsche, the composer made an avowal that sheds light on his development:

"I don't believe that there could ever be a boy or youth so excited about Classical Antiquity as I was when attending the *Kreuzschule* in Dresden. If I was particularly fascinated by Greek mythology and history, then it was the study of the Greek language to which I felt drawn with an almost undisciplinary avoidance of Latin. To what extent I proceeded regularly here, I cannot judge."

Sillig, his favorite teacher, firmly advised him to study classics. However, Wagner's inclinations apparently weren't deep enough; they soon waned. At best, an occasional revival of interest made Wagner aware that his education and environment had suppressed something in him. Still, for all the benefit he derived from Antiquity, he realized that Mendelssohn[13] could no more have written music to Sophoclean dramas than he could. The "reverence for the spirit of Antiquity" would never have permitted him to do so.

In this same letter, Wagner shrewdly expressed the opinion

that "today's Classical philology has no influence on the general state of human education" and "merely supplies philologists, who are of use only to one another."

All the same, the study of Greek civilization, which helped shape young Wagner and made him seem right for a career in classics, had a negligible effect on his life's work. The only thing worth mentioning might be the nationalist element. Wagner evoked the Hellenic model when delineating his concept of the artwork of the future. He felt that this model would make people realize that the art constituting the essence of a nation is born of the needs of that nation and is of the very substance of all who experience the collective crisis.

Nietzsche's evolution was different, and without a nationalistic undertone. His point of departure, which continued to dominate him, was to probe the literary monuments of the Greek intellect. His subsequent inaugural speech at Basel gave voice to the viewpoint that "each and every Classical activity is enclosed and surrounded by a philosophical *Weltanschauung* in which all that is single and isolated is reprehensible and wafts away, and all that remains is totality and unity."

One of Nietzsche's spiritual forebears was Heraclitus,[14] whose principle "all is flux" recurs as the concept of life rhythm in Nietzsche's metaphysics, especially in the adage: "Only he who changes remains akin to me." Likewise, Empedocles'[15] doctrine of the loving and hating of the elements is echoed in Nietzsche's theory that evil, i.e., negation is one of the principles of human and universal growth. Furthermore, early Greek thought inspired Nietzsche's notion, raised to an ethical level, of the eternal return. And then, his *Zarathustra* mirrors the stoics in its insistence on inner freedom, on pride and dignity.

Nietzsche was toying with the idea of going to Paris with Rohde and spending some time there. But in early 1869, these plans were gone with the wind of a great hope. He had wanted "just to relax a bit" before chaining himself to a profession. He had yearned for the charm and gravity of a vagabond life, longed to be an observer just one more time rather than a participant. "I pictured us both, with earnest eyes and smiling lips, marching through the Paris crowds, a couple of philosophical flaneurs whom the Parisians would get used to seeing together everywhere . . . bearing the gravity of their thoughts and the tender sympathy of their togetherness everywhere. . . . Ah, my dear friend, I think a man betrothed feels as I do: Never has our wonderful casualness, our ideal summer vagabondage seemed so enviable as now."

But Nietzsche was being lured by the definite prospect of starting to teach at the University of Basel, imminently, as of Easter. Kiessling, who taught classics, had informed the Board of Education at Basel that he wished to transfer (to the Johanneum in Hamburg); and Ritschl had to answer the inquiry as to whether Nietzsche, "who appears to have a fine educational background," was right for the job. The benevolent teacher sent for his pupil and told him the happy and staggering news. Ritschl then wrote to Kiessling:

"For thirty-nine years now I've watched so many young minds developing before my eyes: but *never* have I known a young man, that is to say, sought to the extent of my power to train anyone in my discipline, who became *so* mature *so* early and *so* young as this Nietzsche."

After seeing Ritschl, Nietzsche strolled about all afternoon, steadfastly singing melodies from *Tannhäuser.* He suppressed any doubts he may have had and accepted the offer. Wagner, in Lucerne, sent his best regards by way of Brockhaus, and Nietzsche's reaction was: "Lucerne is no longer beyond me now." In late January 1869, he took off for Dresden to hear *Meistersinger,* which he looked forward to "more than anything else."

The premiere made an extraordinary impact on him, and before the "great Ash Wednesday" of his career, Nietzsche once again felt that "There is a good part of a musician in my body." His opera experience was "the greatest artistic revelry that this winter has brought me." Later on, he added: ". . . abruptly finding myself in the coziness of my home made everything else I did seem like a faraway mist, from which I had been redeemed." He saw his career as something Philistine, but none of his friends perceived any of these heretical thoughts. They were fooled by the title "Professor" and assumed he was the most contented of mortals.

Right after his return from Switzerland, Nietzsche was invited to a private supper at Leipzig's Hotel de Bologne to meet Franz

Liszt.[16] Nietzsche's advocacy of the "music of the future" had aroused so much attention that the followers of the so-called "New Germans" were "getting pushy" about having him do literary work for their cause. Nietzsche, for his part, didn't much feel like "cackling in public." Even at this early stage, he already objected that the brothers "in Wagnero" wrote stupidly and in a bad style. He believed there was little connecting them with this genius; all they seemed able to see was the surface. And he added: "None of those fellows are ready for the book *Opera and Drama.*"

The draft to this theoretical opus had been finished by Wagner on January 10, 1851, when he had already broken off all relations with Jessie Laussot and was again going back permanently to his wife Minna in Zurich. Nietzsche read a copy of the second edition, for which Wagner had written a "Foreword" in Lucerne, on April 26, 1868. Nietzsche found this book complicated, somewhat liberal with historical facts, but well argued, and mainly concerned with the kinship of music and dramatic art.

The classicist Nietzsche must have been fascinated by what Wagner said about the essence of Greek theater. The composer believed that when Greek drama died and was absorbed into European culture, it split into a number of single arts. He feared that the utmost limits of disintegration had been reached; and a general desire for at last reintegrating the arts was apparent. The salvation of such a new totality could only lie in a work of art whose true author was "the nation." People should call to the nation as to the legendary Wieland: "Weld your wings and soar away!"

Wagner hoped to solve this problem with his future *Gesamtkunstwerk,* total artwork, with its words-and-music oscillation and with the orchestra being given an expressive power to musically convey what the words could not. Wagner grandiosely defined the synthesis of verse and its (assigned) melody. It is obvious how close Wagner is to Schubert in this point. The verse as a poetic component provides the conceptual substructure. It determines the melodic dynamics of the composer. The latter is then charged with making verse and music congruent by applying his notion of emphases, rhythmics, pitch, and the linking of notes. The modulation and timbre of the orchestra and the dramatic expressivity of the singers, or rather the singing actors, support what happens on stage.

For Nietzsche, the revelation of nineteenth-century music culminated in the works of Richard Wagner. In his hands, he felt, Romanticism had gained the power to make the world believe in the artist as the Redeemer. "Thus the operatic composer fully became the Redeemer of the World, and the deeply inspired composer, irresistibly swept up by a self-lacerating visionary zeal, must be recognized as the modern Messiah, the lamb of God, bearing the sins of the world." Thus spake Richard Wagner, of all people, about Meyerbeer[17] in *Opera and Drama*. What was meant as irony and even scorn, changed into an evangelium when it concerned Wagner himself. This was a self-portrait *malgré lui*. With an arsenal of arts and effects, with the nimbus of a philosopher and the ecstasy of a saint, Wagner attempted to subjugate the world to his artwork. And Nietzsche ultimately had to stand up to him and, recognizing the danger of Romanticism, seek the salvation of music, which he too saw as the highest thing, although in a different sense.

3

SCHOPENHAUER

Nietzsche, the admirer of Schopenhauer, may have deliberately chosen to ignore the fact that Wagner's philosophical
theories rested on a shaky foundation. For it wasn't until 1854
that Wagner got to know Schopenhauer,[1] in the magnum opus
The World as Will and Idea. (That was, incidentally, the same month
in which the first conception of *Tristan* took shape.) Music as the
loftiest and as the most liberating form of art, able to express the
essence of the metaphysical with no mediating representation—
this viewpoint changed Wagner's earlier thesis that the arts are
directly and impersonally gathered under the dominion of the
word, a notion stemming in turn from his interest in Communism
during the Dresden years. Meanwhile, Wagner's faith in the possibility of Communism had vanished, along with the art theory it
had produced. Intuition and his grasp of music led him to regard
music as predominant in opera. Modulation as a function of the
poetry (postulated in *Opera and Drama*), this very mirror of constantly changing emotions, was bound to result in those random
sequences of keys within the overall structure—a technique that
Nietzsche flatly rejected later on.

Equally contrary to Nietzsche's viewpoint was the dedication of
the second edition to Konstantin Frantz, a political writer who
greatly excited Wagner. Nietzsche, the composer's young admirer, could not have known about Frantz's theories of anti-
Semitism, Francophobia, and his nationalistic support of a
German Reich. The fact, however, that Wagner championed
Schopenhauer so unreservedly must have been taken by the
younger man as confirming his own direction.

Schopenhauer was an important factor for both Wagner's and
Nietzsche's intellectual development. When Wagner, at forty-

one, read Schopenhauer's chief work, he described it to Liszt as a godsend in his solitude. He said the author was the greatest philosopher since Kant and made Hegel and other thinkers look like charlatans. Anyone who understood Schopenhauer would have to disregard all previous philosophy and its prejudices. In a letter to the painter Lenbach,[2] whose portrait of Schopenhauer was the only picture above Wagner's desk, the composer wrote: "I have this *one* hope for the civilization of the German spirit: that the day may come when Schopenhauer is made the law of our thinking and knowing."

In an addendum to his essay *Religion and Art*, Wagner recommends making Schopenhauer the basis of all spiritual and ethical culture. The experience of this philosophy may not have been the most important event in Wagner's life (who can weigh such superlatives?). But Schopenhauer's impact on him was lasting and powerful, though not unqualified.

No missing components of Wagner's musicianship were brought to his evolution by Schopenhauer. The *Ring* libretti had been completed in 1852, two years before his encounter with Schopenhauer's writings. However, the *Ring*, like the *Flying Dutchman*, did artistically express attitudes for which Schopenhauer now supplied conscious formulas.

Thus Wagner could write to Liszt that "Schopenhauer's dreadfully earnest main thought, the finite negation of the will to live" was "naturally nothing new" to him, although he had made it clear to himself with the philosopher's help. Understandably, Wagner's pessimism deepened under that influence. The victorious thrill of his *Nibelungen* draft became inwardly alien to the composer. He confessed to Liszt that he had decided to finish the libretti only for the sake of a life's dream such as young Siegfried. But in the same letter he also admitted being absorbed in a new poetic work more in line with his present mood:

"Since I have never in my life enjoyed the unique happiness of love, I want to raise a monument to this most beautiful of all dreams, a monument in which love will simply sate itself from beginning to end: I have sketched a *Tristan and Isolde* in my mind, the simplest, but most full-blooded musical conception. I want to take the black flag that waves at the end and cover myself with it —in order to die."

Schopenhauer likewise gained admission to Wagner's prose,

for instance, in his essay on Beethoven. There he says that for the relationship of music to the forms of the phenomenal world and to the notions drawn from objects, there could not possibly be anything more resplendent on the subject than what is to be read in Schopenhauer.

The philosopher Schopenhauer (and this was the peak of his influence) offered the artist Wagner the key to a deeper under-standing of his own work than he previously could have had. A proof is Wagner's statement to Röckel: "Rarely has man been so peculiarly divided and so self-alienated in his views and notions as I was, and I have to avow that I only really grasp my own art now with the help of another man, who supplied me with notions cognate to my own views, so that I seized my art with my powers of conception and made it clear to my reason."

Still, the congruence with Schopenhauer remained fragmen-tary. The chief distinguishing feature is the optimism that ulti-mately dominated Wagner's nature. Contrary to Schopenhauer's bio-anthropological pessimism, which sees man as "at bottom, a wild horrifying beast," Wagner regards "true human nature" as good. Although not denying the "degeneration of paradise," which is how he sees our world, his essay *Religion and Art* speaks of attempts at restoring paradise. These include such reformist strivings as vegetarianism, protection of animals, temperance, socialism, and last but not least, the regeneration of mankind through art. He praises Schopenhauer as "a philosopher who fought an absolutely merciless fight against all inauthenticity," and demonstrated that "compassion, rooted in the deepest part of human will, is the only true basis for all ethics." Such evalua-tions are based on ideas that also made Nietzsche a disciple of Schopenhauer's.

Dealing with this philosophy made Wagner think differently about his own art. Earlier, he had looked upon music as a means of expression, requiring for its realization an object to which it lends expression: drama. But Schopenhauer's theory of music brought him to a different view. The will, which lives in all things, is in any other art embodied merely in reflections, ideas. Music, however is not a mere image of the will; in music the will can manifest itself directly. What Schopenhauer heard in music as a tiding from the world beyond, Wagner wanted to bring forth in his own music. Later, Nietzsche, in the *Genealogy of Morals,* made fun of this goal: "He kept talking—that ventriloquist of God—he talked about metaphysics: no wonder he eventually began talking about ascetic ideals." But by this time, Nietzsche had escaped from Romanticism. He left Wagner behind in the struggle against his era.

Nietzsche, too, first discovered Schopenhauer in the throes of a depression, during 1865, when, disappointed by his semester in Bonn, he came across *The World as Will and Idea* in a second-hand bookshop in Leipzig. The event was recorded in his diary:

"I don't know what demon whispered to me: 'Take this book back home.' At any rate, it happened contrary to my usual habit of not buying a book hastily. At home, I threw myself into a corner of the sofa with the acquired treasure and began to let that energetic, somber genius work upon me. Here, every line cried renunciation, negation, resignation. Here I saw a mirror in which I beheld the world, life, and the personal spirit in dreadful grandeur. Here I was stared at by the fully indifferent solar eye of art. Here I saw disease and healing, exile and refuge, hell and heaven: the need to know myself, nay, gnaw myself asunder, took violent hold of me. Witnesses of that upheaval are still the restless melancholy days, the diary pages of that time with their undemanding self-accusals and their desperate desire for the healing and reshaping of the entire human essence. Hauling universal characteristics and aspirations before the forum of a gloomy self-scorn, I was bitter and unbridled in my hatred of myself. Nor did I leave out bodily torments. For fourteen days in a row I forced myself not to go to bed until three A.M. and then to get up at precisely six o'clock. A nervous excitement had me in its clutches, and who could say to what degree of foolishness I might have proceeded if the lures of life and vanity, and the compulsion for regular studies had not intervened."

The impact was so powerful that Nietzsche, in the third *Untimely Reflection,* lauded Schopenhauer as his teacher and educator. *The Cheerful Knowledge* holds him up as the "first avowed and unyielding atheist that we Germans have ever had." *The Twilight of the Idols* simply designates him as the last German "who can be taken into account—who is a European event, like Goethe, like Hegel, like Heine, and not merely a local, a national one."

Thus, it wasn't Plato[3] or Aristotle,[4] familiar to him from his studies of Antiquity, who brought Nietzsche to philosophy. It was the world of Arthur Schopenhauer.

The first thing to enchant the word-artist Nietzsche may have been this philosophy professor's outstanding style, unlike that of most of his colleagues. The clarity and logic of his thinking were so vivid and graphic as to far outshine Kant and his successors. In contrast to Kant, Schopenhauer's emphasis lay on the scornful rejection of reason, which, for him, could not reveal the essence of things nor provide man with any goals. He saw reason as a mere tool of the will for reaching its aspirations.

But what most attracted Nietzsche to Schopenhauer was his pessimism: Life is not worth being affirmed. Salvation (Wagner's favorite theme, incidentally) can only lie in the ability to renounce the drive and instincts as the blind work of uncontrolled will. Schopenhauer includes compassion as another form of selfishness. Man can attain salvation from himself only in educating the will towards renunciation, in ethical behavior, and particularly under the action of beauty. Among the arts, which he took for granted as belonging to the concept of beauty, Schopenhauer gave music a special place in so far as it seemed to directly express the reality and form of things. Music may not be able to convey any rational knowledge, but for the duration of its performance, all temporal, spatial, causal, and final needs are taken from us. Wagner's enthusiasm for this thesis shows the believer in the future to be a child of his century, since before and after Schopenhauer, there have been entirely different attitudes about the position of music.

Nietzsche's lone-wolf religious independence was, as we have said, drawn to Schopenhauer's pessimism, which points out that even the experience of beauty is not lasting and offers no redemption from drudgery and the natural compulsions. Not even the altruist's absorption in the welfare of others can offer a way out. To morals and rationality, Schopenhauer opposed the asceticism of the individual. Renunciation and mortification of the (for him unfortunate) will may, possibly, lead to an escape from this existence, which stands under the curse of the wrong constellations. Knowledge through reason or virtuousness, such as the Christian ideal, does not signify, for Schopenhauer, any progress out of this misery.

When Nietzsche, two years before meeting Wagner, had to spend twelve months doing military service, he endured the inevitable with a stiff upper lip and with Schopenhauer: "Sometimes, hidden under a horse's belly, I whisper: 'Schopenhauer, help!' And when I come home exhausted and covered with sweat, a single look at his portrait on my desk calms me down."

The influence of the philosopher Feuerbach[5] on young Wagner was weakened by Schopenhauer. Likewise, the latter's effect on Nietzsche was not always consistently intense and unqualified. First and foremost, Nietzsche gave Schopenhauer's atheism a reverse outlook on life. This shows how an identical metaphysics can permit a completely opposite attitude. Nietzsche transformed pessimism into a metaphysical optimism and raised himself to an affirmation that finds its utterance in: "The ideal of the most exuberant, the liveliest, the most world-affirming man, who had not only come to terms and learned how to live with what was and is, but actually wants to have things that way, as they were and are, calling 'encore' insatiably till the end of time, and not only to himself but to the entire play and production." *(Beyond Good and Evil.)*

Characteristic, beyond this, is Nietzsche's radical abjuration of the morality of pity, which he made an effort to overcome or at least to purge of anything woebegone and narrow-minded.

During the closing phase of his work, Nietzsche then turns vehemently against any pessimistic art à la Schopenhauer. He regarded such art as a contradiction in terms, since it makes art "a means of salvation from life."

And Nietzsche was no less disturbed by Schopenhauer's definition of the tragic as a path to resignation. This concept of tragedy as a negating art and a symptom of degeneracy was, according to Nietzsche, "one of those awful counterfeitings, which little by little devastated Schopenhauer's entire psychology . . . the psychology of a man who drastically misunderstood genius, art itself, morality, pagan religion, beauty, knowledge, and just about all arbitrary things."

Those were the eventual words of Nietzsche, the admirer of Schopenhauer, at a time when he was already a long distance from Wagner.

4

TRIBSCHEN:
"Isle of the Blessed"

Four weeks after first meeting Wagner, Nietzsche wrote to his friend Rohde: "Wagner, as I know him, is a living exemplar of what Schopenhauer calls a genius. . . . I wish we could read his poetic writings together. . . . We could walk the bold, nay, dizzying path of his subversive and constructive aesthetics together, we could let ourselves be carried away by the emotional sweep of his music, by this Schopenhauerean ocean of sound, whose most secret undulation I can sense, so that my listening to Wagner's music is a jubilant intuition, nay, an amazed finding of myself." These lines reflect the excitement kindled by an encounter of the two most important minds of their century.

If something improbable did come true, i.e., another meeting very soon, in Lucerne, between the classics student Nietzsche and the renowned composer, then the offer of a teaching position for the twenty-four-year-old at the University of Basel was a full-fledged miracle. On February 13, 1869, he was appointed "Associate Professor of Classical Philology and teacher of the Greek language in the highest class of the Paedigogium." He had neither a doctorate nor a habilitation (a post-doctoral title usually required for a teaching career at a German university).

Ritschl, on January 11, wrote to Profesor W. Vischer, the chairman of the Board of Education: "Your kind letter of the fifth of this month was truly a boon . . . for this is the first time that I have seen an official agency ignoring 'formal insufficiency' in the clearly recognized interest of the spirit of the law. Such a thing could simply never happen in *Germany*. . . ."

With no examination or dissertation, solely on the basis of what he had been publishing in the *Rheinisches Museum*,[1] the Leipzig faculty awarded him a doctoral degree. And on April 17, Nietzsche could confirm his "release from the Prussian union of underlings." He became Swiss, leaving Naumburg on April 12, 1869 and traveling via Cologne, Bonn, Wiesbaden, Karlsruhe, and lastly Heidelberg, where he wrote down his inaugural lecture. On April 19, he arrived in Basel, holding the lecture on May 28: *Homer and Classical Philology.* In the interim, he made his first visit to Tribschen on Lake Vierwaldstätt.

At this point, we ought to mention a fact that is generally unknown. It was Nietzsche who, at this early time, first brought the later Wagner-apostle Hermann Levi[2] into close contact with his idol. What happened was that on Sunday April 18, while en route to Basel, Nietzsche overheard a passenger say that the Royal Theater in Karlsruhe (where the train would soon be stopping) was playing *Meistersinger.* Nietzsche interrupted his trip to attend the performance. It was under the baton of Chief Conductor Levi. A short time later, in Wagner's home, Nietzsche talked about this excellent production, making Wagner anxious to meet Levi. The conductor was invited to Tribschen.

Levi, that astonishing mediator between the hostile Schumann and Wagner camps, was one of the few who succeeded in having the best of both worlds. On the one side, he remained friends with Clara Schumann, an inveterate enemy of Wagner, and he conducted the premiere and a few subsequent mountings of Schumann's opera *Genoveva.* Yet on the other side, he was one of the foremost champions of Wagner's work. Wagner even suggested that he stage the premiere of *Tristan* in Karlsruhe, a plan that didn't work out because the first performance ultimately took place in Munich.

One glorious spring morning, right at the start of the semester, Nietzsche arrived on the shore of Lake Vierwaldstätt. He overcame his qualms as to whether the master's invitation last fall was really still valid, and, asking directions here and there, he made his way to the villa on the jutting bank. Soon, he was standing below the windows. Someone inside was playing the piano. For a long while, the young man remained stockstill, listening to an oft-repeated chord. Wagner was composing Brünnhilde's lament in *Siegfried:* "He wounded me who made me awake!" Words that would soon bear significantly upon the eavesdropper.

Upon ringing, Nietzsche was told by the butler that Herr Wagner was working and could not be disturbed before two P.M. But the young man could leave his card if he wished. And the servant stepped back into the house. Turning and leaving, Nietzsche heard the butler running after him. Herr Wagner wished to inquire whether the Herr Professor was the same Herr Nietzsche whose acquaintance he had recently made in Leipzig, at the home of his sister, Frau Brockhaus. Nietzsche said he was and promptly received a luncheon invitation, but had to beg off since he was already committed. He was asked instead to spend the day after the next in Tribschen.

Nietzsche noted in his diary: "Meanwhile serene days with Ochsenbrüggen, Lontius, Echsner and his sister, at the *Imhof Pension.*"

Whitmonday turned out to be "the first of those delicious days that eventually became the bliss of my soul and my comforting solitude." When Nietzsche took his leave of Wagner, the composer gave him his photograph and accompanied him back to Lucerne.

The older man was destined to arouse Nietzsche's personality and play a crucial part in his development as one of the most important modern thinkers. Of course, the collision with such a completely opposite temperament as Richard Wagner's left the worshipping Nietzsche a shattered and despairing man. It was Nietzsche's fate to overthrow idols.

But naturally, no one could foresee these things at the lake, during those sunny and peaceful days, which only intensified Nietzsche's adoration of the Master. He was delighted to steal time from his duties in Basel for these visits. And it is significant that long after his complete break with Wagner, he was able to write: "As for the rest of my relationships, I can take them or leave them; but I would never give away the days at Tribschen for anything in the world, the days of intimacy, of serenity, of sublime hazards—of *profound* moments."

Wagner, thirty-one years older than Nietzsche, headed a rather unconventional household kept by Cosima. She was still married to Wagner's friend, the conductor Hans von Bülow, and was a daughter of Franz Liszt. Wagner and Cosima lived in a common-law marriage and had already had two children. In 1866, after the death of his first wife, the composer had moved from Munich to

Switzerland, in one of his customary escapes from political, financial, and scandalous difficulties. Cosima had followed him there with her children Daniela and Blandine von Bülow. Even little Isolde, who was fathered by Wagner, had come along. The year 1867 brought the couple another daughter, Eva-Maria; and two weeks after Nietzsche's arrival, their third child, Siegfried Helfferich Richard, came into the world.

Nietzsche now had a chance to unabashedly speak out his accumulated gratitude, and it is obvious what a strong effect he must have had on Richard and Cosima. The young scholar felt he owed his best and loftiest moments to Wagner. There was only *one* man he could honor with the same devotion: "Your great spiritual brother" Schopenhauer.

His friend Rohde as usual found out what was moving Nietzsche: "The things I learn and see there, hear and grasp, are indescribable. Schopenhauer and Goethe, Aeschylus[3] and Pindar,[4] are still alive, believe me."

Wagner and his intelligent wife seemed to have a deep understanding of Nietzsche's works. According to Wagner, Nietzsche came into the house like a messenger from a better and purer world. Cosima told Nietzsche that his presence dispelled "doleful moods;" he had a cheering influence on Wagner.

On the composer's birthday, May 22, Nietzsche admitted with a sense of pride: "If it is the fate of the genius to be just *paucorum hominum* for a while, then these *pauci* really ought to feel particularly fortunate and honored for being privileged to see the light and warm themselves in it while the mass remains freezing in the cold fog. Nor do these special few have the enjoyment of genius merely drop effortlessly into their laps; they have to struggle with all their might against the omnipotent prejudices and their own resistiveness; so that, having carried the day, they ultimately have a sort of conqueror's claim to the genius."

Nietzsche later became a fierce enemy of racism, which was one of the reasons why he tried to get away from his sister Elisabeth. At this point, however, he was still under the sway of Wagner's pamphlets against the Jews when he continued:

"I have now been so bold as to reckon myself among these *pauci* after perceiving how incapable all the people we associate with prove to be when it comes to grasping your personality as an integral whole, and feeling the uniform and deeply ethical stream that passes through your life, your writings, and your music—in short, they are unable to sense the atmosphere of a more earnest and soul-felt *Weltanschauung* such as we poor Germans have lost overnight through all manner of political miseries, philosophical mischief, and pushing Jewry. It is your and Schopenhauer's doing that I have managed to cling fast to the Germanic earnestness of life, to a more profound observation of this so enigmatic and precarious existence.

"I would rather tell you in person how many purely scholarly problems have gradually been clarified for me because of your so unique and memorable personality; and likewise, I would much have preferred *not* having to write all that I have just written. How delighted I would have been to appear in your lake-and-mountain solitude today if the wretched chain of my profession had not held me in my Basel kennel." (This is an allusion to the awful apartment in which Nietzsche was domiciled for several weeks.)

Because of this adoration, the composer and Cosima yielded to a growing intimacy. Nietzsche was soon more or less a part of the liberal household. They were always glad to see him and even assigned him two rooms permanently; he could come and go as he pleased. Nietzsche, for the first time since childhood, had something like a home. A non-bourgeois atmosphere and Wagner's spell-binding nature, which always showed itself from its best and most engaging side here, made him feel vastly at ease. Even Cosima, who never truly took to Nietzsche, deployed her entire repertoire of charms. She was wrapped in mystery, her reserve and coolness fascinated her friends as well as her father Liszt, whom she likewise so closely resembled in appearance. What had made her seem unattractive as a girl, her boyishness, now in league with the intellectual brilliance and motherliness, so enchanted the rather callow young man that he fell head over heels in love with her.

Under Cosima, a steadiness had come into Wagner's creativity. She pushed away his socialist and revolutionary ideas, supplanting them with anti-French and anti-Jewish influences, although some of Wagner's most intimate friends were Jews like Porges,[5] Tausig,[6] Mottl,[7] and later Neumann[8] and Levi.

Nietzsche did not merely remain passive and receptive in

Tribschen, he was soon expounding his own ideas. Proudly he sent his friends his inaugural lecture *Homer and Classical Philology*. Wagner had Cosima write him: "This evening, in between Goethe, Schiller, and Beethoven, we read your lecture with utmost interest. Herr Wagner gratefully wishes to say that he can only concur in all your views on aesthetic issues and, in regard to the topic of your lecture, he congratulates you on having correctly presented the problem, which is, after all, the beginning, and perhaps the end, of all wisdom and is most often ignored."

However, the outer peacefulness of the Tribschen days was deceptive. Richard and Cosima were greatly upset about the *Rheingold* production in Munich. Wagner considered it damaging to his projected four-part festive drama and he wanted to keep Ludwig II from mounting the premiere, despite their contractual agreement. The ruler, of course, hesitated to accept Wagner's artistic reasons for interfering. And naturally, Wagner's anxieties about the authenticity of production also played their part. Thus, he wrote to Peter Cornelius:[9] "The king loves my music; but he doesn't care how it's performed." Embarrassing things occurred, intrigues began, about which Wagner lamented to Cornelius: "The things we have all had to suffer and endure are beyond imagining."

In this situation, Nietzsche brought some solace into the house. At first, Wagner saw the Munich business in a kindlier light since he still hoped his friends there would do something about the production. The singers playing Wotan, Loge, and Alberich reported to Wagner in Tribschen for criticism of their acting and vocals, and he corrected wherever he could. Once they were gone, he set all his hopes on the 107-piece orchestra, which, led by Hans Richter,[10] hopefully would prevent the worst. But open and secret enemies in Munich dashed even these hopes. Richter was not being allowed to conduct. At first, the premiere was postponed, which made everyone at Tribschen breathe easier. Next, Wagner took a secret trip to Munich. But the king's secretary, with whom he prudently spoke, made it clear that there were bound to be insults and injuries if Wagner were to stop the production or insist on having Richter conduct.

For better or worse, Wagner let things run their course, and Cosima complained to Nietzsche: "I could take all these disgraceful things in stride if the Master's health weren't so dreadfully affected by them." Ignoring the king's actual feelings and motives, she went on: "And it's not because his work has been so wretchedly dishonored, but because the last fine hope of his life has been irrevocably lost in this conflict! I think you understand: I know nothing of a *rupture*—but there *is* a rift, tacit and beyond recovery, with one side unaware of anything, and the other side feeling it all the more painfully.—And now he's supposed to work on his *Siegfried.* I am still banking on our solitude in Tribschen to calm down the shaken stamina—if only all tongues could stop wagging."

Nietzsche got involved in the tumult; he was taken into confidence. He also listened when Hans Richter suddenly showed up to report on the intrigues. Eventually, the production did go over the boards, and Cosima wrote to Nietzsche: "You've probably heard more about the *Rheingold* than we have; everything printed about it seems to be unanimous in finding the performance splendid and the work unbearable. You can imagine how dismal and melancholy our hearts and spirits are."

Now, this wasn't just the standpoint of the press. The audience had included such people as the Russian novelist Turgenev,[11] who, as a lifelong friend of the singer Pauline Viardot-Garcia,[12] was not only interested in, but very open and sympathetic to, music. More than anything, he adored Mozart, Beethoven, and Schumann. But he lacked any feel for Wagner in those years. Thus, he summed up the premiere in a terse sentence: "Music and text are unbearable." Nonetheless, this was said by someone equally unresponsive to the "oldies" of grand opera à la Meyerbeer, although some of them contained Viardot's most brilliant roles.

Cosima, seven years older than Nietzsche, often made use of his services for the household. A few examples: Private letters of Wagner's had been published without his knowledge. And Nietzsche was asked to put an advertisement in a well-known newspaper, saying these publications did not have the approval of the Master. Another time, Wagner asked him to locate a picture of his uncle in Leipzig. With Christmas around the corner, Cosima had Nietzsche run a huge number of errands for her. He purchased a good part of the presents in Basel, not only Dürer engravings, antiques, and extremely elegant furnishings, but also a puppet theater and other toys. Cosima always acted embarrassed at such times, claiming the Master was indignant at her taking advantage of Nietzsche in this way. But still, she forgot that Nietzsche was a professor, doctor, and philologist; all she saw in him was the young man of twenty-five. What with his being rather impractical, she tried to make the errands easier. He was merely to hand in notes with detailed descriptions at the shops. But "Fritz" did not take his task so lightly; he critically examined books and art objects, and even toys. Thus, with the marionettes, he objected that the king didn't look genuine enough and the devil wasn't as black as he ought to be. He felt that an angel he found in Basel wasn't dressed in accordance with heavenly custom, and he ordered a garment from Paris instead.

The Master recognized Nietzsche's gift for writing. And he too profited from the younger man's devotion by asking him for all sorts of help. Thus, he gave Nietzsche the opening chapters of *My Life* for revision, but soon took them back. Was he afraid that the well-bred Doctor Nietzsche might be disillusioned by this autobiography? Something similar had happened with King Ludwig, whom he had sent part of the manuscript. The monarch's amazement at the way Wagner reacted to his Munich plans grew with the malaise he felt upon getting to know the composer more closely in his life story.

Wagner's intention of exploiting Nietzsche's literary talent for his own cause was concealed from the unsophisticated scholar. The concordance of the two men in regard to Schopenhauer actually deluded Nietzsche into believing there might be some philosophical gains. He wrote to Carl von Gersdorff: "What's more, I've found a man who, like no one else, reveals the image of what Schopenhauer calls *genius* and who is completely imbued with that wondrously introspective philosophy. This man is none other than Richard Wagner, and you mustn't believe any judgments about him in the press, in the writings of musical scholars, etc. *No one* knows him and no one can judge him because the rest of the world stands on a different foundation and is not at home in his atmosphere. He is filled with such an absolute ideality, such a deep and poignant humanity, such a sublime earnestness of life, that when I'm in his presence I feel I'm in the presence of the divine. How many days have I already spent at the charming country estate on Lake Vierwaldstätt, and that wonderful personality of his is always fresh and tireless. Thus, only yesterday, I was reading a manuscript he had given me, *On State and Religion;* a long, deep essay, meant to enlighten his "young friend," the little king of Bavaria, about his own position on the state and religion. Never has a king been spoken to in a more dignified and more philosophical manner; I was perfectly uplifted and profoundly moved by this ideality, which seemed to have sprung directly from Schopenhauer."

This essay, written in July 1864, was supposed to outline Wagner's political stance after his participation in the Dresden uprising. The dedication, sounding opportunistic, hails the king as the "Representative of Pure Human Interest." Wagner solemnly declares that he has been misrepresented as a revolutionary, the slanderers have been taken in by appearances. Such a thing could never happen to Ludwig the statesman. His assurance of henceforth refraining from any political activity whatsoever passes into the definition of his musical drama, "which, albeit not really and fully taking us out of life, nevertheless, while we are within life, raises us above life and makes it seem like a play to us, which, though seemingly earnest and terrible, is ultimately shown to be a mirage."

Delusion as Schopenhauer's conception of reality—such utterances had to appeal to young Nietzsche, just as they convinced the young king that Wagner's intentions were harmless, even if the composer was working on the *Meistersinger* with its nationalistic finale.

Wagner's friendly and receptive mood in the Tribschen years was probably bolstered by the birth of his only son, who, hopefully, would look after and continue his work. Wagner's fatigue after completing *Meistersinger* had long since vanished. He was in the "idyll" of Tribschen, together with his beloved, who had moved in with him during November 1869 after Hans von Bülow's final separation from her. Wagner could gather his strength and start afresh, with a process of creativity that surprised even him.

For ten years, the composer had been hanging fire on the *Ring*, concentrating instead on *Tristan*, then on *Meistersinger*. Now he once again took up the thread of the *Nibelungen* tetralogy. Shortly before the birth of his son ("out of wedlock" because Bülow's lengthy divorce proceedings were still dragging on in Berlin), Cosima wrote in her diary:

"They will pull us into the mire. I will gladly put up with anything, just to stand at his side. Let them calumniate me far into the next world, so long as I have helped him, so long as I could give him my hand and say: I will follow you into death if need be. My only prayer is some day to die with Richard at the very same moment."

Her wish was not to come true. She outlived Richard by almost fifty years, notorious for her scrupulous guardianship of his estate. In 1930, the same year that her son Siegfried died and only three months before him, she passed away.

Siegfried was born on Sunday, June 6, 1869 at four A.M. In his euphoria, the father finished the score of *Siegfried* the very same day. Sending the news of both events to his friend Pussinelli[13] in Dresden, he added: "It's unbelievable! No one really thought I would make it!" These words actually refer to both events. Prophetical, he went on: "Siegfried will inherit his father's name and keep his works alive for the world."

On the day Siegfried was born, Nietzsche was present in the house without realizing what was happening. Wagner had invited him on June 3, thanking him for his well-wishing letter:

"Dearest friend—please accept my deepest and heartiest, albeit belated, gratitude for your beautiful and meaningful letter!—If I wished for your visit then, let me now vociferously repeat the open invitation that I extended to you verbally when we took leave of one another in front of the Rössli.—Do come (just drop us a line to let us know), say, Saturday afternoon. Spend Sunday here and go back Monday morning. Why, any common laborer could do that, and how much more so a professor.—You can stay in my home and sleep both nights in the Tribschen entail-house. —Now let us see what sort of person you are. My experiences with fellow Germans haven't been all too blissful. Restore my not fully unshaking faith in what I, along with Goethe and several others, call German freedom.—All the very best from Yours Truly Richard Wagner."

Nietzsche complied with the invitation and remained until

Monday, leaving at the crack of dawn because of his class. After-wards, he was informed of Siegfried's birth that Sunday night, and he took the news as a happy omen for the friendship.

An immediate account of his overnight visit went out to Rohde: ". . . Recently, I was indiscreet enough to read to him personally a lovely passage from your earlier letters about W.; he was very touched and asked for a copy. Do him (and me) a favor soon and write him a detailed letter. By now, you're certainly no stranger to him. His address: Herr Richard Wagner in Tribschen by Lu-cerne. I recently spent two days there and felt astonishingly re-freshed. He makes anything we could ever wish for come true; the world doesn't know the human grandeur and singularity of his nature. I learn so much in his presence: this is my practical course in Schopenhauer's philosophy.—Being near Wagner is my sol-ace."

And while the new-born Siegfried filled the house with his powerful bawling, Wagner began the orchestral sketch to *Götter-dämmerung,* the fourth and last part of the tetralogy. Not even an annoyed letter from the Bavarian king, who was jealous of both Cosima and the baby, could dispel the mood of creativity. The letter arrived after the performance of *Rheingold,* which Wagner had expressly forbidden, but the monarch had ordered, by invok-ing his contractual rights. The twenty-four-year-old sovereign wrote to Richard:

"I think you imagine my job (if I may term it that) to be easier than it is. Standing so fully, so absolutely alone in a bleak, joyless world, alone with my views, misunderstood and distrusted—is no small matter. . . . Pity those who have to cope with the masses, lucky those who can deal with individuals as you do. Oh, I have gotten to know mankind, believe me; I came to them with true love, and was rejected, and such wounds take a long time to heal."

Ludwig the adolescent dreamer no longer existed—the iso-lated misanthrope grew more and more distant to his idol Wagner. They had little contact with one another, socially or intellectually, until the Bayreuth Festival—eight years later. Only meager and conventional letters were exchanged.

When summer vacation began, Wagner wanted Nietzsche to spend most of it in his home; but this didn't happen because the younger man preferred to wander through the mountains. Wagner's annoyed and joking reaction was: "We don't see much of the Professor nowadays."

Still, the Tribschen household kept abreast of Nietzsche's summer excursions, as revealed in Cosima's letter in late July 1869:

"We have truly suffered along with your irksome Pilatus adventure. After your decreeing on Sunday evening in Stanza, at a peasant nine-pins match, that you would have fine weather, the whole kit and caboodle of us, servants, children, old people, woke up on Monday truly terrified. It spread like wildfire through the rooms, from the kitchen to the nursery: 'What is Professor N. going to do?' Isolde came to me and said: 'But Uncle Richard's man is up there.' That was Monday; on Tuesday, with the sun shining, we assumed you must have remained up there, and we were expecting you for lunch. Well, it wasn't until much, much later that it occurred to us, you had been punished for treating us so wretchedly and refusing to put off your Pilatus trip for even one day. But penalty or destiny, it was certainly dreadful."

Nevertheless, Nietzsche was promptly invited back: "And I'm to ask you whether you would care to spend Saturday and Sunday at Tribschen again. The bad weather is more easily borne here than on Mount Pilatus, and you know that your presence here is always welcome. Herr Wagner assures you of this, and sends his best wishes. He had a letter from Professor Brockhaus last week, announcing he was leaving and might visit us at Tribschen."

This time, of course, Nietzsche didn't want to hurt Wagner's feelings; so he went. And then, when the composer's brother-in-law and sister arrived from Leipzig, he was again hastily summoned. Wagner wired: "On 8/27/69, the Brockhauses are lunching with us tomorrow (Saturday) 2 p.m., please do join us, promise you total freedom for Sunday afternoon. Wagner."

They expressed a desire for Nietzsche's presence at every turn. And even the servants appeared delighted: "Do visit Tribschen again soon, you know Jacob likes to do everything, and hopefully you're even more certain how welcome you are to the Master and myself."

Along with the two cozy rooms, they gave Nietzsche the small parlor, which was named "Thinking Room" in his honor. But Wagner and Cosima most likely failed to realize how much valuable time Fritz was giving them, not only with running all kinds of errands, but because they disposed of his only free days and invited him to Tribschen as often as possible. Nietzsche was fairly overladen with his many courses and his highly taxing private labors. Only a man for whom work was a necessity could satisfy such demands. His sister confirms: "That was the only thing my brother complained about a bit, that Wagner and Frau Cosima had no idea how overburdened he was."

At Christmas 1869, Nietzsche was once more a guest at Tribschen, "a most beautiful and inspiring memory," as he wrote to Rohde in January 1870. Wagner read the great *Parsifal* draft aloud, which undermines a later theory that Nietzsche was surprised by his religious metamorphosis in *Parsifal*.

Wagner had thus found a new "Walther von Stolzing" in Nietzsche, who could be of use to him.

In April 1870, the University of Basel and the Swiss government awarded the young man a full professorship in Classical Philology, which dazzled the composer, if for no other reason than because he had never received much attention from scholars. The writings of this young genius Nietzsche would make it possible for him to spread his own thoughts into academic circles. And Wagner was no less drawn personally to the sensitive but intellectually very active youth. The two of them had exhaustive conversations, and not just on artistic themes.

Thus, together with a classmate from Leipzig, Carl von Gersdorff, Nietzsche had once accustomed himself to a vegetarian diet. Meanwhile, he became convinced that the whole thing was just a fad, and a rather questionable one at that. The composer had previously been a vegetarian for years, and now Nietzsche could discuss the pros and cons with him. Wagner, subsequently a passionate opponent of vivisection, became all worked up and vociferous about the split between theory and practice in vegetarianism. Nietzsche realized this was obviously a part of that optimism constantly cropping up as socialism, or cremation of the dead, or vegetarianism, or any number of other ideologies, "as though abolishing something sinful and unnatural could bring about happiness and harmony. Whereas our sublime philosophy teaches that wherever we may reach, we will merely find complete corruption, the pure will to live, everywhere, and thus all palliative remedies are nonsense. . . . Living purely on vegetables is possible for us too, for particularly strong, *physically* active men, but only with a violent rebellion *against* nature."

Wagner felt that nature evens the score in her own way, as he had found out personally. One of his friends had been the victim of a vegetarian experiment, and he himself believed he would no longer be among the living had he stuck to that diet.

The two men concluded, "Intellectually productive and emotionally intense natures require meat."

Nietzsche called out to his friend Gersdorff: "Let us fight, and, if possible not for windmills. Let us recall the struggle and asceticism of truly great men, Schopenhauer, Schiller, Wagner!" Wagner's total change of heart on this issue, as shown in *Parsifal,* must be mentioned.

5

LIFE WITH FRIENDS

Schopenhauer's view of the world exercised more and more control over Nietzsche's thinking. After his first semester, he was quite satisfied with his academic work, even in terms of his scholarly area. His students showed their interest and sympathy by frequently asking his advice. Nor did he lack invitations at first, and he even enjoyed dances and parties. But soon, as in the past, he found it hard to adjust. Above all, he missed his "dearest friend" Rohde. To be sure, the Brockhauses visited him in Basel and went out to Tribschen with him. And the holidays he spent there at Christmas 1869 were lovely and heart-warming.

But withal, he felt like a hermit and called out like a sick man to Rohde, who was staying in Rome: "Come to Basel!" He told him: "As soon as you come here, we'll take a trip to my friend Wagner. If you return home by way of Lago di Como, you'd be able to do us an enormous favor. We, i.e. the Tribscheners, have an eye on a lakeside villa, near Fiume latte, called Villa Capuana, two houses. Couldn't you inspect this villa and let us know what you think?"

The year 1870 began with a great deal of work for Nietzsche. He had agreed to give two lectures at the Basel Museum, on January 18, and February 1, on *The Greek Musical Drama* and *Socrates and Tragedy.* Tribschen had stolen so much time from his duties that he now had to hurry along in preparing himself.

Since, as a result, he delayed sending a thank-you note for his Christmas sojourn, Wagner quickly expressed a jealous impatience. He wrote: "My dear friend! I find your silence astonishing: but I pray you will dispel my astonishment.—For today, in passing, a request! Reading old family letters, which arrived as a Christmas present, I stumbled upon a chronological mistake in my biography. Hopefully, the first folio has not been printed definitively yet, and so may I ask you . . . to correct the chronological data on these pages.—Please do not take it amiss! I, as the one remaining behind, had planned not to contact you until you, who went forth, were heard from. But since the chronology ordained it, I must, peripherally, tell you that here at Tribschen things are at sixes and at sevens. Coughs, running noses, katharrhs (sic)— or however it's spelled—have laid everyone low. Meanwhile, I've taken up the Norns afresh. And the king, in his wild wonted way, has gotten in touch with me again; it is *possible* that I will produce *Rheingold* and *Valkyrie* this year—that everything will happen as I want it to; but it is not probable. That's how things stand.—The academics came from Berlin: I told Jacob to receive only those who ask for 'Herr Full-Outside-Member R. W.' That's my newest title.—But not another word, you've become rather dubious for me. Your R. W."

Nietzsche answered by return mail. Even Wagner seemed to have guessed that one should not be overdemanding with him. Cosima, however, proved to be quite far from this insight, for she wrote: "I was not angry with you, but now I would like to be, for I was really worried you might be ill; however, I am quite glad to see my neverending distrust of destiny unfounded, and I do not care to have my good mood spoiled in any way. Besides, the Master has told me how busy you are."

Reconciled and in high feather, Wagner wrote: "My dear unscrupulous friend!—There are still people around with some scruples. That will take care of itself. For the moment, I wish you all kinds of good deliveries and I enclose the two latest installments of *On Conducting* to ease your labour pains.— The coat-of-arms turned out very well; we have every reason to thank you for your meticulous care. But here my old *vulture* draft has risen anew, the bird of prey that everyone takes for an eagle until told that scientifically there is such a thing as a 'cinerary vulture,' closely resembling the eagle. Now, since, because of the relationship, the 'vulture' absolutely has to be recognized at once; may we ask you to prevail upon the engraver to give our bird its characteristic ruffle—using any available picture of the beast. This probably won't work without a change in the neck, but perhaps it will come out all right."

The drawing in question had been suggested by Nietzsche as the emblem for Wagner's memoirs.

Nietzsche's sister Elisabeth was likewise harnessed into finding an effigy of a vulture, but at first she simply couldn't grasp that there would be no eagle carrying the coat-of-arms. Nietzsche therefore divulged that Wagner referred to his stepfather Geyer (German for "vulture") as his real father. There is no reason to discredit that statement made during the days of greatest intimacy, which is why we cannot go along with the conjectures still being voiced about the "secret," even in the last great Wagner monograph by Robert Gutman.[1] Nietzsche's awareness of Wagner's Jewish descent dates back to that time of friendship. In his polemical The Wagner Case, Nietzsche merely touched upon this point again; but it was written off by others as implausible because of his "partisanship." Geyer, incidentally, was a man of parts. He painted, authored a comedy entitled The Murder of the Innocents, and was known to be musical. His father was an organist in Eisleben. Gutman rightfully points out that nothing more clearly attests to Wagner's familiarity with his Jewish background than his hysterical anti-Semitism, powerfully egged on by Cosima.

Nietzsche's lectures at the Basel Museum had kindled "dread and misunderstandings" in the audience. Wagner's comfort and support showed him to be a far-seeing, if not fully unselfish, encourager of Nietzsche's writing, for which the younger man lacked self-confidence: "Scholarship, art, and philosophy are so intergrown in me that some day I am sure to give birth to Centaurs."

Nietzsche promptly sent manuscripts of the two lectures to Tribschen, where they provoked some excitement. For the first time, more thorough and precise than in conversation, they developed the ideas on the ousting of the old Dionysian tragedy by Socrates[2] and Euripides.[3] Wagner had to put Cosima's mind at ease; she felt that Nietzsche had been rather cavalier in his surprisingly modern treatment of the sublime Athenians. The composer expressed his own reaction to the friend: "I, for my part, was startled by the boldness of your presenting so tersely and positively such a new idea to an audience that was scarcely in an educational frame of mind; for the sake of your absolution, one could only reckon with their wholehearted lack of understanding.

Even those people who are initiated in my thinking would be caught off guard if such ideas brought them into conflict with their belief in Sophocles and even Aeschylus. I personally can exclaim: It is so! You have hit the nail on the head and made the real point with utmost accuracy, so that I can only look forward in wonderment to your further evolution, to your doing away with the common dogmatic prejudice." However, he advised him not to articulate these thoughts in short papers that were easily sensationalist, but instead to gather himself for a comprehensive work.

Nietzsche's replies to the two Wagner letters were unfortunately destroyed in Wahnfried, a particularly painful loss considering Wagner's echo. The composer writes: "Dear friend! It's good being able to write such letters. There is no one I could be so serious with—except for Her, the Only One. God knows how I would go about it otherwise! Whenever I, in the throes of depression, ultimately go back to my labor, it often puts me in a good mood, because I can barely understand it and I have to laugh. It instantly dawns on me what the reasons are, but then I promptly feel that to pursue my insight and turn it into Socratic knowledge, I would have to have all the time in the world and nothing better to do. For—making the knowledge of such reasons comprehensible to others necessitates forgoing all creativity. Thus, a division of labor is good. You could take over a good portion, indeed a full half, of what I am meant to do. And you might thereby be wholeheartedly pursuing what you have to do. You can see how miserably I have come to terms with Classics and how good it is that you have done more or less the same with music. Had you become a musician, you would more or less be what I would have become had I been bent on philology."

As hard as this unwittingly left-handed compliment may have struck Nietzsche, he most surely must have smiled at the thought of pulling himself together for a major work. Eloquent as he may have acted in daily intercourse, he never emerged with completed plans until they had ripened in private.

The amazement of the Wagners at Nietzsche's new ideas also had a cheering effect, which Cosima describes: "The manuscripts you sent and our perusal thereof have brought a change of mood to Tribschen. We were so downhearted we couldn't even read in the evening; our pilgrimage, thanks to you, to the most beautiful era of humanity had such a beneficial effect on us that the next morning the Master, to the accompaniment of the boldest and merriest violin figure, had his Siegfried blow a cheerful theme on the Rhine, and the Rhine Maidens, upon hearing it, joyfully and hopefully sounded out their motif, broad and strong." This is a reference to *Siegfried's Rhine Journey*, the interlude in *Twilight of the Gods* after he takes leave of Brünnhilde.

The "melancholy" in Tribschen was mainly due to the imminent presentation of *Valkyrie* in Munich, on which the king, unmindful of Wagner's arguments, insisted, citing his contractual option. But what made the Master resign once and for all was the refusal of the theater to go by his wishes. The composer wrote to Karl Klindworth:[4]

"That would consequently be the price I must pay for purchasing enough civil peace of mind to at least carry out my projects."

With energetic words, he unburdened himself to Nietzsche, branding the Munich production. Anyone attending it would have to reckon with Wagner's anger, and that included Liszt, who was setting out for Munich with a swarm of admirers. Unhappily, the *Meistersinger* productions in Vienna and Berlin brought little joy. The Beckmesser serenade was hooted by the Viennese, who had learned that Wagner meant to parody an old synagogal chant. From Berlin, Nietzsche received Frau von Schleinitz's[5] and Gersdorff's report on a great success, but also "colossal defects."

Nietzsche's friendship with the Wagners could hardly ease the young scholar's tensions, generated by his awareness of his uncompromising intellectual insights that made him a social outsider. Hence his efforts to lure Rohde, his "dioscuri twin" (as Ritschl used to call him), to a chair at Basel, while he himself was aiming for the *cathedra* of Philosophy. Although unable to persuade him, he at least soon had the pleasure of greeting him in Basel.

Nietzsche also missed Gersdorff. The friend at first felt no rapport with the Wagner passion. By March 1870, however, he appears to have been won over, for Nietzsche confirms the receipt of a letter as a "proof that we belong together."

As always around an impact-making genius, pro- and anti-Wagner parties had been forming, and even Nietzsche required some stamina not to lose his bearings in the general hue and cry. He couldn't comprehend why so many important men refused to side with Wagner. The composer's Schopenhauerean gesture of "renunciation" encouraged Nietzsche to cerebrally put himself above this conflict. The philosopher found solace in the thought that Wagner's incredible hard work and his intellectual approach to artistic expression must have been as much of a *bête noire* to most people as Schopenhauer's asceticism and his denial of the will.

At the same time, Nietzsche initially overlooked the imponderable surges of emotion that secretly determined Wagner's idealistic habitus, which reminded the young professor of Schiller.

"This ardent, generous struggle to make the day of noble spirits come at last, in a word, the chivalresque, which is so in opposition to our plebeian political noise of the day," and which he sensed in Wagner, led Nietzsche into his youthful adoration. Any man in disagreement with the Master's opinions and music was, for Nietzsche, indolent and incapable of studying hard to understand such a towering artist and such epoch-making artworks. Nietzsche thus behaved exactly like the Wagnerites, whom he came to despise. He was delighted, for instance, when Gersdorff fervently pored over Wagner's *Opera and Drama,* which Nietzsche had sent him; and he promptly informed his Tribschen friends about this "event."

Nietzsche had good cause to conclude: "Getting to know such a genius is an unbelievable enrichment of one's life. For me, the best and the most beautiful things in the world are linked with the names of Schopenhauer and Wagner, and I am proud and happy to be of one mind in this matter with my closest friends." Nietzsche sent two of Wagner's papers to all his acquaintances, *Art and Politics* and *On Conducting,* and he considered the latter on a par with Schopenhauer's essay, *Philosophy Professors.*

In early April 1870, Nietzsche's mother and sister visited their Fritz in Basel. The three of them traveled out to Lake Geneva, where they spent several lovely spring days at the Ketterer Pension in Clarens-au-Basset. The brand-new Full Professor had a hearty *bon voyage* from Tribschen. Wagner was relieved; his friend had taken the unpleasantnesses that winter too much to heart, he had even wanted to give up his professorship and devote himself body and soul to defending his beloved Master. Wagner would occasionally discourage such plans, for he was more than anxious to be defended by a university professor; position and title were terribly important to him. When Nietzsche came back from Geneva, reconciled to his teaching position, he focused on a new scholarly task; Wagner, at the close of a letter, expressed his satisfaction after complaining about all his problems with the printers: "I'm so delighted that your outing to Lake Geneva managed to cheer you up. The same places you passed through and observed also made a deep impact on me in various periods of my life. At the Hotel Byron in Villeneuve, I experienced a peculiar catastrophe of my fate; in Montreux, I had a strange experience with a young, highly gifted friend; in Vevey, four and a half years ago, I sought refuge during the winter and discussed German politics while strolling with the Grand Duke of Baden, etc.—Now that (as I see) philology, 'gray and in the flesh,' has become your rule in life, and even diverting excursions into the realm of 'style' would be difficult for you, let me also ignore tomfoolery: perhaps I contribute to bringing you away from certain bewildering impressions forcing themselves upon you from a sphere in which another can—or must—feel called upon to see the world with all his will.—I am laboring slowly but 'surely' on my works and basking in the comfort of knowing that *Meistersinger* was my last contact with the theater and with opera. I greet you from the bottom of my heart. Yours truly, Richard Wagner."

A short time later, Wagner was quite surprised at seeing Nietzsche in such high spirits after his trip to Geneva, and he gave voice to his amazement, listing other times when Nietzsche had conspicuously and rapidly overcome pessimistic moods.

In the year 1870, the friendship reached its zenith. Wagner, well aware that he would not be able to watch over Siegfried's education until the boy became twenty-one, briefly toyed with the idea of making his friend the legal guardian.

As in the previous year, Nietzsche's professorial duties kept him from visiting Wagner on the latter's birthday. He dispatched a letter and twelve blossoming rosebushes to Tribschen. But he wanted to bring the *pièce de résistance*, Dürer's *Melancholia*, personally. He felt he could not just *send* this gloomy picture on the Master's birthday. Enclosing his photograph in the letter, he wrote on May 21:

"Pater seraphice, just as it was not given to me last year to attend the celebration of your birthday, so, once again, an unfavorable constellation is detaining me; the plume pushes reluctantly into my hand today, whereas I had hoped to be able to undertake a May journey to you.—Permit me to restrict the circle of my wishes as narrowly and personally as possible; others may venture to utter their congratulations in the name of sacred art, in the name of the finest German hopes, in the name of their most personal wishes; but for me, let the most subjective of all wishes suffice: may you remain for me what you were last year, my mystagogue in the arcana of art and life. Although at times the gray fog of philology might make me seem somewhat remote from you, it is not so, my thoughts are always with you. If what you once wrote (to my proud delight) is true, i.e. that music conducts me, then you in any event are the conductor of my music; and you yourself have told me that even something mediocre can, if *well* conducted, have a satisfying effect. In this sense, I express the rarest of all wishes: let it thus remain, let the moment linger: it is so beautiful! All I ask of the coming year is that I may not prove unworthy of your inestimable sympathy and your courageous appreciation. Please accept this wish among the wishes with which you are beginning a new year! One of the 'blissful boys.' "

Nietzsche eventually regretted not having gone to Tribschen when he heard all sorts of marvelous things about the celebration. Cosima had transformed the house into a flower garden, and the four little daughters, in white frocks and wreathes of roses, stood about as living blossoms. At eight in the morning, forty-five soldiers stationed in the garden played the *March of Homage.* Cosima had previously gone to the barracks and painstakingly supervised the tempi. Wagner was so moved he couldn't say a word, and they were almost sorry about the arrangement. Then came an unforeseen misfortune. Cosima's oldest daughter Daniela wanted to set her five beloved birds free again. Reciting a few lines of poetry, she let four of the birds fly away. The fifth one, however, refused to leave the cage. Ultimately, after being placed on a bush, he sprang to the ground, whereupon the dog grabbed the bird and chewed it to death. Richard and Cosima were so saddened that Cosima felt Nietzsche could have gone right ahead and sent them the *Melancholia.*

Wagner thanked Nietzsche: "My dear friend! A precious hand has already informed you how welcome the 'blissful boy' was to the 'Pater seraphicus.' I am certain that you least of all have any doubts about that. You were also told about the blissful quarter-hour whose impact will remain with me as long as I have any feeling. Hence I will not report on all the 'bliss' and will only tell you what is required by another sphere of life."

He was talking about Pussinelli, the publisher of his memoirs, and again he asked Nietzsche to "survey" what was happening with the publication.

Wagner didn't fail to add that "you have also been chosen by me to be a guardian of these remembrances of me beyond my death.—Everything is going well here. Tomorrow I intend to finish the sketches of Act I of Siegfried (I nearly said Götterdämmerung). The day after, I am celebrating my son's first birthday and also the 'memorial day' of your first visit in my home. May the stars look down kindly upon this double anniversary! At that time, I felt you had brought luck to my son.—Since then, we have had a difficult but inwardly joyous year, and at last I feel we have to take my zodiac sign into account, Taurus the Bull: Perseverance will come into its own. In just a few months I hope to wed the magnanimous mother of my son.—My very best wishes, and keep up your good spirits.—In the ancient, and not modern, Greek way!—From the bottom of my heart, Yours Truly, Richard Wagner."

From June 11 to 13, 1870, Nietzsche visited Tribschen with Erwin Rohde, who was "on the road" for fifteen months. Rohde described those days as the high point of his grand tour of Europe.

After this visit, Nietzsche likewise wrote rapturously to the "most honored Baroness" Cosima: "I can understand why the Athenians put up altars for their Aeschylus and Sophocles and gave Sophocles the heroic name Dexion for having received and entertained the gods in his home. This sojourn of the gods in the house of genius aroused that religious mood I reported to you."

During those days, Wagner, heartened by such enthusiasm prevailed upon his young admirer to consider giving up his professorial duties for a few years and accompanying the Master to the Fichtel Mountains, to help him prepare for the Bayreuth

Festival. But Nietzsche could only hope for a temporary release from his academic fetters.

The Tribscheners had a lively discussion about how excited they had been by Nietzsche's reinterpretation of the Greek mind. It turned out that they only had fragments of the first of his two lectures, *The Greek Musical Drama*. Nietzsche assiduously made fresh copies of both, inscribing them to Cosima. She thanked him all the more emphatically, because Wagner had reproached her for jumping the gun: she had expressed her admiration prematurely and excitedly without really knowing Nietzsche's drift.

Cosima wrote him: "How moved I was by the dedication of the lectures which you were so kind as to send me. . . . I read the lecture on the musical drama during these past few days and can only repeat that I consider it an indispensable portico to the edifice of your Socrates, and that I could have spared myself my very superfluous excitement had I but known the prelude, that warm and lively description of Greek art." Of course, Cosima always had an eye out for whatever could be useful to the Bayreuth project. "You write your book in Bayreuth, and we do honor to the book. And if these are castles in the air—should your radiant picture, as a protecting roof, favor the growth of the most splendid plant, always endangered by outer tempest, then I will cultivate it and make it fruitful, such as has never happened with anything truly good."

Munich was a particular danger and a thorn in their flesh. In spite of the Master, who feared for the first-performance rights of his Festival Theater, the Bavarian National Theater mounted the successful and unusually popular premiere of *Valkyrie.* Wagner had done everything in his power to prevent it, even calling upon the king for help: "I implore you once again, have the Valkyrie put on for yourself alone, but leave out the public." Nevertheless, Franz Wüllner[6] conducted the alternating performances of *Rheingold* and *Valkyrie* to full houses, and Wagner had no way of stopping such people as Brahms, Liszt, and French friends from attending.

Nietzsche's presence once again calmed the jangling nerves at Tribschen. And this was the first time he could see "Fidi" (the parents' pet name for Siegfried), who had always been concealed upstairs. His crib stood beneath the high poplars or between the fruit trees in the meadow. The scholar, while not too interested, found the baby "healthy and hopeful." Cosima held back any opinion of their holiday guest Rohde and cited her husband's feelings when she wrote to Nietzsche: "These days are fixed in our memory, the Master was very fond of your friend, he so greatly liked his virile earnestness, his significant participation, and the genuine friendliness that sometimes shone through his severe features. If he does teach in Freiburg" (as Nietzsche wished) "then the two of you can always come together to Tribschen, for 'two's a company' says our authority."

Wagner was soon expecting *Kapellmeister* Hans Richter at Tribschen, to help him write out the score of the *Ring*. Invitations describing musical sessions in the house made Nietzsche's mouth water. Because of the scholar's many obligations, Wagner was not pressing him, but Nietzsche of course did know how welcome he was at any time. The professor had to confess with a sigh that his duties were depriving him of the enjoyment of art.

In late June 1870, Nietzsche's mother left Basel after a long visit with her son, while Nietzsche's sister remained. Letters and packages went to and fro between Tribschen and Basel; the Wagners mostly sent requests. But Nietzsche had twisted his ankle and had to lie still. So Elisabeth procured whatever Wagner jovially telegraphed for: "At Tribschen, Dutch herrings are greatly in demand. . . . *Kapellmeister* Richter has moved in with us. The professor? Wagner." Nietzsche was to come as soon as he could.

On July 15, the Swiss Day of Independence, when all the schools and universities are closed, Elisabeth and Friedrich went to Lucerne. Friedrich continued on to Tribschen, while Elisabeth cautiously stayed with the family of a professor, who owned a villa straight across the lake from Tribschen. The host and hostess peered at the peninsula through a telescope, and one day, according to Elisabeth, they announced: "Your brother and another man are coming here in a skiff and he probably wants to take you along." But could one go to such unseemly people as the Wagners? The sister asked the family for advice. "Wherever your brother goes, you can go, too," was the answer.

Elisabeth's heart pounded as she sat in the boat which Hans Richter rowed across to Tribschen. Wagner and Frau Cosima welcomed her cordially at the pier. At first, Elisabeth was confused because Wagner was so short and Frau Cosima towered above him. Although the visit didn't last very long, the furnishings of the old and simple mansion made Elisabeth rather uneasy. A Parisian "meubleur" had been unpleasantly lavish with pink satin and amoretti. But she found Wagner and Frau Cosima esteemable and the children delightful, especially little Siegfried, whom her brother had never mentioned to her. She rightly suspected that Nietzsche was tremendously relieved that the visit had gone so well and that she hadn't embarrassed him with a thoughtless question. Afterwards, the brother and sister traveled to the Axenstein and the Maderan Valley.

A blast of thunder disrupted the Tribschen idyll. While the Wagners were on a family outing on Mount Pilatus, Kaiser Wilhelm I broke off negotiations with France about the candidature for the throne of Spain. The communiqué that Wilhelm issued in Bad Ems was drastically abridged by Bismarck. Its publication caused enormous agitation in France. On July 19, 1870, France declared war on Prussia, "and our whole threadbare culture is leaping to the breast of the most dreadful demon" (Nietzsche to Rohde). The spokesman of the declaration of war was the French politician Emile Ollivier, Cosima's brother-in-law. Wagner's French friends Mendès,[7] Gautier,[8] Villiers de l'Isle-Adam,[9] Saint-Saëns,[10] Duparc,[11] and Joly,[12] arrived in Switzerland on the way back from the Weimar and Munich presentations of Wagner and stopped off at Tribschen. Tense as the political conversations may have been, there was easy communication about artistic matters. Saint-Saëns, on the piano, accompanied Wagner singing selections from the *Ring*.

Nietzsche volunteered for military service but he only spent two months in the war, as an orderly. The canton authorities would not allow a Swiss citizen to serve actively in the Prussian army. He therefore requested a "leave for medical duty," which was granted. On August 12, in Lindau, he met his Hamburg friend, the painter Mosengel,[13] and the next day they went to Erlangen for training as nurses.

Earlier, upon his return to Basel, Nietzsche had paid a brief call at Tribschen, finding time to read aloud his paper *On the Dionysian World-View*. He mentioned his war plans only hypothetically to Cosima and Wagner, for, exhilarated as they were about the war, they didn't want to lose their friend. They said this wasn't 1813, after all, when young men like him had formed a Lützow Corps. But the Wagners, hearing the government was only allowing him to serve as an orderly, no longer objected.

However, just as Nietzsche's early military training had been quickly terminated by a fall from a horse, he once again had to interrupt his service because of illness. While accompanying a convoy of wounded men, he caught dysentery and diphtheria, and recovered very gradually, first in Erlangen, then at his mother's home in Naumburg.

While still bedridden in Erlangen, Nietzsche learned about Wagner's marriage. Five weeks after the announcement of the divorce (coincidentally on King Ludwig's birthday), on the 25th of August, at 8 A.M., in the little Protestant church of Lucerne, the wedding took place between Richard Wagner and Cosima, née Countess d'Agoult, the divorced wife of Hans von Bülow. The witnesses were Malwida von Meysenbug,[14] and Hans Richter, replacing Nietzsche.

At the time of the ceremony, Cosima was assailed by conflicting emotions. There was no word from her father, nor from her mother Countess Marie d'Agoult,[15] who was in a state of mental decline; and there was no word from old Frau von Bülow, who felt resentful and scornful towards the "fallen woman." But what troubled Cosima most was the hatred of Princess Sayn-Wittgenstein,[16] her father's mistress and lifetime companion, a cold, nasty woman who grew more and more sanctimonious with age, apparently forgetting that she herself had once abandoned family, money, and honor for Liszt.

On the other hand, Cosima could now legally regard Wagner as the object of her "fulfillment of duty." In her diary, she wished: "May I be worthy of bearing Richard's name. My devotion has focused on two points: Richard's well-being, that I may always promote it; and Hans's happiness, that it may be given to him, far from me, to lead a serene life." A more pious than realistic prayer.

Malwida von Meysenbug, in her *Reminiscences,* tells how blissful Wagner was to have order at last in his domestic situation. He keenly regretted Nietzsche's absence "since no one would be as delighted as he." For Wagner had confided to Malwida that his "beloved friend" came from a family that could look upon several utterly virtuous generations, and that he "suffered terribly" from Wagner's illicit position.

One can believe that during this past year of close friendship, it must have cost Nietzsche a great deal of self-control to frequent such a liberal household. Naturally, he saw Wagner and Cosima as far beyond all other mortals, not to mention middle-class conditions. In those days, it had some significance when Nietzsche wrote:

"Our artists are living more bravely and more honestly; and the most striking example we have before us, Richard Wagner, shows that the genius need not be afraid of flying in the face of conventional forms and orders if he wishes to bring to light the higher orders and truth dwelling within him."

But then again, Nietzsche believed that special natures find a strong shield in convention in order to rise all the higher in the world of the spirit, unhampered by everyday struggles. Wagner was well aware of this, and in consideration of Nietzsche's character and feelings, he concealed many embarrassing things, especially from the last few years before their friendship, which is why he relieved Nietzsche of proofreading his autobiography.

And yet there were times when Wagner was rankled by Nietzsche's delicate virtuousness; at such moments, he would suddenly make gross jokes about himself and Cosima. A second later, he would severely renounce his own vulgar streak, brought down as he was by Nietzsche's look of dismay. But soon, Nietzsche, by himself, revised his transfigured image of Wagner's life and character.

The no-longer-youthful bridegroom felt proud and relieved. Now, no one would train binoculars on the peninsula to sneak a glance at the two adulterers. Boatloads of tourists and coaches would stop trying to invade their property. And the neighboring community of Horw, which had been making moralistic efforts to drive the couple out of Lucerne, could now rest easy. And little by little, the flood of poison-pen letters ebbed off.

It was to a court toady rather than the king that Wagner broke the news of his nuptials "after the removal of all obstacles to the contrary." Self-possessed, he prophesized to Hans Richter: "The world, I think, will some day come to a realization of what it owes this good fortune. . . ."

Cosima was the one who wrote to Nietzsche about the wedding. He, for his part, in the Erlangen military hospital, let the bridal pair know what had been happening with him. His manifold duties had brought him as far as the environs of Metz. In Ars-sur-Moselle, he and Mosengel had nursed some wounded men and then started back to Germany with them.

Those three days and three nights with critically injured men were the most strenuous time of all. Nietzsche had to supply bandages and food for six wounded soldiers lying in a miserable cattle car. It struck him as a "miracle" that he could sleep and eat in that pestilential atmosphere. But no sooner had he brought his transport to a military hospital in Karlsruhe than he felt the first serious symptoms of illness. He just barely made it to Erlangen to hand in his report, whereupon he had to take to his bed:

"Thus I made the acquaintance of two of those notorious plagues of military hospitals: they so rapidly weakened and disempowered me that I now have to give up all my plans for helping the army and am forced to think of nothing but my health. . . . As for the German victories, I would rather not say a word about them: they are fire signs on the wall, intelligible to *all* nations."

On September 2, the French surrendered at Sedan. In November 1870, Ludwig II signed the document asking the Prussian king to accept the imperial crown. Meanwhile, Wagner was adapting *The Capitulation, A Comedy by Aristophanes,* which he completed as *A Capitulation, Comedy in the Manner of Antiquity.* He then offered his modest effort to Richter, asking him to score it and suggesting the style of Offenbach. But after a theater in Berlin rejected it, he put the manuscript aside. The play mocked a beaten France and included such characters as Perrin[17] and Hugo;[18] but it also made fun of the German public that surrenders to the Paris operetta.

When Nietzsche had regained enough strength to travel, he went to convalesce at his mother's home in Naumburg. But the disease marked him physically for life, especially because the harsh medications weakened his previously healthy stomach. Moved by a sense of duty, a love of scholarly work, and the hope of being revived by his studies, he made the mistake of trusting in his constitution and returning to Basel only half cured.

Once there, he was joyously welcomed by colleagues and students. In early November 1870, Wagner sent him the manuscript of the article *Beethoven* as a present; he had finished it only two months earlier.

"Here we have an utterly profound philosophy of music, closely tied to Schopenhauer," said Nietzsche, believing that Wagner had thus paid Beethoven the greatest honor that the nation could offer him. Nietzsche's own contacts with Beethoven's music were limited to what was played at Tribschen. Now and then, Friedrich Hegar's[19] string quartet would come to Tribschen from Zurich and perform Beethoven's chamber music. Wagner was very fond of the final quartets; he always tried to demonstrate that Beethoven, deprived of his hearing, was unconcerned about form: "He could have stopped here just as well as there." That was one of Wagner's pronouncements as reported by Nietzsche in 1883 to Peter Gast. An exception to this tendentious approach was the very last quartet, which the Wagnerites promptly labeled "regressive."

Wagner's words characterize *himself* more aptly than Beethoven, particularly since they can apply at best to movements in the form of variations, which Beethoven in the end so frequently employed for his most sublime revelations. Thus, all the adagios of that period are variations. But these very pieces prove that Beethoven, even in his concluding days, was beholden to form.

Nietzsche considered Wagner's musical theorizing as *the* philosophy of music. As for his own essay of the previous summer, *On the Dionysian World-View,* he demoted it to a preliminary study for thoroughly grasping Wagner's reflections on music. He did this even though he at times saw Wagner's ideas as "far-fetched" and was amazed at, and slightly estranged by, the discussion of Beethoven's peculiar nature.

In his thank-you note of November 10, 1870, Nietzsche expressed the following anxiety to Wagner: "The aestheticians of these days may look upon you as a sleepwalker, whom it would be ill-advised, nay, dangerous, and, above all, impossible to follow. Even the vast majority of those who are versed in Schopenhauer's philosophy will be incapable of translating into concepts and feelings the profound harmony between your thoughts and those of their master. Only he 'to whom Tristan is unsealed' can follow the thinker Wagner."

These lines may have flattered Wagner, but at the same time they indicate mixed feelings on the part of Nietzsche the reader. He too, like Wagner, was busy with a major work reflecting the happiest time of their rapport. Richard Strauss regarded this as one of the crucial moments of the century.

One may wonder, of course, how far Nietzsche's allegiance to Wagner really went at this point. Naturally, Nietzsche must have been delighted to find in *Beethoven* a style that he himself had encouraged. And Wagner's poetic approach to Schopenhauer generally mirrored the conversations at Tribschen. But could principles of opera really be tacked on to such philosophical foundations with which they were not in agreement? Schopenhauer's notions were being applied to things far removed from his taste and mentality. Thus, in *Beethoven*, Wagner tied his theory of the *Gesamtkunstwerk* to Schopenhauer's views of the symbolism of dreams and visions. Because of its clairvoyance, music is celebrated as being superior to all the other arts; its kinship to poetry is scorned as "purely illusory." Wagner postulates that in the fusion of words and music the text is always fully subordinate. By way of proof, he points out that in the *Ninth Symphony*, Schiller's verses were set with no regard for the words. At bottom, the listener is swept away by the hymnal melody, which quite characteristically is at first played only by the orchestra. The text can at best put the composer in a mood favorable to inspiration. A piece of music retains its character no matter what lyrics are sung with it. The article closes with an interpretation of Goethe's "Eternal Feminine" as the genius of music, which alone is capable of redeeming the poet.

The fact that Nietzsche had similar ideas at that time was later castigated by him in his first "impossible book," as a "youthful peccadillo." But for now he regarded the knowledge of Wagner's music philosophy as a "costly distinction available to very few at this moment."

The man tentatively dealing with issues of music had already attained everything in Classics that could be the goal of an academic career. The statements and judgments of the highly respected young scholar were taken seriously, if not always without protest, by the learned world. Nietzsche was a good teacher to his few students. Earlier than other men, he had reached the top of the university ladder with his professorship and could lead an independent life. He also had real friends. But for him these factors were just peripheral conditions for his own intellectual and human realization. The rather narrow scope of his duties and his assured livelihood left him time for his own works.

He conceived a series of books which were soon to put him at extreme odds with social conventions, contemporary scholarship, and philosophy. For the time being, however, he was spared the dreadful loneliness of his later years.

He continued to participate in the happiness of the Wagner family in Tribschen and delighted in the lectures of, and a friendship with, Jacob Burckhardt.[20] Meanwhile, war was flickering into the distance even though Wagner was spoiling to "fight for Prussia." This was their first conflict, for a deep hatred of war was growing in Nietzsche. He told Rohde how worried he was about the imminent future in which he foresaw a disguised Middle Ages. He found Prussia obnoxious and uncivilized, a place "where underlings and clerics sprout like mushrooms, and their miasma will soon darken all of Germany for us."

Wagner, in contrast, would have given anything to meet Bismarck and Moltke. Cosima noted that he wanted to do it "without their knowing who he is. He would like to be near them as a completely obscure subordinate."

However, Wagner's chauvinism abated slightly after Prussia's easy victory. Richard said to Cosima: "By right we can only maintain silence regarding the terribly great thing that has occurred: no boasting about victories, no lamenting about sufferings, a deep, silent, realization that God is ruling."

Tribschen was thus filled with a patriotic mentality. And Wagner, who hoped that the victory of the Germans would bring the victory of his art, was excitedly working on his *Imperial March*. The children had to learn the national chorus in it, and they caroled out their "Heil dem Kaiser!" throughout the villa, not always to the delectation of visitors, such as Cosima's mother. Countess d'Agoult, according to Wagner, had that French quality known as "heroic frivolity." Nevertheless, she was fanatically French. Nietzsche was unable to show any sympathy with the "great German emotion" of the Wagners. Nationalism was completely alien to him. His letters to Tribschen speak of anxieties about the future; militarism was going to crush everything. The master would flare up: "I can take anything, policemen, soldiers, a throttling of the press, a reduction of parlamentarism, but *no* obscurantism."

Cosima's birthday on December 25, 1870 was celebrated in a special way. Richard had been preparing a surprise for weeks. Telegrams were dispatched all over the world. Nietzsche received an invitation. There were negotiations with musicians, and in the Hotel du Lac in town there was talk of secret meetings. Wise and devoted, Cosima pretended not to notice anything.

On the morning of the birthday, at the crack of dawn, when it was still dark over the lake, the first orchestral draft of the *Siegfried Idyll,* which had been completed on December 4, swept through the air. Nietzsche, although freezing, soon became oblivious of the harsh morning as he listened.

Cosima's diary goes: "There is nothing I can tell you about this day, my children, nothing about my feelings, nothing about my mood, nothing, nothing. I will only narrate the events, drily and matter-of-factly. As I awoke, my ears caught a sound, it kept swelling up, I could no longer think I was dreaming. Music came forth, and what music! When it was over, Richard and the five children came to my room and handed me the score of the symphonic birthday poem. I was in tears, and so was the entire house. Richard had stationed his orchestra on the stairs and thus our Tribschen was hallowed forever."

Nietzsche once again had bought a reproduction of a Dürer engraving for a Christmas present, this time his own favorite, *Knight, Death, and Devil.* As he told his mother and sister, a happy fluke had brought it into his hands. From now on, this copper engraving recurred more and more often in his life. The theologian Franz Overbeck[21] received it as a friendly gift to recall and confirm their joint knighthood in the spirit of truth. When Elisabeth migrated to Paraguay with her husband many years later, Nietzsche could find no more encouraging wedding and going-away present than that engraving.

The earliest sign of his love for Dürer's picture is in *The Birth of Tragedy.* Because of this book, a grateful reader in Basel had sent him the engraving, and the passage in question was the one that Cosima most admired. It outlines precisely the meeting of

Schopenhauer's philosophy and Wagner's creative will in Nietzsche's mind:

"A lonely and desolate man could choose no better symbol
than the knight with death and the devil, as Dürer drew him, the
armored knight, with the hard, steely eyes, who knows how to
follow his course of terror, unerringly, past his dreadful compan-
ions, and yet hopelessly, alone with his dog and his mount. Our
Schopenhauer was such a Dürer knight; he lacked all hope but he
wanted truth. He is without peer."

This quote corresponds to the sentence in Nietzsche's letter to
Rohde in October 1868: "I relish in Wagner what I relish in
Schopenhauer, the ethical air, the Faustian fragrance, the cross,
death, the tomb . . ."

On Christmas Eve, Nietzsche came over from Basel for just a
few hours but stayed longer than planned. For the second day of
Christmas, he handed to Wagner Cosima's birthday gift, the manuscript of the *Genesis of the Tragic Idea*. Cosima was thrilled:

"The depth and grandeur of these views, expressed with such
utter terseness, is amazing. We pursue his thoughts with the
greatest and liveliest interest. I am particularly glad that Richard's
ideas in this area could be expanded."

These hopes seemed justified, and Cosima did not stop reproaching Nietzsche about the way he delivered his thoughts. She
said that anyone could have bright and great ideas, but it was
crucial to express them in a decisive and developed form. Nietzsche listened loyally. He was imbued with the truth and justice of
her views.

The hours of his visit grew into days, and thus Nietzsche remained through the holidays. On December 28, the Master felt
a strong urge to read the third act of his *Tristan* to the others, and
they wandered from room to room, declaiming. It was cold down-
stairs, Nietzsche was living in the "thinking room," and so they
went upstairs, where "Fidi" was sleeping. Wagner lowered his
voice so as not to wake the child. "A dreadful impact of greatness
on me," wrote Cosima in her diary.

The campaign in France came to an end, Paris fell, and the
German Empire was proclaimed in Versailles, of all places. All
this while, Wagner was finishing the score of *Siegfried* in Tribschen. With the actual composition terminated, the orchestration

required a long, difficult, and responsible labor, which he brought to a close on February 5, 1871.

That spring, Nietzsche was still not in the best of health. Every other night, he couldn't sleep a wink. He yearned to leave the whole academic business, partly to have more time for his book. He finally obtained a leave because he complained about periodic exhaustion and wanted "to follow the voice of his nature" at last. The authorities announced: "Granted a leave of absence for the winter semester for the purpose of restoral of health."

At Tribschen, they were alarmed about Nietzsche's condition, for Wagner had hoped his friend would come every Saturday and Sunday to take part in the Beethoven Quartet evenings, which Hans Richter had arranged, and scheduled on the weekends out of consideration for Nietzsche.

"Must it be?" asked Nietzsche with the notes of Beethoven's Quartet in F Major, and necessity demanded: "It must be." (This is in Beethoven's Quartet manuscript.)

6

TRAGEDY
AND MUSICAL DRAMA

The doctor, Professor Liebermeister, had opposed Nietzsche's premature return to teaching. Now, in spring 1871, he insisted that Nietzsche take a long vacation on the Italian lakes.

Nietzsche went to Tribschen to make his good-byes, and then traveled on to Lugano. His sister accompanied him until early April, but since any further voyaging was too strenuous they stayed at the Hotel du Parc in Lugano. They also had bad luck with the weather.

Nietzsche was bothered that no measures had as yet been taken in Basel to give Rohde his Classics chair. He wrote him that he was annoyed and unhappy about it, and he also complained: "I've been in Lugano for over six weeks now and haven't even seen Lake Como or Lago Maggiore. The weather is by and large quite un-Italian; I've sensed nothing of a spring that was anything more than our German spring."

But his anxieties were interrupted by better moods. He would then work on his "philosophical justifications," a piece on the "Origin and Purpose of Tragedy," which was to both prepare his leave-taking from Classics and be useful to his labor on the bigger book.

He devoted himself more and more steadily to his philosophic work. The main features of his philosophic conception were outlined. "Why, even if I'm to become a poet, I'm quite ready." However, he was still wavering as to what route he should take to his goal. First he would turn to a piece of new metaphysics, next to a new aesthetics, and then again to a new principle of education with a total rejection of all contemporary high schools and universities.

"More than anything I feel the growth of this private world when I, calm but not cool, review all the so-called world history of the past ten months and employ it as a means for my good intentions, with no exaggerated reverence. Pride and madness are really far too weak expressions for my spiritual insomnia. This condition enables me to look upon my entire university position as something irrelevant, nay, often embarrassing, and that philosophical professorship really attracts me only for your sake, since I can regard even this professorship as merely something provisional" (to Rohde).

It was only the summer of 1871 that saw an abatement of Nietzsche's complaints—insomnia, hemorrhoids, and a taste of blood. He promptly read parts of his book aloud at Tribschen. The title was to be: *Origin and Purpose of Tragedy.* To Nietzsche's great dismay, Wagner revealed a slight disappointment. There was too little that bore on his own work. With all his enthusiasm for Wagner and his art, Nietzsche's scholarly conscience resisted taking in any ideas that were contrary to the theme of the book.

The draft, which he had handed to Cosima at Christmas as a birthday gift, presented a Wagner disciple par excellence, such as Nietzsche himself scarcely realized. Now came revision upon revision. His sister later described his first book as arising out of "aesthetic problems and answers that had been fermenting in him for years."

Two lectures delivered in early 1870 had accompanied his planning. He now privately published one of these lectures in 1871: *Socrates and Tragedy.* The skepticism of the Wagners towards this essay had already been voiced when Cosima maintained that one cannot oppose the rationalism of Socrates and Euripides to the tragedy of the Greeks. Nietzsche rapidly included a glorification of Wagner's musical drama in his theories on Greek tragedy. With full conviction and most likely in all honesty, the author now claimed that tragedy, which had once arisen out of music, had been reborn with Wagner.

Early in 1872, the piece came out with a new title: *The Birth of Tragedy* or *Hellenism and Pessimism.* Two years later, there was a second edition, partly revised, with a long epilogue praising Wagner and his *Tristan.*

Whatever may have been the basis of this book, which Nietzsche eventually described as "dubious," it nevertheless treated certain issues of prime importance to him and bearing on his entire existence. The era in which it defiantly appeared, the time of the Franco-Prussian War, demonstrated this all too clearly. While Europe reverberated from the booming of the Battle of Worth, Nietzsche was off in "some corner of the Alps . . . at once worried and not worried," and setting down his ideas on the Greeks. A few weeks later, he found himself "under the walls of Metz, having still not shaken off the question marks that he put after the alleged 'serenity' of the Greeks. . . ."

Various things contributed to Nietzsche's development: The study of the Greeks, the devotion to music (not creative at that moment, but always present through Wagner's works), and the passionate worship of Schopenhauer. This unfermented blend of philological labor, his own philosophical cognition, and utmost admiration ultimately evolved into Nietzsche's lonesome position in modern intellectual history. In many great minds of the past, including Goethe, Schiller, and Heine, Nietzsche found the polarity of "Apollonian" and "Dionysian," two concepts acquiring a key function in his thought.

For Nietzsche, the antithesis of the two notions became a synthesis in Greek drama. The hostile Greek gods Apollo and Dionysus joined into a necessary interdependence. It was *Tristan* that helped young Nietzsche confront the Dionysian, forcing him to think about those aspects. In the heady and orgiastic language of *Tristan*, woe seemed to conjure up weal, and weal woe.

The new *Foreword to Richard Wagner* scarcely needed to mention that the book was first sketched when the Master was working on his tribute to Beethoven. The text crackles throughout with the intellectual exchange between these two men. Thus Nietzsche writes:

"Under the spell of the Dionysian, not only is the alliance between man and man restored: but Nature, estranged, hostile, or subjugated, celebrates anew her feast of reconciliation with her prodigal son, Man. The earth freely offers her gifts and peacefully the beasts of prey draw near from rock and desert. The scales of Dionysus overflow with blossoms and wreaths: the panther and the tiger stride beneath his yoke. One can transmute Beethoven's *Ode to Joy* into a painting without restraining one's imagination when the awe-struck millions sink into the dust: That is how one can approach the Dionysian. Now, the slave is a free man, now all the rigid and inimical distinctions are smashed, the boundaries which misery, arbitrariness, or 'impudent fashion' have established between men. Now, with the gospel of world harmony, each man feels . . . as one with his neighbor, as though the veil of the Maia had been torn to bits and only shreds of it were fluttering about before the mysterious Primal One. Man expresses himself singing and dancing as part of a higher communion: he has forgotten how to walk or speak and is about to soar balletically into the air. Enchantment speaks forth from his gestures. As now the animals speak and the earth gives forth milk and honey, so too does something supernatural resound from him: he feels like God, he himself goes about as ecstatic and transported as he saw the gods striding in his dreams. Man is no longer an artist, he has become an artwork: the artistic power of all Nature, for the highest blissful satisfaction of the Primal One reveals itself in the thrills of intoxication. The noblest clay, the costliest marble are kneaded and hewn here, Man, and the chisel strokes of the Dionysian world artist are accompanied by the call of the Eleusinian mysteries: 'You plunge down, you millions? Didst thou sense the Creator, World?' "

In early Greek culture, Nietzsche saw two forms of art, tragedy and music, that can be characterized as Apollonian and Dionysian. Both of them converged in Attic tragedy, Dionysian wildness tightened into Apollonian rigor. The Dionysian chorus, in Nietzsche's opinion, evolved into tragedy, and music nourished myth which the theater tamed in performance. Nietzsche, to Cosima's vexation, viewed the dreadfulness and mystery of the tragic, which revealed itself in Hellenic theater, as the opposite of the skepticism and criticism of enlightening philosophy since Socrates. For Nietzsche, the question of science, the analysis of problems, carried the death seeds of all culture. Today's imminent impoverishment of Western art through a purely scientific perspective of the world was already looming, and young Nietzsche hoped against hope that a new form of art would save mankind. The revival of music, naturally through Wagner's genius, would infuse new life into the moribund tragic myth. The self-complaisance and self-righteousness of technology might thus be ousted from the field. But so might the dogmatism of faith, as in senile Christianity.

This was Nietzsche's first open polemic against the Church. He put down Christianity as just another form of Socratic analytical disintegration. Morality could hardly justify the world anymore; mankind had to get beyond Schopenhauer's demand for renunciation and beyond compassion as the quintessence of Christian doctrine. Nietzsche's thoughts were thus germane with Wagner's, but from a stance rooted in philosophical frustration. The world was no longer to be morally justified—a new beginning from the paraprimitive aboriginal state: Dionysus was to be helped back to power.

Nietzsche recalls the spring rites of the ancients in the intoxication of sexual excitement, the subjective vanishes in self-oblivion, the covenant between man and man is renewed, in an attempt at reverting to the primal unity.

That is the concept of the spell cast by the Dionysian. Its antithesis is the Apollonian: a shaping domination of poetic fancy in dreams, as a limitation, a liberation from wildness. On the one side, mystical self-alienation; on the other, awareness of the individual condition, whose unity with the innermost basis of the world is revealed as a metaphor in the dream image.

The Dionysian finds utterance mainly in music; the Apollonian in plastic and literary art. Expressionism of the essence of the genre and impressionism of the individual phenomenon—Nietzsche sees them as wed and jointly giving birth to the tragedy of the Greeks. Thus, when he speaks about Greek serenity, we do not encounter an optimism akin, say, to the self-satisfaction of modern civilization; instead, this serenity is the necessary counterpoise to tragic knowledge. The illusion of sensual pleasure conquers the terror of world pondering. "Here, nothing recalls asceticism, spirituality, or duty; here, all that speaks to us is a triumphant existence, in which all that exists is deified, no matter whether it be good or evil."

How did Nietzsche feel Greek tragedy had come into being? He says: From the tragic chorus. To understand, let us trace the origin of the word. The original use of "chorus," as a delimited area for dancing, widened into the meaning of a circular dance combined with singing, and performed at festivals to honor a deity. Ultimately, the term was restricted to this singing.

In this connection, there is an interesting avowal by Schiller: "Emotion initially has no definite or lucid object for me; the object forms only later. A certain musical mood precedes, and the poetic idea only comes after."

We can likewise picture the musical performance at Dionysian festivals as a communion of the feelings leading to self-oblivion. The communion was at first expressed in dance and song, and then intensified until the music became well-nigh visible to the disciples of Dionysus.

From this perspective (the origin of tragedy in the Dionysian chorus), the orchestra in front of the stage gains a deeper significance. For originally, the stage and the action were the contents of the singing.

Wagner similarly explained the relationship between music and action; except now the orchestra rather than the chorus had to fulfill the creative mission of the music: "It (the music) sounds and what it sounds you can behold up there on the stage."

Nietzsche's prophecy focuses on the removal of the genius of music from tragedy, which he regards as menaced by optimistic dialectics. Socrates, as the grand maintainer of the anti-Dionysian, is, for Nietzsche, the prototype of the theoretical man who seeks redemption not in the subconscious of artistic creation but in the conscious of scientific cognition. The hope of seeing the spirit of German music restore the Hellenic feeling deceived both Nietzsche and Wagner. Precisely because Nietzsche guessed that the era of Socratic man was far from over, he exclaimed: "Just dare to be tragic men!" Wagner's faith in his personal future success could not shake Nietzsche's later realization that man was doomed to science.

Nietzsche, to his astonishment, found himself in his first book, and it was only now that he saw his tasks and possibilities. His work is a monument to the intransience of such moments, one of the strangest love documents of all times, and perhaps even today it remains Nietzsche's purest, though not most important, effort.

Right after visiting Tribschen at Christmas 1870, Nietzsche, homeward bound from Lugano, read what the grateful composer had written him: "I have never read anything finer than your book!" And on January 18, 1872, after the work came out, Cosima explained: "In this book, you have conjured spirits that I thought were only at our Master's beck and call."

Such a response instantly had the desired effect. On April 15, 1871, Richard and Cosima started out on their first trip into the "Empire," together with Hans Richter, who left them in Augsburg. They arrived in Bayreuth on April 16, as evening was gathering. Meanwhile, Nietzsche, reluctantly staying behind, was wondering how he could collect a phalanx of pugnacious friends to actively aid him in realizing the Bayreuth Festival project. He was fully committed to the idea of having Bayreuth generate new impulses for art.

In line with this plan, Wagner had decided in summer 1870 not to permit his operas to be mounted anywhere else. As long as a perfect staging could not be achieved, he preferred renunciation. At the same time, however, he energetically proclaimed his demand for a theater of his own. Thus he wrote to Ludwig:

"People must understand that for my works, which outer chance has flung into the genre of 'opera,' I would have to have my very own playhouse, to which not the indolent opera public, accustomed to utter trivia, would be invited, but only such people who hitherto remained away from those shallow entertainments."

This statement in May 1870 was the first definition of the modern festival idea, which in our time has reached a point of absurdity with an almost endless number of imitations. For a long while, Wagner had been hoping to carry out his plans in Munich with the king's help. This hope, partly through his own fault, had to be abandoned. He thought of shifting the *Festspiele* to Nuremberg but then decided against that. The locale could not be a metropolis or an industrial center; he was seeking the idyll of a small town.

Wagner had seen Bayreuth twenty-five years earlier, prior to his marriage with Minna Planer or his maiden opera *Das Liebesverbot*. When still a little *Kapellmeister* under Theater Manager Bethmann (who played Magdeburg in winter and Lauchstädt and Rudolstadt in summer), Wagner had come to Bayreuth by chance. He felt love at first sight for this sleepy margravial town. For several decades, his memory of it receded before the restlessness of his life. But now, realizing he had to secure his work for posterity and refusing to have anything to do with pedestrian stages, he looked upon this Franconian town as a wish come true. Hence, "sub rosa and unnoticed," he and Cosima traveled from Switzerland to Germany, where he hoped to find a location for his own playhouse.

He inspected the renowned margravial opera, one of the last in pure Italian Baroque on German soil. And he instantly recognized that this building was out of the question for his purposes. It was too small, the stage too primitive, and there was no way of expanding it. But "the characteristic features and the position of the friendly town" were just what he was looking for. Cosima, in her journal, crowed that the populace of Bayreuth had simply been in a state of turmoil during Wagner's sojourn.

In late fall, Wagner took another trip to Bayreuth, this time to start negotiating with the authorities. He was bowled over. Unlike Munich, all doors opened up to him. His daring enterprise, as he states in his biography, elicited "an eagerness to please surpassing all expectations." With a farsightedness unusual for municipal bureaucracies, Bayreuth foresaw the historic importance of Wagner's project. The minutes of the Bayreuth Town Council on November 16, 1871 contain the sentence: "The Town Council is unanimously in favor of giving every possible support . . . to Richard Wagner's grandiose undertaking." Words soon became deeds. The town presented Wagner with "an incomparably beautiful and generous piece of land, not far from town, for the purpose of erecting a theater."

Meanwhile, Wagner and Cosima traveled on to Berlin, partly in order to pay their respects to Chancelor Bismarck, who was extremely reserved about King Ludwig of Bavaria. Although Bismarck received Wagner cordially at his home, he seemed quite uncharmed by the lively little Saxon.

The main reason for the journey, however, was to mobilize the Berlin Patronage Association, of which Nietzsche's friend Gersdorff was a member. They met for preliminary discussions, especially with Carl Tausig, the ad hoc manager of the projected Festival, and Marie Countess von Schleinitz, the influential and indefatigable promoter. In 1863, as Marie von Buch, she had met Wagner in Breslau, and now she was married to a court official, who carried out his beautiful wife's every wish for the composer. She made Berlin the business center of the Bayreuth undertaking.

Tausig succeeded in enlisting the necessary number of patrons for Wagner, whom he fervently admired. Unhappily, this highly gifted pianist died just half a year later, of typhus, at the age of twenty-nine. Now the main pillar of the action was Frau von Schleinitz.

Later, Wagner admitted that he actually owed the creation of Bayreuth to this woman, who was so greatly lionized in the new society of the *Reich.* Tireless, she agitated and solicited, not without having to endure the smirks of people and the open mockery of the press. For no one could believe that such wishful thinking would ever come true, that a composer would have his personal theater, which, remote from the big cities, would perform his operas for just a few weeks every couple of summers. The venture seemed absurd, the risk enormous. But it was hard to withstand the enthusiasm of this woman. By spring 1872, Wagner, with no help from King Ludwig, had at his disposal a capital of some three hundred thousand thalers (worth many times that amount today). The first few subscribers of the Patronage Association included Kaiser Wilhelm I and the Khedive of Egypt.

And now the move to Bayreuth was at hand. Simply impossible things had come to fruition in the year after the Franco-Prussian peace treaty. Wagner's planning had more of a goal than ever. During the plenary session of the Prussian Academy of the Arts, he was permitted to read his essay *On the Aims of Opera.* At the Royal Opera House, before the Kaiser, Empress Augusta, and the court, he gave a benefit concert for the King Wilhelm Association, placing the *Imperial March* next to Beethoven's *Fifth Symphony* and selections from the *Kapellmeister*'s own music dramas.

The Wagners also stopped in Leipzig. Clemens Brockhaus told them the awkward news that Nietzsche, originally dedicating his essay *Homer's Contest* to Cosima, had now inscribed it to his sister with the same accompanying poem. Cosima felt offended in her claim to exclusivity:

"I had to laugh at first, but then, discussing it with Richard, I took it as a dubious thing, a kind of mania for betrayal, to ensure himself, as it were, against making a great impact."

Mannheim also had a Wagner Association, founded by the piano-maker Heckel; and in September 1871 Wagner conducted there. Nietzsche, coming from Basel to attend, told Gersdorff: "I know of no higher or more sublime state than I lived through here!" And to Rohde, with whom he was corresponding about the outer form of the book, he wrote: "What are all other artistic experiences measured by these last ones! I felt like a man for whom a premonition has at last come true. For music is just that and nothing else! And just that and nothing else is what I mean with the word 'music' when I describe the Dionysian!"

Heckel's son Karl had reported what took place in Mannheim a week before Christmas 1871: It was getting on towards midnight, the town was fast asleep. But the railroad station was all a-bustle. Friends were boisterously greeting and hailing one another, curiosity-seekers clustered in groups. They were excitedly awaiting a train from the East. When it pulled in, out climbed a short, colorful figure with uncommonly nimble movements. A cheer broke out: "Richard Wagner, *hoch, hoch, hoch!*"

"For goodness' sake!" the celebrity cheerfully exclaimed in a Saxon accent, "I'm no prince!"

And then he shook hands with the numerous members of the just recently founded Wagner Association. He explained that he had inspected the building site in Bayreuth on the previous day and that the announcement of his Mannheim concert had boosted his faith in the project.

Shortly after Wagner's coming, Frau Cosima also arrived from Tribschen. Her escort, who helped her out of the train, was a young man of medium height, with dark brown hair and a bushy moustache. His spectacles made him look like a scholar—which was apparently contradicted by his careful wardrobe, his quasi-military bearing, and his clear, bright voice. The next day it turned out that Nietzsche had come to Mannheim expressly for the concert. He didn't miss a single rehearsal and was one of the few guests when Wagner performed the manuscript of the *Siegfried Idyll,* which thus had a sort of premiere in Mannheim.

Nietzsche, as Karl Heckel relates, occasionally joined the Wagners when they visited old Heckel, and deep conversations took place between Wagner, Cosima, and Nietzsche. Mainly they seemed to revolve around the Greeks and Schopenhauer, but also the state of culture in Germany. Young Heckel's interest was aroused in the Basel professor, who was truly devoted to Wagner and had such deep sympathy for goals of the Wagner Association. (When, after Wagner's departure, the news spread that the Master was dangerously sick with typhus in Tribschen, Nietzsche instantly wired Emil Heckel: "Rumor totally unfounded; best news from Tribschen. Happy New Year's wishes to the Wagner Association.")

Before leaving Mannheim, Wagner warmly invited Nietzsche to come with his sister and spend the Pentecost holidays in Tribschen. Elisabeth's account of their last evening there is interesting for its period coloring:

"The sun was setting, but the moon already stood full and clear above the radiant snowfield of the Witlis; as the brightness of the sun gradually passed into the wan light of the moon, as the lake and the so picturesquely formed, sharply outlined mountain grew more and more delicate, gossamer, and transparent, more and more spiritualized as it were, our lively conversation halted, and we all sank into a dreamy hush. The four of us (actually five) were strolling down the so-called Brigand's Road, on the very edge of the lake, with Frau Cosima and my brother in front, Cosima in a pink cashmere frock with wide genuine-lace facings down to the very hem; a large Florentine hat with a wreath of pink roses hung from her arm; behind her, dignified and ponderous, strode the gigantic coal-black Newfoundland Russ, followed by Wagner and myself, Wagner in a Netherlandish painter's costume: black velvet jacket, black satin knickerbockers, black silk stockings, a pale-blue satin cravat richly pleated, with fine linen and lace in between, and the artist's beret on the then still luxuriant brown hair.

"I can still clearly see the light falling through the trees upon the various shapes as we strolled in silence, peering across the silvery lake; we harkened to the gentle murmur of the lapping waves, and to each of us, there sounded from this sweet monotonous melody, as from the notes of a magic horn, the song of his own thoughts.

"The goal of our wandering was the hermitage, a bark cottage on the highest point of the estate, affording, in the almost sunny moonlight, a delicious view far across the lake and the surrounding chain of mountains. Gradually the spell of silence was broken; Wagner, Cosima, and my brother began talking about the tragedy of human life, about the Greeks, the Germans, about plans and wishes."

Wagner seemed to embody what Schopenhauer had prepared

in Nietzsche. The last thin partition between Nietzsche's intellectual world and his musical alter ego appeared to have toppled. This is a major reason for the disciple's deep gratitude to his master for the creative torrent of works, which (and not just in the author's opinion) were full of music: *The Birth of Tragedy* and the writings encircling it. Wagner allowed Nietzsche an intensive part in his life and the labor in his artistic studio that the younger man, overcoming his inhibitions as a barely trained musician, found the courage to release the verbal instrumentalist in himself. And the later Nietzsche, inwardly aloof from Wagner, never forgot this about the "great benefactor of my life."

In summer 1871, Nietzsche's interest concentrated on *The Birth of Tragedy*. For a long while, the Leipzig publisher Engelmann was shrouded in silence. Finally, he informed the author that an expert had felt "a slight shudder" at reading the essay. Nietzsche impatiently took back the manuscript, though subsequently it turned out that Engelmann had been quite ready to accept it. Thus, when Nietzsche was celebrating an exuberant birthday with Gersdorff and Rohde in Naumburg during autumn vacation, the friends resolved to spend a few days together in Leipzig. A keyboard piece was to preserve the "transfigured remembrance of the happiness of his fall holidays." To copy the music, Nietzsche employed a man in straitened circumstances. Wishing to help out, he recommended the copyist to Wagner, who never reacted.

The friends pleaded with Nietzsche to submit his book to Wagner's publisher E. W. Fritzsch, who, as director of a music publishing house in Leipzig, would surely not be taken aback by the "modern problems." And Fritzsch, after some delay, did accept the work. Wagner, initially perturbed by the choice of a *music* publisher, wrote in autumn 1871:

"My dear worthy friend! I beg you fervently to tell me point-blank, as your true friend, the reasons that moved you to offer your promising manuscript, so highly regarded by me, to the music businessman Fritzsch. Your having withdrawn it from Engelmann makes me conjecture certain things, in regard to which I desire, out of pure and sympathetic interest in you, to hear your confident information." Nietzsche's explanation was then followed by Wagner's recommendation to Fritzsch.

Nietzsche could not comply with the invitation to spend Christmas 1871 in Lucerne; he needed rest and solitude to work out six lectures *On the Future of Our Educational Institutions.* To make up for his refusal, he sent Cosima a birthday present on the first day of Christmas: his early piece for piano and violin, *A New Year's Eve*, with a dedication. "I am anxious to know what I will hear about my musical work since I have *never* heard anything competent." That can hardly come as a surprise, for almost nothing in Nietzsche's music is reminiscent of Wagner. If anything, the influence is Schumann's; later details anticipate Mahler and von Webern. These filigree, unextravagant compositions were certainly alien to Wagner's taste. In 1886, Cosima wrote to Felix Mottl:

"Just think, my dear Felix, that I once received *New Year's Bells* in Tribschen. I sat down and played. Jacob Stock, my then butler, who would always say to me throughout the various vicissitudes of life: 'One just has to be *fin,* ' stopped setting the table, listened attentively, and finally turned away with the words: 'Don't like it.' I must confess that I laughed so hard I couldn't play any further."

But contrary to such opinion, Nietzsche's musical talent was extraordinary, and a crucial part of his thought and philosophy. Hence, it was especially musicians who first felt they understood him. The Dionysian in particular, from Nietzsche's new perspective, was closer to their creative aims than the conceptual world of the philologist, moralist, and biologist. Of course, his musician friends, too, failed to realize that his Dionysian approach was meant to go beyond art. In a vision of the future, he really saw the overtowering man of affect, such as he had pictured when, in the *Birth of Tragedy*, he measured the prototypes of world-negation and intellectualism on him. Though the ultimate consequences of these ideas might elude the conventional understanding of music, we can still assume one thing. These ideas arose from the same impulse leading in future decades to the dithyrambic music of a Gustav Mahler or Arnold Schönberg: that ecstasy and visionary exultation which generated a mounting musical expression. But even Nietzsche's psychological analysis of art must be viewed in analogy to his sense of music and his joy in polyphony. His urge to plumb the depths of the psyche is like the musician's desire to bring to light those spiritual processes which can be depicted only through music.

Nietzsche's book *The Birth of Tragedy* was a creative aid to knowledge here. This maiden effort often affected unprepared readers like a musical experience. Nietzsche himself called it "music for those who are baptized for music, who are bound together from the very start in collective and unwonted experiences of art."

The most willing reader at first was Richard Wagner, whom the author had sent a still-unbound copy on January 2, 1872. The Master could regard it as written *pro domo sua,* albeit not in the shape originally intended. Early in April 1871, Nietzsche, on the way back from Lugano to Basel, had dropped in at Tribschen, only to find Wagner in despair about his projects in Germany. The young scholar resolved to publicly take his friend's side, and in addition to the *Birth of Tragedy,* which picked up on Classical themes, he would evoke the rebirth of tragedy from the spirit of German music as well.

Nietzsche also added something to the manuscript, describing it to Rohde as follows: "The entire last section, as yet unknown to you, will most certainly astound you; I have ventured a great deal, but in a quite tremendous way I can call to myself: *Animam salvavi;* which is why I recall the piece with great satisfaction and won't worry, even though the book may be utterly offensive and actually arouse a few screams of indignation when published." He was more right than he realized.

The letter to Rohde also makes it clear how many personal opinions he had suppressed for Wagner's sake:

"No one has the foggiest notion of the way a book like this comes into being, the effort and torment to keep oneself pure to this degree in the face of all the ideas flooding in from all sides, the courage of the concept, and the sincerity in the execution: and perhaps least of all, the enormous task I had to perform for Wagner and which truly provoked many and heavy contristations within me."

Wagner didn't know to what extent the new version referred to him. During Nietzsche's last stay in Tribschen, they had only discussed publishing problems. Prior to the Whitsuntide visit, Nietzsche didn't want to reveal how much homage he had paid to Wagner. We can credit his sister's statement that she was strongly urged not to drop even the slightest hint. And thus, Wagner's letter of November 21, concentrates on Nietzsche's position in regard to the honorarium and merely adds: "Lots of luck with epigraphy and Plato, whom we are now also dealing with at Tribschen."

Nietzsche had to swallow his pride in a thousand different ways merely for the happiness of existing for the sublime couple. The Master would say "My Nietzsche" to him, and this "My" was the loftiest dignity he ever bestowed.

The added "Interference of the Most Modern Things" to the book shifted the audience. Nietzsche had chiefly wanted to win over Classicists and historians to his view of the Greeks. But they drily declined. Instead, Wagner's followers swarmed to the work, mistaking the side issue for the main issue and ignoring the basic difference between Nietzsche's and Wagner's attitudes on art.

No doubt, Hans von Bülow, too, clung to the book's glorification of Wagner. He still believed in the idol of his life and passionately recommended him to others. There is no detailed written utterance by Bülow on *The Birth of Tragedy*. But he must have discussed it with Nietzsche while sojourning in Basel towards the end of March 1872. Nietzsche always thought back to that day with delight, for Bülow, as a token of gratitude, asked if he might play a few pieces, including, to Nietzsche's great joy, Chopin's *Barcarole*. Nietzsche's letters variously mention Bülow's enthusiasm for *The Birth of Tragedy*.

To Rohde, he wrote on April 11, 1872:

"Hans von Bülow, whom I didn't yet know, has called here and inquired whether he might dedicate his translation of Leopardi (the result of his leisure hours in Italy) to me. He is so excited about my book that he travels about with countless copies to give away."

On the very day of his visit, Bülow sent the book to the composer Felix Draeseke,[1] to whom he wrote five days later: "Did you receive my greeting from Basel in the guise of Nietzsche's *Birth of Tragedy*? You've got to read it—it's absolutely smashing. The author, a propos, is a charming person, still rather young."

Nietzsche's esteem for Bülow went back well into the 1850's. With his flair for the extraordinary, he had recognized Bülow, who wrote and concertized, as courageous and clever. He also discovered a polemicist in the virtuoso and conductor. Every recital, every pronouncement of his was, for Nietzsche, a blow against sloppiness and philistinism. Bülow's zeal was not only for introducing new things (recall his promotion of Tchaikovsky in Western Europe); he also knew how to draw new values from old masters.

However, a closer personal relationship never could mellow between him and Nietzsche. After Basel and a meeting in Munich during March 1872, the two men never saw one another again. This is all the more regrettable as Bülow would surely have been fine company for the philosopher. He was earnest, almost severe on the inside; but on the outside, full of exuberant humor that could also shine in aggressive jokes. What happened was that in those very years, 1871–72, Bülow was starting his virtuoso tours —primarily, no doubt, to insure a private fortune for his daughters. He traveled up and down the Old World and the New, ultimately becoming Royal Concert Master of Hanover in September 1877. Still, Bülow was one of Nietzsche's few readers whose appreciation the philosopher valued at the end of his life as much as before.

Frau von Schleinitz, too, was spellbound by Nietzsche's book. Cosima urged her to convey her impression to the author, "for he has laid the book at your feet of his own accord, without our having asked him to do so. And it is certainly fair that those who sympathize with him impart their appreciation, since he garners little joy from *school*—as one might have expected."

His desires for relaxing and working in Basel were thwarted when Romundt and Overbeck came to visit. They all sat in Nietzsche's apartment, sometimes joined by Wagner. Together they read Gottfried Keller's *People of Seldwyla*, and when Nietzsche described himself and his friends as the "three Kammachers," Wagner laughed until tears came to his eyes. Mention must be made that in those days Keller, whom the philosopher later knew casually, didn't have very gracious thoughts about Professor Nietzsche. At the appearance of the third *Untimely Reflection*, he wrote:

"Nietzsche, they say, is a young professor barely 26 years old, a student of Ritschl in Leipzig, and a Classicist, driven by megalomania to make a splash in other fields. Otherwise not untalented, he has supposedly gotten all mixed up with Wagnerania and Schopenhauerania and formed a cult in Basel with others who are similarly mixed up."

In point of fact, except for the approval of the Wagners, Hans von Bülow, and the author's closest friends, *The Birth of Tragedy* at first had scarcely any positive echo. Nietzsche's colleagues did not go along with his friends; they held back or else maintained an icy silence. On New Year's Eve 1871, the manuscript was given to Professor Ritschl by the Leipzig publisher. But the scholar did not care for the book, he shook his head in disappointment—and maintained his silence. In reply to Nietzsche's agitated inquiry, he wrote:

"You cannot possibly expect a scholar to condemn *knowledge* and see a redeeming and liberating power in art *alone.*"

What Ritschl had jotted down in his diary a month before, "a bright spree," now became the consensus.

The new book made life difficult for the author. A review by Erwin Rohde was turned down flat by the *Literarisches Centralblatt.* And the following May, twenty-four-year-old Ulrich von Wilamowitz-Moellendorff,[2] once Nietzsche's schoolmate at Schulpforta, put out a pamphlet: Entitled *Future Philology, A Reply to Friedrich Nietzsche's "Birth of Tragedy,"* it tried to defend Classical learning against Wagnerite bondage:

"The author has shattered the divine images with which poetry and fine art have populated our heaven, smashed them in order to worship the idol Richard Wagner in their dust."

Wilamowitz faulted Nietzsche for ignoring research and historical data.

Nietzsche's downfall as a scholar and philosopher appeared to be sealed; in the winter semester, not a single student registered for his classes. No one could forgive the so-promising young philologist for turning his first book into a polemic for the dubious Wagner cause. Among established scholars, only Jacob Burckhardt offered him sympathy, although he too rejected the composer. What Nietzsche had to say about the Greeks aroused his admiration.

Wagner defended Nietzsche in an open letter in the *Norddeutsche Allgemeine Zeitung,* but it didn't help. He couldn't refute the criticism from scholars. In his "missive," Wagner flung his polemics at the attacks and challenged his young friend "to reach into the noblest source of the German spirit for revelation and indication as to how German education is to be constituted if it shall help the resurrected nation achieve its noblest goals."

When Nietzsche had sent him the Wilamowitz pamphlet, Wagner had sweepingly commented that he no longer could see why making music was still necessary. The professors, training specialized professors in turn, lacked any humanistic background whatsoever.

In October 1872, Rohde attempted a learned rebuttal of Wilamowitz's attack: *Afterphilologie (Pseudo-Scholarship)*. But his accusal that Wilamowitz had disrespectfully adulterated Nietzsche's intentions got Nietzsche nowhere. Even though his students began trickling back after a while, his scholarly reputation had been deeply shaken. The *Nationalzeitung* actually degraded him into a "literary lackey."

Who can say whether Nietzsche's position would have looked any better without the Wagner propaganda he had added to the book?

But Nietzsche was not dispirited. The above-mentioned lectures went further than the book. He fixed his sights on educational philistinism and professorial narrowmindedness; and surprisingly, he made a hit with scholars. An inquiry came from Greifswald: Would he be interested in a professorship there? Cosima quickly realized that Nietzsche turned this offer down mainly because he didn't want to give up his personal association with Jacob Burckhardt. Wagner was jealous of this scholar whom he unfairly put down as a "cool historian." Here their views diverged, and it was hard for Nietzsche, with his loving heart, to abide on his course and yet at times have a different opinion from his mystagogue. Later he described this conflict as follows:

"I passed my test by letting nothing entice me away from my cause, not the great political movement of Germany, not the artistic agitation of Wagner, and not the philosophical lure of Schopenhauer; yet it was difficult, and at times it made me ill."

His letter to Wagner at New Year's 1872 already sounds like a desperate sticking-to-it. Nietzsche's hope of turning from a scholar into a philosopher (for now, of a Wagnerian stamp) was based entirely on Bayreuth and his activity for the Master. In the same letter, Nietzsche says about his book: "And if I myself believe that I am largely right, then all that this means is that *you* with *your* art must be right for all eternity." Nietzsche viewed the publication of his book as marking out a road that he intended never to leave.

Once again, Wagner felt excited and inspired by Nietzsche's thoughts on composing, as in January 1870, when first confronted with Nietzsche's new opinions in the lectures. Cosima enthusiastically informed the young friend that in the morning the Master was working on the second *Song of the Rhine Maidens*, that they read Schopenhauer together every evening and the *Birth of Tragedy* alone every afternoon. Any time left over was spent discussing the performance of Beethoven's Ninth Symphony at the founding ceremony for Bayreuth. An appeal was made to German musicians to participate without a fee. It was still uncertain whether this latest idea could materialize, "but it almost doesn't matter," added Cosima, "we can only stand for our intentions."

Nietzsche felt under the weather again and feared his condition of the previous year might resume. This prevented him from following an urgent invitation from Tribschen, especially since he was totally involved in the lectures *On the Future of Our Educational Institutions.* Wagner was puzzled. At first Nietzsche had so passionately laid his admiration at his feet, but now he refused to come on demand. Distrustful, he suspected that Nietzsche might already be regretting his book, particularly its publication, and he wrote to him:

"How difficult you make it for me to show any joy over you! The fact that you are ill made me quite unhappy. You must forgive us if we are rather anguished at the peripeties of your developmental stages, so to speak, ascertainment stages of your profession, to the extent that they have bearing upon your inner spiritual life."

Wagner's observations were to the point. Ever since he and Cosima had gotten to know Nietzsche, there had been constant and conspicuous uneasiness. Nietzsche's explanations sounded straightforward, but they always divulged merely the patent rather than latent reasons. Wagner was worried as to how much autonomy the young man had developed aside from his influence. He openly admitted to Nietzsche that his fervent wish had been fulfilled, the yearning "to have something come to us from outside that totally engages us." But if he looked up from the work and at the author, he became fearful: "These illnesses have so often startled us, arousing as they did serious anxieties, not about your physical but about your spiritual condition." These sincere words elicited a "truly poignant" reply, which, alas, has not come down to us. Did Nietzsche already regret his anthem? Would a time come when the book would have to be defended against its own author?

The road to the *Festspiele* seemed paved with obstacles. In January 1872, the purchase of the site on the Stuckberg near Bayreuth met with insurmountable difficulties. As a result, the two divisions of the town council held a joint session, resolving to find another location for the Festival Theater. The new plot was to be under the so-called *Bürgerreuthe;* and it became today's Festival Hill. Burgomaster Muncker and the banker Feustel[3] called at Tribschen to get Wagner's approval for the change. Wagner, ever exposing himself to the vicissitudes of travel, set out on January 24, for Bayreuth via Basel (where he saw Nietzsche), Berlin, and Weimar. Right after his departure, Nietzsche wrote him:

"The moment seems to have come when the bow is finally tautened—after hanging for so long with slack strings. To think that it was *you* who did it! To think that ultimately everything harks back to you! I view my present existence as a reproach and I ask you sincerely whether you can use me." And four days later, to Erwin Rohde: "I have concluded an alliance with Wagner. You cannot imagine how close we are now and how our plans overlap."

In early 1872, Wagner let Nietzsche know he would be stopping off en route to Berlin to pour out his heart to him. He had been summoned to the capital by a message that somebody there wanted to get two hundred thousand thalers together and begin constructing the Master's house and the *Festspiel* theater before the patronage certificates were even signed. The call to Berlin wrenched him from his labor on the third act of *Götterdämmerung,* and his reluctance to go was increased by lack of confidence in the project.

Conversing with Nietzsche (as Gersdorff reports), the composer gave vent to complaints, worries, and annoyance "that everything was put upon him, that no one stood at his side in such matters." Nietzsche, deeply troubled to see his friend suffer, comforted him since, unlike Wagner, he believed in the fantastic possibility of last-minute help, especially since good news had just come about the patrons. Nietzsche would have loved to accompany him to Berlin. But prevented by his job, he asked Gersdorff to replace him for Wagner:

"You will most likely be astonished to greet Wagner so unexpectedly in your home. I beg you to do, long for, and feel everything that could be of value to him in such a crucial moment. I am delegating to you for these days everything I feel for him, and I ask you to behave as though you were I."

Gersdorff, according to Wagner's telegram, justified such confidence: "The Alexandrine Gersdorff has become inexpendable." Nietzsche thanked his friend:

"Whatever you may do—just remember that we are both called upon to be among the front-line fighters and workers in a cultural movement that will be imparted to the greater mass perhaps in the next generation, perhaps even later. Let that be our pride, let that give us heart. As it is, I believe we are born not to be happy but to do our duty; we can thank our lucky stars once we know what our duty is."

At his return from Berlin, Wagner unexpectedly was in the best of spirits. His first letter from Tribschen was to Nietzsche. It indicated his qualms about accepting the scholar's sacrifice:

"My dear friend," he wrote on the evening of February 5, "just as your lines were the first to welcome me in Berlin, so too shall you be the first to be greeted by me upon my homecoming (at noon today). I was almost terror-stricken at being so clearly comprehended by you in Basel! Gersdorff has probably reported a good deal to you; everything proceeded openly before him. The only thing he doesn't know is Bayreuth: there I received deeply moving benefaction. It is obvious to me that in terms of the concrete side of my travail, Bayreuth was the happiest discovery of my instinct. If only I could talk to you about it!—Everything is in order, just as I wished it to be. My reign is inaugurated."

He then asks Nietzsche to send certain books to friends, since he has so many letters to write in order to drum up the "elite orchestra" for the *Ninth* in Bayreuth.

Wagner's joyous mood was due to the purchase of the site for his house on Bayreuth's Hofgarten for twelve thousand guldens. Also, the administrative board of the *Festspiele* had been constituted so that now they could start handing out the patronage certificates.

On April 4, 1872, Bülow gave a concert in Munich for the benefit of Bayreuth. On this occasion, Ludwig II expressed the wish that Bülow conduct *Tristan* and *Meistersinger* that summer as in the past. All private events notwithstanding, Bülow came to Munich for three months.

Nietzsche knew about the projected stagings. He was determined to go with Gersdorff and hear *Tristan,* having relied for ten years on the keyboard arrangements and having enthused about the opera in *The Birth of Tragedy.* Together with Gersdorff and Fräulein Malwida von Meysenbug, he attended the June 3rd and 9th performances of *Tristan.* This was seven years after those first memorable "festivals" at the National Theater, in which the title roles had been sung by the couple Schnorr von Carolsfeld—only four times, since Ludwig Schnorr died of typhoid fever. Wagner had despaired of himself and the world; he could never again hope to find such a couple, musically, theatrically, and vocally ideal. But now, in 1872, *Tristan* once more made a deep impact, and once more under Hans von Bülow's baton.

In April 1872, the "Holy Family" decided to move to Bayreuth. Wagner had twelve months of passionate planning behind him. It was not easy taking leave of Tribschen, which had sheltered him against storms for six years and where he had finally joined destinies with Cosima. In addition, he had to give up having Nietzsche nearby.

The scholar, now twenty-eight, had just put out *The Birth of Tragedy* in January. It was a sense of self-sacrifice and not rambunctiousness that drove him to enter the grueling struggle against the intellectual void of his times, even though his sensitivity would seem to have gotten in his way. His keen awareness of this was revealed in an outcry in *The Birth of Tragedy:* "Ah! The witchcraft of these struggles is such that whoever beholds them must join the fray!"

On April 22, Wagner traveled on ahead to Bayreuth, via Darmstadt, arriving on the afternoon of April 24. Cosima was to follow in a few days. On April 25, Nietzsche paid a last visit, his twenty-third, at Tribschen. He found Cosima packing. The two of them wandered through the house as among ruins. "A sorrow hovered in the air, in the clouds, everywhere," Nietzsche wrote to Gersdorff, "the dog wouldn't eat, the servant family were constantly sobbing whenever anyone addressed them. We packed the manuscripts, letters, and books together—ah! it was so dismal! Those three years I spent near Tribschen . . . how much they meant to me! Deprived of them, what would I be! I am happy that in my book I have captured that Tribschen world for myself forever."

In departing from this "Isle of the Blessed," he expressed his melancholy by fantasizing on the keyboard while Cosima walked to and fro. In later years, long after the friendship was over, Cosima still remembered that improvisation. And after the excitement of the opening festival, which did not turn out as perfect as they had hoped, she thought back nostalgically to Tribschen.

On New Year's Day 1877, she wrote to Nietzsche:

"Just think that, of the three evenings without opera, Richter spent twenty-four hours here: he couldn't endure things anymore without seeing us. On the morning of December 31, we reviewed all our past life at Tribschen, with mirth and deep emotion. And we also recalled your visits, and it was as though the *Festspiele* could not even balance the magic of that solitude to which we now look back as to a paradise lost."

7

DISRUPTING A DREAM

It is hard to put a finger on when Nietzsche started having misgivings about Wagner and his works. He must have had qualms as early as during the resettlement in Bayreuth. The atmosphere at Tribschen had kindled good cheer and trust. But the dream was to dissipate in gray and rainy Bayreuth.

Burckhardt's courses and the joyful anticipation of rehearsals at Bayreuth helped to tide Nietzsche over his momentary depression. Next to his work for the summer semester, he found time to play whatever piano reductions existed of the *Nibelungen,* "to make ourselves worthy of such unheard-of things."

On April 27, while Nietzsche returned to Basel from Tribschen, Wagner moved to Bayreuth. The margravial town saluted its new citizen with a radiant spring. Never is Franconia more glorious than when the late spring finally arrives. With an instinct for what befitted him, Wagner registered not in one of the old inns on Market Square, but in the Hotel Phantasie in Donndorf, an hour from the center of town. This temporary residence was a small castle inn, a jewel further in the countryside, after Castle Eremeitage, to the west of the city. Cosima, with the five children and their dog Russ, showed up four days later.

The couple couldn't spend too much time fixing up their provisional home, for Wagner was expected in Vienna on the morning of May 6 to ready himself for conducting a grand concert on May 12, for the Viennese Wagner Association. In preparation for this event, Hans Richter came in from Budapest.

Meanwhile, in Basel, Nietzsche was troubled by shingles on his neck. He hoped however that "a peace would be concluded in time" between his skin infection and his brain function since he "had" to go to Bayreuth. He wrote to Rohde: "Ah! It is truly unbelievable what we are witnessing! And together! A grand day! A Wagner concert in Vienna! And—the day of the *riforma federale* in Switzerland!"

All through May, at an astonishing clip, Wagner hectically drove his project, assisted by the men of the city "who can see the light ahead." He slated the cornerstone celebration of the Festival Theater for his fifty-ninth birthday, the 22nd of May 1872. The old blueprints of the architect Gottfried Semper, once meant for the Wagnerian Festive Temple in Munich, were revised or replaced by the designs of Otto Brückwald from Leipzig, who instantly grasped what Wagner had in mind.

It was not to be an ordinary theater; they would have to do without the usual "opera and ballet tinsel-style." What Wagner desired was a "stage fully capable of performing even the most complicated scenic events." The auditorium would have neither boxes nor balconies, and the orchestra would remain out of sight. These features would be regarded as upheaving innovations in the history of European theater construction. There had never been anything of the sort since Antiquity, and Wagner wanted such a renewal of ancient ideas to underscore the ritualistic impact. After all, the Baroque tradition of boxes and balconies in nineteenth-century opera houses served the self-presentation of the public more than the events on stage.

Wagner defined the innovation thus:

"The spectator, as soon as he takes his seat, finds himself actually in a 'theatron,' that is to say, a room which is calculated to do nothing else than have him look—more precisely, look to where his seat indicates. Between him and the image that he must behold there is nothing distinctly perceptible, only a space showing him the remote image in the aloofness of a dream vision, while the music, phantasmally welling up from 'mystic depths,' puts him in that inspired state of clairvoyance in which the scenic image he beholds turns into a genuine image of life itself."

There was no question that Bülow would not come to the founding-day ceremonies. But what about King Ludwig, considering his recent coolness? And Franz Liszt, Richard's father-in-law and only two years his senior? Wagner must have cared a great deal about the presence of both men. The letter of invitation to Liszt, a week before the event, concludes: "If I tell you: 'Come!', I am saying: 'Come to me!' For here you will find your-self. I bless you and love you no matter what you decide!"

What did these words refer to? What had caused the still op-pressive falling-out between the two men?

A closer friendship between Wagner and Liszt had begun when the latter was Royal Concert Master in Weimar. After meeting in Paris during 1841, they had seen one another just sporadically; most of Wagner's letters were pleas for money. In early 1849, with the production of *Tannhäuser*, Liszt began documenting his admiration of the other man's genius. Wagner had been unable to attend the opening in February, or any subsequent perfor-mances, managing only to sneak into a rehearsal, because the police were after him for his part in the Dresden Uprising. Liszt concealed the refugee, got him a passport made out for "Doktor Widmann," and brought him to Paris via Zurich. Letters of recommendation would open all doors for him. Further support came from Liszt's article on *Tannhäuser*, thanks to the journalistic initiative of Hector Berlioz.[1]

Liszt not only supplied Wagner with a huge portion of musical material, he was also one of the first to recognize his brilliance, and strongly contributed to his recognition. Self-sacrificingly, he often made his own work take second place, and he always gave in to Wagner's requests for money whenever he could, not with-out being exploited. Anyone desiring to be Wagner's friend had to take him without reservations, just as he was; and this was true for Nietzsche as well. Wagner's friendship with Liszt outlasted his friendship with Nietzsche; it endured for twenty years despite all the efforts of Liszt's jealous companion, Princess Sayn-Wittgen-stein, to drive them apart.

With the 1850 premiere of *Lohengrin*, Liszt opened a new chap-ter in the history of music—with the limited means of the Royal Theater in Weimar. Though not as successful as *Tannhäuser*, *Lo-hengrin* did call the attention of the music world to the bastion of the New German School. Liszt's support of Wagner became par-ticularly crucial when Wagner lived in Swiss exile. Liszt nego-tiated for Wagner's works and tried to obtain his pardon. Though hardly ever seeing one another, the two friends did correspond frequently, both usually commenting on Wagner's music.

They met again in 1853, when Liszt, with Princess Sayn-Witt-genstein and her daughter, traveled to Basel and then took Wag-ner along to Paris. There, under the tutelage of a governess, lived Liszt's children Blandine, Cosima, and Daniel, whom he hadn't seen for eight years in deference to the wishes of the domineering princess. It was here that Wagner first met the girl who was to become his wife seventeen years later.

In the sequel, the temperaments and artistic goals of the two men diverged so sharply that they had to clash. Their correspon-dence ebbed perceptibly, the possessive princess was not only jealous of Wagner, she resented his failure to speak up for Liszt. But by now this made no difference, Wagner had his protector in the person of King Ludwig. Cosima's decision to leave Hans von Bülow and marry Wagner led to an open rupture between the friends. The princess put the sole blame on Wagner, Liszt like-wise took the husband's side, and for several years now the great musician of Weimar had not had anything to do with either his daughter or his friend.

Notwithstanding, Liszt did send a kindly reply to the invitation for the Bayreuth ceremonies, and the friendship resumed hesitat-ingly, though under different conditions. The former "lion of the podium," who had recently taken his first vows, came in the cowl of an abbé to a Wagner who was universally acclaimed. Liszt submerged in the throng of Wagnerites. Of course, the two men now got along much better, for Wagner could express his thank-fulness, without demands, for all the good deeds of the past. Thus began again the friendship, which had ground to a halt when Cosima deserted Hans von Bülow.

On the other hand, the royal friend, Ludwig, was evidently more annoyed than anyone might have expected at what Wagner had attained without his help. The maecenas had been left behind and alone by his protegé.

On the morning of the great ceremony, it rained on Bayreuth's Green Hill. Art lovers and prideful patrons opened their umbrel-las. Boards had been placed upon the softened earth, and singers, conductors, journalists, political celebrities, and admirers of the Wagner canon must have reveled in their martyrdom for the Holy Cause. The group of the faithful around the Renewer of Art demonstrated their strength: Thousands had poured in. Alas, only a few of the old friends, including Nietzsche, of course, plus a few "recruits."

Under the lowering sky, the *March of Allegiance* for the absent king turned out quite poorly. Still, a telegram arriving from the sovereign in the nick of time said: "From the utter bottom of my soul, I express my warmest and sincerest congratulations to you, dearest friend, on this day of such great moment for all of Germany. Now more than ever I am one with you in spirit." As the capsule holding the symbol of the document was joined into the stone, a lugubrious silence prevailed. Wagner had penned the words of the document, which have lost nothing of their truth today:

> *Hier schliess ich ein Geheimnis ein,*
> *da ruh es viele hundert Jahr:*
> *so lange es verwahrt der Stein,*
> *macht es der Welt sich offenbar.*

> *Here I enclose a secret*
> *for hundreds of years to remain:*
> *as long as this stone shall keep it,*
> *the secret to all shall be plain.*

If Wagner's face was pale and tears made his voice tremble, this was no pose. "Be blessed, my stone. Stand long and keep solid!" he tried to call out during the first three blows of the hammer. Wagner's speech was directed, as could obviously be discerned, to Germany—nay, the whole world could hearken. "People recently depicted our enterprise as the erection of a National Theater in Bayreuth. It is not incumbent upon me to acknowledge this statement as valid. Just where is the Nation that is allegedly constructing this theater for itself?" He went on to say that he only owed it to the friends of his so particular expression of art, the devotees of the effects of his individuality, who had actively responded to his plea for assistance, and the foundation had been fashioned only with such a personal relationship to bear upon itself the edifice "of the noblest German aspirations."

Nietzsche, Gersdorff, and Emil Heckel were in the carriage bringing Richard and Cosima back to town, and the sensitive

Nietzsche, in his subsequent account *Richard Wagner in Bayreuth*, cast about for words to describe the composer's introspection during that ride:

"On this day, he was starting his sixtieth year: The entire past was a preliminary to this instant. We know that in a moment of extraordinary danger or even in a crucial decision of their lives people compress all their experiences in an infinitely speeded inward review and recognize with unwonted sharpness things both near and far."

Witnessing such a lonesome gaze signified, for Nietzsche, that he might be one of the few to understand Wagner's action and, with such understanding, vouchsafe its fruitfulness.

At five in the afternoon, at the opera house, Beethoven's Ninth Symphony soared forth under Wagner's direction. Wagner had dubbed it the "Wonder Symphony" and exerted much thought to the problem of performing it. The symbolism of such a festive program emphasized Wagner's commitment to Beethoven as the "Dionysian musician." Beethoven, acknowledged to be the greater, was to consecrate the new building. Before picking up the baton, Wagner turned to Cosima and the children with a smile, motioning them to come on stage from their boxes. He wanted them at hand in this hour between the pit and the soloists.

At this concert, Nietzsche first met Fräulein Malwida von Meysenbug. She was born in Kassel in 1816 as the daughter of Phillip Rivalier, who had been made Baron von Meysenbug by Electoral Prince Wilhelm I of Hessen-Kassel. Through her love for a Doctor Althaus, Malwida had been initiated into the revolutionary ideals of 1848, and even at an advanced age she still spoke about this love and her political ideals, that ran counter to the era. Expelled from Berlin, in 1852, she fled via Hamburg to London. Here she met Alexander Herzen,[2] the Russian adept at German revolutionary philosophy, whose children she raised after the death of Herzen's wife. She grew particularly fond of Olga, the youngest daughter, and took her into her own home as a foster child. For Olga's children, she was a grandmother, affectionately known as Mou-Mou.

This passionate Wagnerite lived in Florence, where Cosima had made her aware of *The Birth of Tragedy*. She promptly read the book aloud to friends, and the enthusiasm ranged high. In her essay *Individualities,* Malwida wrote: "True delight filled me at the thought that there was such a splendid young personality, both scholarly and creative, near the project coming to fruition in Bayreuth." The old lady naturally attended the Beethoven performance that afternoon. During a rehearsal break, Cosima approached Malwida with the young professor to introduce him. "What? *The* Nietzsche?" exulted the tiny lady. "Yes, *the* Nietzsche!" laughed the others.

Just a few weeks after the cornerstone was laid, they came together again for *Tristan* in Munich, and the acquaintance with Nietzsche turned into a friendship, lasting with its ups and downs until the appearance of *The Wagner Case.* Malwida, in her book, quotes a remark of Nietzsche's after the performance, "This drama of death does not sadden me at all, on the contrary, I feel happy and redeemed!"

When Malwida moved to Bayreuth, Nietzsche never failed to drop by when in town and play the piano for her, mostly free improvisations, about which Wagner once joked: "No, Nietzsche, you play much too well for a professor!"

Brockhaus, Wagner's brother-in-law from Leipzig, also came into Malwida's home and said something to the effect that Schopenhauer's works had been lying in his attic for long years, unsellable. He had been on the verge of pulping them when all at once Schopenhauer's star arose.

In the evening, after the festive performance at Bayreuth, a smaller circle gathered for dinner at the *Sonne,* a cozy hostelry. Wagner knocked on his glass and, trying to bridge the gap between himself and his royal friend, he spontaneously formulated his gratitude for the realization of a dream:

"For me, he is still more, still infinitely more than for any other person in this land. What he means to me goes far beyond my own existence. What he has encouraged in me and with me constitutes a future that shall bear upon us in huge circles going far beyond what we call civil and political life: a lofty, spiritual culture, a start towards the highest thing destined for a nation and expressing itself in the wondrous relationship about which I am talking here."

Someone busily wrote down what the Master pontificated. The truth about this long-terminated friendship was camouflaged.

On June 22, 1872, just a short time after those days of such importance for Wagner and Nietzsche, the composer's open letter to Friedrich Nietzsche was run in the *Norddeutsche Zeitung*. It is quite conceivable that Nietzsche's grateful note, subsequently destroyed, contained all kinds of tributes. The scholar must have at least been relieved not to ascertain any further hindrance to his position in the scholarly world. But Wagner had no illusions about the damage Nietzsche had done to himself by his partisanship for the composer; he even feared that his "missive" wouldn't avail very much.

On June 25, he wrote from the Hotel Phantasie in Donndorf:

"Oh, friend, now you are only causing me to worry, simply because I think so highly of you! To be exact, after my wife you are the only benefit that life has brought me; now, happily, I also have Fidi; but between him and myself I need a link that only you can form, somewhat like the son to the grandson. . . . I would want your quite ordinary well-being since everything else strikes me as being assured with you. I have been reading the *Birth* once again, morning for morning, quite attentively; and I kept saying to myself: 'If only he remains quite healthy and if everything goes quite well for him—for it cannot go very badly!' . . . I do not perceive from my Open Letter that I have been breaking any ground for you and can only assume that all I have done is to leave you with a fine burden on your back; nor did I think that you should 'mature' for your mission, but only that you will be occupied with it all your life. *Tristan* must needs be interesting to you; only— off with your spectacles!—All you may hear is the orchestra. — Farewell! Dear, precious friend! We'll soon be meeting again, will we not? . . ."

Now *Tristan* was always Wagner's most fascinating opera for Nietzsche. In 1888, after their break, he could still write: "I am yet seeking a work of the same perilous fascination, of the same dreadful and sweet infinity as *Tristan*, I seek through all the arts, in vain. All the strange things about Leonardo da Vinci lose their spell at the first note of *Tristan*. This work is certainly the *ne plus ultra.* "

When Nietzsche was about to write down his impression of the *Tristan* production at Munich and dispatch it to Bülow, it struck him that he could express his gratitude not just in words. He had his symphonic meditation *Manfred* copied and then dispatched it to the conductor with a warm inscription. In the accompanying letter, Nietzsche talks about his "questionable music": "Ridicule me, I deserve it!" Nietzsche's composer friend Peter Gast, upon hearing the piece, was obviously biased when he characterized it as "an outstanding symphonic accomplishment in every respect, inventiveness, contrast, structure, detail, technique, and of a veracity and grandeur of expression as could only belong to the future creator of *Zarathustra.*"

Bülow's response was different, and he pulled no punches. Nietzsche, he said, was certainly just an empiricist and dilettante in musical matters; there were mistakes, breaches of musical orthography. He spoke about luxuriant reminiscences of "Wagnerian sounds" and gave the probably correct advice to compose vocal music and let the word lead the way. Still, he did ascertain that one could sense "an unusual and, despite all the veneration, a distinguished spirit."

Nietzsche was candid to his friends about Bülow's letter. Thus, he wrote to Rohde in August 1872:

"I have at last received some real criticism of my most recent composition, which I played for you in Bayreuth at Whitsuntide; Bülow's letter is inestimable for me in its honesty. Read it, laugh me to scorn, and believe me that I was so terrified of myself that I haven't been able to touch a keyboard since."

Nietzsche didn't answer the conductor's letter until October. But when he heard comments, echoing Liszt, that Bülow was a "very desperate critic," he wrote to him, gently saying that he believed "you would have judged me a shade (just a tiny shade, of course) less harshly had I but played that non-music for you in my way, badly, but expressively: a number of things in it, because of technical awkwardness, reached the paper so askew as to offend any true musician's sense of propriety and purity. Just imagine that until now, ever since my earliest childhood, I have been living in the most insane illusion, *greatly* delighting in my music! It was always a problem for me to determine whence my delight derived. There was something irrational about it, I could make neither head nor tail of it, the delight remained. Precisely this Manfred music gave me a grim, nay, snide and high-flown feeling, it was the pleasure of a diabolical irony! The very title was ironic—for Byron's *Manfred,* which I admired almost as my favorite poem when I was a boy, is to my mind nothing but a mad, formless, monotonous humbug."

However, an extant draft to this letter does not coincide with the final version. Nietzsche, in that draft admits how far he is from the "semi-psychiatric musician's emotion" of judging and venerating Wagner's works. He indicates that Bülow's critique is making him submit his musical knowledge to a "therapy":

"Generally, the whole thing is a highly instructive experience —the question of education, which I am dealing with in other areas, has been thrown up for me in the field of art with particular strength. The individual is now exposed to such dreadful confusions!"

Regarding such an outcry, we must bear in mind that Nietzsche's musical theory came solely from his private study of Georg Albrechtsberger,[3] who had once taught Beethoven. The endless writing of fugues let Nietzsche feel he had reached a certain level of purity. His craft, not really mastered, occasionally made him defiant and ironic. Seriousness, irony, and caricature intertwined as in other composers who quickly followed him in our century. In music, too, he anticipated the coming discords.

In summer 1872, while construction workers were busy on the Bayreuth Hill, Nietzsche started coping with the Wilamowitz-Moellendorff pamphlet. His self-confidence is astonishing:

"I'm truly sorry for the young man, and, like you, I feel real pity when I think of his good name. It's no use! He has to be openly punished" (to Gersdorff).

We can leave aside the question of Nietzsche's sincerity when he claimed he was now progressing into the future more fit and more courageous. Nevertheless, the "Bayreuth mutualities" brought the friends closer together, even if it was a heady possessedness. Rohde authored his pamphlet against Wilamowitz that summer. Nietzsche otherwise spent his time on philological and psychological studies of the Greeks, and the quiet work made him happy.

Meanwhile, Wagner also had to put up with attacks. He was furious about Doctor Puschmann's article, which accused Wagner of delusions.

The setting in which the mutual affairs of the friends would be shown was only a temporary accommodation, for Wagner from the very outset regarded his *Festspielhaus* as provisional; private funds did not suffice for erecting a German National Theater in Bayreuth. His hopes centered on eventual subsidy from the State. To be sure, the really essential wherewithal has never come through till this very day, except for a modest revamping of the playhouse, restaurants at intermission, and the overhauling of unbearable seats into merely strenuous ones. The hand-to-mouth budget has prevented any new edifice. Even the "thousand years" of the Third Reich and the friendship between Winifred Wagner,[4] the "Mistress of Bayreuth," and Hitler failed to make the dream come true. As it happened, in 1939, the dictator planned to build a new "representative" theater. Architect Emil Mewe's blueprints, which would preserve the stage, orchestra, and auditorium for the "unique acoustics" were finished; but the observer of the pageantry architecture of that era can only feel relief at what the war spared posterity.

In the Hotel Phantasie, Wagner got back to work on Act III of *Götterdämmerung.* It was completed on July 22.

Nietzsche, in Basel, was just returning compositions he had gotten from his old schoolmate Gustav Krug. He found it difficult to part with them; in his totally emotional attitude to music, he was hopelessly enamored of them. Merely reading a score didn't help him much, and he desired a lovely, four-handed arrangement, "to savor with greater ease." His friend's notes (we have to believe him) signalized "grace and melancholy." Krug's vocal line and counterpoints made Nietzsche see his own fortissimi and tremoli as gross and lubberly. After all, since the *Manfred Meditation,* he hadn't composed a thing for six years. But his musicality all at once made pure thought look foolish; his "Apollonian" and "Dionysian" struck him as insipid next to what he considered "real producing." Indeed, a man would have to have a "calling" to prevent him from "dolefully lazing about on his belly like an indolent bear." Yet he was rankled by his previous musical productions, which, even for those times, were full of fantastic ugliness and improper debauchery. He felt obliged to warn his friend Krug "against this bad music of mine. Let no false drop come into your sense of music, least of all from the barbarizing sphere of my music." He certainly wanted no part of conventional "good taste." And he must have been quite aware that, musically too, he was forging ahead on virgin soil.

Much of modernity (which Nietzsche was incapable of writing, and not just technically) could be heard in *Tristan*. Hence the final words in his letter of July 24, 1872, to Krug: "It has just crossed my mind that I haven't told you that you absolutely have to hear *Tristan*. It is an immensely marvelous work, giving us the utmost happiness, the utmost sublimity, the utmost purity." A judgment to which he stuck all his life, though at times with great effort.

The year 1872 has often been labeled a turning-point in Nietzsche's life despite a lack of any outstanding event. He was filled with disquiet. His tendency to spread himself thin was intensified by the removal of the Wagners and the irritation of public hostility; his feeble constitution did the rest. Whenever he could get away from teaching, he would travel.

Nor was Wagner in the best of health; he was putting his affairs in order. This included the resumption of his friendship with Liszt, which had paused for many years. In early September 1872, he and Cosima went to Weimar, concluding a difficult peace with her father. The restlessly active master pianist and Grand Ducal Music Director appeared to have gotten on in years. He promised to visit Bayreuth for a few days in October.

No sooner had the Wagner family returned than they moved from the Hotel Phantasie in Donndorf to the city. To be sure, the spacious house at number 7 Dammallee was just another transition. Wagner wanted to build his own home; and King Ludwig had given him a tract on the outskirts of the *Hofgarten*. This from the king who avoided any personal contact with Wagner and—still paid out of love.

When Liszt did appear in Bayreuth, his mood was conciliatory, but he insisted that Wagner and Cosima had Hans von Bülow on their conscience. When Cosima tried to show understanding for what her father was saying, the husband and wife had a falling-out, and Cosima left Wagner alone for the evening.

Liszt also caused the Master grief by refusing to settle in Bayreuth, despite all coaxing. Actually, Wagner didn't like this man, whom he had once styled "half Franciscan, half Gypsy." The Protestant Wagner bristled at the toady of Rome, the bourgeois as the eternal Bohemian, the blunt German as the cosmopolite from Hungary. And yet he was piqued at Liszt's unwillingness to retire to Bayreuth.

On October 24, Wagner informed Nietzsche:

"We had Liszt visiting us for a week; we have come to cherish him afresh; good-byes once again dissolved into longing. How much we have learned from him again about the world, which we do know quite well, but are mortally frightened at reviewing in detail. He was able to tell us many things, since people thought we were at daggers drawn and hoped to please him by saying nasty things about us."

In the meantime, Nietzsche's attempt at touring Italy petered out. In Bergamo, after the beautiful valleys of the High Alps, he was seized with a quirky dislike of anything Italian, and more than ever he felt like warming himself in his room at Basel against the coming autumn. All sorts of indignant or scornful reactions to his widely distributed book were reaching him. Nietzsche realized how terrible Wilamowitz's attack had been when he thought of Rohde's hesitance at publicly defending him.

The young scholar was deeply reluctant to get along without the Wagners. He perused the Master's latest essay *On Actors and Singers,* and saw this theme as a newly discovered province of aesthetics. A number of ideas here from his *Birth of Tragedy* struck him as "fruitfully applied." The few friends whose enthusiasm for Wagner was really due to Nietzsche's attachment were likewise competing, he assumed, for nobler goals. But his allegiance to the composer took first place. The effort to please him impelled Nietzsche "harder and higher than any other force" (to Rohde). And if that was difficult since the Master made his demands point-blank and the devotee complied while knowing better, then Nietzsche reinterpreted Wagner's criticism as a "good conscience, punitive and rewarding."

On his own birthday, October 15, Nietzsche poured out his heart to Wagner. Unfortunately, all that is left is Wagner's response of October 24, which implies that Nietzsche expressed a mood now common to everyone interested in Bayreuth. Wagner writes:

"One might almost call it an anxiety following the disgust at everything we perceive, an anxiety with which we then come back to ourselves, perhaps with the question as to what connection we have with this scandalous world? . . . All in all, I mainly sense that

I know my contemporaries less and less: that may be necessary though, if one is to create for posterity. But I often feel peculiar, like an only just awakening tyro! Individual solitude is boundless when one simply labors into the elements. I can quite comprehend what has so often stifled and almost crushed you: you were still casting about a great deal. It's all a matter of seeing and not seeing! If one relinquishes hope one is also rid of despair. In the end, one feels that this is the only way of becoming conscious of oneself, by quite decisively distinguishing oneself from contemporaries, namely in a strict effort to wipe out their badness. I at least have reached the point of not mincing my words with anyone: and if Empress Augusta herself were to get in my way, I would give her what she deserved."

In Munich, Nietzsche had met the General Music Director of the Geneva Orchestra, Hugo von Senger, who soon asked him whether he would like to adapt Flaubert's *Salammbô* into a libretto. Nietzsche declined, explaining he was neither a poet nor a musician, but a philosopher. He conveyed to Senger his own thoughts about musical development, especially the composition of musical dramas. Wagner, he said, must be defended against the accusation of having wiped out classical forms of music. The claim that the end of pure music had come with Wagner did not mean that composers necessarily had to turn to theater music.

Nietzsche then foreshadows the negator of Wagner:

"If the highest form of art has been invented, then, to my mind, the lesser ones, down to the very least, are all the more urgent so that artists can express themselves in their different ways without constantly being overthundered. The purest devotion to Wagner is certainly shown by the creative artist who gives way to him in his own province and, instead, enlivens, and inspires another form, a *smaller* one, nay, the very smallest, in his own spirit, I mean with ruthless self-severity, with the energy of giving at every moment the highest that he can give."

Towards Wagner, Nietzsche pooh-poohed his letter to Senger as a "wise epistle," underlining a jab against Mendelssohn that was to be especially pleasing to Wagner: "I very much advised him against it: let him compose a good cantata, namely Goethe's *Walpurgis Night* afresh, only better than Mendelssohn! I wonder whether he will follow my advice."

On an "inspection tour of Germany," Wagner had a look at

what the opera stages were doing, and the close view did not lift his spirits. Along the way, he gave recitals to raise new funds for Bayreuth, but they brought him more trouble than money.

He announced a visit to Nietzsche for a week in mid-November —the "ultimate visit": Wagner and wife. Nietzsche felt he owed his special thanks to the renowned Basel dentist whom Wagner intended to consult. He suggested the couple lodge at the Hotel of the Three Kings, where he had enjoyed a pleasurable summer day with Malwida von Meysenbug and her recently engaged foster-daughter, Olga Herzen.

But Nietzsche and Wagner didn't see each other until November 22. "After long telegraphic preliminaries," Nietzsche, one Friday, betook himself to Strasbourg, where they spent two and a half days together, with no other business, talking, walking, making plans. They seemed to have every reason for enjoying the heartiest fellowship. They discussed Nietzsche's dismay that no student had shown up even though the winter term was already well underway. Both in letters and in person, Nietzsche was open to Wagner about this circumstance, which he had been too embarrassed to divulge to anyone else. His correspondence reveals how troubled he was to have hurt his little university.

Nor had the like ever occurred before. Until the past semester, his students had increased constantly, but now, this winter, they failed to come. This was perfectly in keeping with the jaundiced condemnations to be heard at other universities. One student, for example, who had wanted to transfer to Basel for Nietzsche, had been held back in Bonn until he told his Basel relatives that he thanked God he hadn't switched to a school where someone like Nietzsche was teaching. Nietzsche felt obligated to apologize to Wagner for any hatred or disfavor he might suffer as a result of Rohde's public defensive. The dreamy-eyed fan seemed to be ignoring the fact that Wagner had gotten him into this dilemma in the first place.

Wagner was overjoyed to hear him describe his essay *On Actors and Singers* as "splendid." Nietzsche fervently wished "that someone would work out a digest of your aesthetic investigations and conclusions, so as to show that meanwhile all pondering of art has been so altered, deepened, and determined that at bottom nothing is left of traditional 'aesthetics.' "

That summer, on the Splügen, Nietzsche had been weighing

the choreographic side of Greek tragedy, the connection between mimicry and the sculptural, and the grouping of the play-
ers. He now felt that Aeschylus himself had been an example of
what Wagner was realizing in his virtually gestural music. Wagner's dramatic style seemed to set a standard, goal, and measure
for a musical theater movement which would endure for a long
time. After such preparatory thinking, Nietzsche saw the essay
with the programmatic aesthetics of acting and singing as a revelation.

Wagner seemed in good cheer and satisfied with his trip. Conditions were bad on provincial stages, but he had found capable
voices and willing people, which made his spirits soar. In Mannheim, he had recruited Louise Jaïde as his first Erda and Wal-
traute at Bayreuth. He planned to keep hunting all winter,
scheduling a three-week stay in Berlin. But this was reduced to
three days in January 1873. During this time, in the home of
Minister von Schleinitz, he recited the text of *Götterdämmerung* to
a select group, which included Field Marshal Count Moltke and
Adolph von Menzel.

On the other hand, he did not get around to inspecting La Scala
in Milan. In Karlsruhe, he obtained an audience with Grand Duke
Friedrich I. Next, he traveled through Cologne, Düsseldorf, Hanover, Bremen, and Magdeburg, stopping in Dessau, where he
discovered the choreographic director for the first two festivals,
Richard Fricke, the ballet-master in that city. The new year
brought him to Dresden, where he attended a performance of
Rienzi and called upon the Wesendonks,[5] who had settled here.
After two concerts in Hamburg, the Wagners caught a production
of *The Flying Dutchman* in the Schwerin Theater, which was known
for its fine achievements. Karl Hill sang the title role, and Wagner
promptly hired him for the part of Alberich.

Returning to Bayreuth, Wagner had renewed symptoms of a
heart disease and a general exhaustion. The balance sheet of his
tour of Germany consisted mainly of harsh criticism. His only
positive experience had been Gluck's *Orfeo* at Dessau: "I openly
bear record that I have never witnessed a nobler and more perfect
overall achievement in the theater than this performance."

By implication, he didn't seem to have valued the epoch-making Wagner productions on the Weimar stage. Nietzsche had
attended *Lohengrin* there, under Liszt, on December 26, 1872.

Like *Tannhäuser*, he had never seen it produced before. "Never! How incredible! And I have always lived in Europe!"

At New Year's 1873, Nietzsche did not accept Wagner's invitation to Bayreuth, thereby irritating the thin-skinned composer. At their last meeting, Wagner had repeatedly said that their separation might cause misunderstandings. Nietzsche did not contradict so urgently as Cosima wished, for early in December 1872 she concluded a letter to Nietzsche with these words:

"Believe me, no estrangement can take place here any more than a misunderstanding; I, who am usually so nervous, am cheerfully convinced of that."

It is worth noting that the year 1873 began with a serious misunderstanding. Nietzsche, spending a brief vacation with his mother in Naumburg, was absorbed in his new articles. Unexpectedly, the above invitation arrived, asking Nietzsche to utilize his return trip for a visit in Bayreuth. The scholar, however, had no intention of curtailing his short, quiet working time. He failed to foresee the hurt feelings in Bayreuth. Later he heard how incensed Wagner had been when Peter Cornelius turned down his request to come to Munich because he wanted to finish working on his opera *The Cid*. "As though he couldn't have written it in Munich," grumbled Wagner, who could never realize how greatly his charisma interfered with the work of his loyal followers. Soon, however, highly amical letters drove away the clouds, although Nietzsche could not fully grasp that his behavior had unleashed any annoyance.

In February, fleeing the Lenten drums of Basel, he sought refuge in Gersau on Lake Vierwaldstätt. Fog and rain made it impossible for him to go on walks. "Fairly ill-humored, but at least undisturbed," he wrote Gersdorff for his opinion:

"I cannot imagine how one can proffer more allegiance to Wagner in all important matters and show deeper devotion than I do. If I could imagine how, I would do it. But in minor, less relevant points, and in a virtually 'salubrious' abstention for *more frequent* personal association, I am bound to maintain a freedom, really only to be able to continue that loyalty in a higher sense. There is nothing to say about that, of course, but one can feel it, and despair, when that involves annoyance, distrust, and silence. In this instance, I never would have dreamt that I had given such offence; and I always fear that such experiences will make me even more apprehensive than I already am.—Please, my dear friend, your honest opinion!"

The friend's comforting must have been powerful. He must have temporarily relieved the stupid "myopsis" tormenting Nietzsche. The latter was now planning to surprise Wagner on his next birthday with a part of the *Untimely Reflection* entitled *The Philosopher as Cultural Physician*. Olga Herzen's imminent marriage with a Monsieur Gabriel Monod[6] inspired him to compose again. *Une Monodie à deux,* as a piano piece for four hands and a preview of a good marriage, went out to Malwida's home in Florence.

For Cosima's birthday, on December 25, Nietzsche had dispatched small essays, calling them "Five Prefaces to five unwritten books by Friedrich Nietzsche": 1. *On the Passion of Truth.* 2. *On the Future of Our Educational Institutions.* 3. *The Greek State.* 4. *On the Relationship of Schopenhauer's Philosophy to a German Culture.* 5. *Homer's Contest.* Attractively bound and supplied with forewords, the bundle bore the inscription: "For Cosima Wagner in deepest devotion and as a response to personal and epistolary questions, penned with great pleasure during the Christmas days of 1872."

A thank-you note never came, nor the customary New Year's greeting. Nietzsche was not bothered at first, since he had been told that the Wagners were on another concert tour of Germany in January 1873. His devotion was as strong as ever. This can be seen in a short, aggressive article which, though polemics were contrary to his nature, he authored against an opponent of Wagner, a mental specialist, who had tried to demonstrate in "refined parlance" that Wagner was insane. Nietzsche, in his retort, even conformed his style to Wagner's.

The Master, whatever his vexation, didn't, of course, wish to drive away his apostle. So Cosima put out conciliatory feelers on Wagner's behalf. Her letter to Nietzsche does admit that she "cannot make head or tail" of the words "penned with great pleasure" in the dedication on the New Year's present. (She had never observed such bliss of scholarly labor in her own husband. His gesture of creativity was usually theatrical, even histrionic.)

Nietzsche's efforts to avoid any estrangement are shown in his asking whether he and Rohde might visit the Wagners during the Easter holidays. Wagner wired back: "Sensible suggestions are always a joy, especially in the form of heartily accepted announcements of a visit, so until Sunday. Richard Wagner."

The professor in Basel began having a difficult time with the burden of demands from Bayreuth. Just why was the Master always dissatisfied? How could one serve him with greater devotion?

After an exchange of telegrams between Heidelberg, Nurnberg, and Bayreuth, Nietzsche was sitting in the train for Bayreuth, poignantly thinking that every step would mean a memory of utterly happy days. There had been something in the air in Tribschen, something he would never sense again, something "ineffable but so rich in hope." Then, however, his joy struck him as foolish. How could he think that everything would be so beautifully restored "that even a god could not wish for anything more." He dutifully desired that his visit might atone for what his absence at Christmas had caused.

In Wagner's provisional lodgings on *Dammallee*, they talked a great deal about Malwida and Gersdorff, whom Wagner spoke of as a "cavalier wandering through the labyrinth of love." Nietzsche had a chance to read aloud his manuscript *Philosophy in the Tragic Age of the Greeks,* still far from its definitive shape. This was already the fourth version, but it did not as yet satisfy his self-criticism. He had had to undertake "the most specialized studies," some mathematics as well as mechanics, chemical atom theory. . . . "I have once again convinced myself in the most splendid way as to what the Greeks are and were. The road from Thales[7] to Socrates is tremendous."

He also told Wagner that Gersdorff had happened to meet Wilamowitz. Tableau! The "scoundrel" had followed his pamphlet with a second one "full of invective and sophistry and not worth a refutal. With its sights trained on Rohde, the pamphlet finally moves away from the two 'corrupt minds' and concludes with generalities; David Strauss's comments against Schopenhauer are applied to me verbatim, and altogether I am made to look like a Herostrates, a desecrator of temples, etc. The document is dated in Rome. Recently, a periodical referred to me as 'Darwinism and materialism translated into musicality,' the impure was compared to 'Darwin's primordial cell': I supposedly teach the 'developism' of the 'primal slime'! I find that my honored opponents are starting to go crazy. A certain Bonus Meyer recently opined about Wagner's works that even the 'brutal building frenzy of the Romans' had never dared to go so far. Hatred seems to be flaming brightly" (to Gersdorff, April 5, 1873).

There is no reason to assume that these things weren't mentioned in Bayreuth. Wagner probably realized afresh how urgently he needed Nietzsche for propagandistic assistance and how dangerous it was to make this enfant terrible of all people into his mouthpiece, particularly since the scholarly world appeared to be so hostile to him.

"Not content" is an expression in Nietzsche's thank-you note of April 18, characterizing Wagner's mood during the visit. Nietzsche defines his aloofness from Wagner's ill-humor, which was caused by financial worries and his shock at the younger man's critical attitude toward the times. Unexpectedly, the two interlocutors were no longer in concord. At a loss, Nietzsche avowed to his friend: "I understand it all too well, but without being able to change anything; for I learn and perceive very slowly, and every moment I experience something with you that I hadn't thought of and would like to retain. I so often desired at least a semblance of greater freedom and independence, but in vain." For the sake of a good rapport, he would gladly have gone back to the role of pupil, "if possible with a pen in hand and notebook in front of me."

Wagner, about to petition Bismarck for financial aid, was alarmed at Nietzsche's misgivings about the Prussian cause. This skepticism had supplanted his youthful veneration for the new imperium.

Hitherto, next to the continued Classical studies, there had been no trace of current political critique in Nietzsche's writings. This evidently changed when he saw himself elbowed into scholarly isolation during 1872. Nietzsche now displayed little ambition to advocate his convictions within the framework of Classics. Still, the path he chose may have been determined to no small extent by the marked deterioration of his health. The strenuous illnesses had their consequences.

Nietzsche thus always had a dismal memory concerning the manuscript he had read to the others in Bayreuth. He announced his hope of "affording pleasure by reading a new manuscript."

But Wagner merely registered disappointment at being confronted with something as remote as *The Philosophy of the Greeks,* which had nothing to do with the practical present, the foes of his work, or the Bayreuth plans. How far afield from the Wagner theme!

The composer seemed to clearly sense the tightness in Nietzsche's behavior during that visit. Upon receiving the above-mentioned humble letter of April 18, he replied: ". . . Your letter is not to be answered by me: You yourself must know how keenly it touched me, and there is nothing further to say about it except perhaps that you should not discourage yourself with painful notions about yourself; by all means, continue to be a 'burden' as often as you please in the same way."

Citing Nietzsche's essay on the religious thinker David Friedrich Strauss,[8] Wagner commented: "Re your Straussiana, all I feel is torment since I can't wait to see it. Ergo: out with it!—Yesterday, after ten days of travel tumult, we came home to *Dammallee,* not planning to leave it again for quite a spell. Tomorrow—God and Strauss willing!—the cornerstone shall be laid for the instrumentation of *Götterdämmerung.*—The latest about Fidi is that when I was moving my books, he hung about attentively, and when I called to him: 'Fidi, hand me Creuzer's *Symbolism,*' he handed me Creuzer's *Symbolism.*—Greetings from everyone. This morning Eva and Fidi played 'Nietzsche and Rohde.' And my very best wishes to Rohde. It was really fun having you both celebrate Easter in my home!—With all my heart, Richard Wagner."

The work on the *Untimely Reflection* ground to a halt since ocular pains made Nietzsche's increasing myopia even more unpleasant. Gersdorff hurried over to help him with his labors. He also accompanied Nietzsche to the specialist, who at first diagnosed only a weak-sightedness in the right eye and the top degree of short-sightedness in the left eye. The condition demanded inactivity. The doctor prescribed eye washes plus absolutely no reading or writing for two weeks. The pause was then extended until summer vacation. But atropine and tender care through inactivity did improve Nietzsche's vision just a bit.

Between 1873 and 1876, Nietzsche's *Untimely Reflections* came out singly. The four finished ones, mutilated as they were out of consideration for Wagner, are certainly not among Nietzsche's crucial statements. But against the background of his life, they acquire a powerful meaning and indicate both a metamorphosis of thought and new goals. They run parallel with the change in his relationship to Wagner.

Nietzsche was still hoping to please Wagner with the manuscript he was then working on. The essay *David Strauss, the Confessor and Writer* dealt with the serious impact that this man's work had made on Nietzsche's youth. The Protestant minister Strauss, at twenty-seven, had penned his book *The Life of Jesus,* which had unleashed controversies and ultimately made him forsake theology. The new version, "revised for the German Nation," aroused Nietzsche's protest. Strauss had hammered together a scholarly pseudo-religion for himself; and an accommodating optimism interpreted the world as fine and reasonable. To make matters worse, Strauss's late writings lacked any appreciation of Wagner. Nietzsche was furious at the "dull mind and baseness of the author and thinker." He simply cleaned the floor with Strauss, who was universally respected as classic, by garnering a collection of "the most repugnant" examples of Strauss' style.

The very opening of Nietzsche's essay sounds fresh even today and is virtually independent of the occasion (did Nietzsche, incidentally, realize how far his political thought now diverged from Wagner's?):

"Public opinion in Germany would seem to prohibit speaking of the evil and dangerous consequences of war, especially a successful war: but people are all the more willing to listen to those writers who know of no more important viewpoint than that public opinion and therefore zealously vie to praise war and jubilantly inspect the powerful phenomena of its impact on ethics, culture, and art."

Nietzsche rashly thought of presenting the manuscript to the Master on his sixtieth birthday. But the onslaught of work in the new semester kept him from revising it. A further reason can be gleaned from the rather conventional letter of congratulations on May 20: ". . . especially with my suffering from sudden and painful weakness of the eyes and being quite worried about it."

On Wagner's sixtieth birthday, four friends were calling at Nietzsche's home in Basel to honor the Master by playing the Ninth Symphony (for four hands) and Wagner's insipid *Imperial*

March. These guests were Gersdorff, Overbeck, Romundt, and Rée[9]—teaching colleagues, auditors, all of whom Nietzsche had converted to Wagner.

Meanwhile the Master was celebrated by his "New German" apostles with a "Festive Performance" in Bayreuth's margravial opera house. Peter Cornelius contributed an arrangement of Wagnerian compositions sporting the up-to-date title of *Artist Consecration.* Next, the Wagners immediately took off for Weimar to finalize their reunion with Liszt by listening—albeit disparagingly—to the first unabridged rendering of the oratorium *Christ,* with the composer himself on the podium. When the couple came home to Bayreuth, the celebratory wreath marking the erection of the roof timbers was perching atop the *Festspielhaus.* On August 2, for the *Hebefest* (the traditional entertainment for the workers when the carpentry on a house in completed), Wagner himself indited the workers' rhyme.

Meanwhile, the summer had seen the growth of the other house, which would become an oppressive home for generations of Wagner children. Its symbolic name *Wahnfried,* "illusive peace," became a by-word in the world of music. After donating the site, Ludwig added the building. His gesture was all the more generous, considering his jealousy and skepticism about the Bayreuth idea. Wagner had driven himself out of all his previous heavens: the refuge in Zurich, the house on Brienner Strasse in Munich, and the "safe harbor" of Tribschen. He now saw his lasting home in the Festival Theater and in the house on the *Hofgarten.*

Accordingly, he prepared a tomb for himself and Cosima. With the king's permission, he was able to use the *Hofgarten,* and he wanted to be buried on the line between the royal park and Wahnfried.

In June he wrote to the king: "How ineffably gladdened we are by the thought of precisely knowing and daily cultivating the place that is to receive us for divine rest, on the soil which we owe to the generosity of Your love and which shall some day be handed down to my son as his inalienable home."

8
WORRIES AND DOUBTS

The celebratory wreath and the gaudy ribbons could not conceal the delays in the project. Large donations, which had recently been promised by the "Patrons," never came or were slow to arrive. Were people regretting their generosity? Losing faith in the fantastic idea? Wagner made a thundering appeal to his Germans. They didn't hear. A letter, long, servile, and unusually awkward, accompanied a copy of *German Art and German Politics* to Prince Bismarck. There was no reply. A premiere of the *Ring* in any metropolis could have brought the necessary funds, providing Wagner dropped his Festival plans. But with his tenacity, that could hardly be expected. He did however have to put up with a one-year delay of the production, which had been slated for 1875. Meanwhile, along with Frau von Schleinitz and a tiny number of devotees, he continued trying to drum up interest.

Nietzsche, feeling affectionate solidarity from Basel, shared the anxieties and was impressed by Wagner's courage. On October 29, 1873, he traveled to Bayreuth, having been asked to compose an *Appeal to the Germans* for the *Festspiele*. The great friend needed help; he was not refused. Members of the Bayreuth Patronage and delegates of the Wagner associations were now entrusting Nietzsche, of all people, with inditing a call to the wider masses to pledge contributions. Those gentlemen were using for this eminently political task a man whose mere name met with indignation or unfamiliarity and who was as unsuitable as could be for such a mission. Emil Heckel once suggested to Wagner that they place signature lists for patrons in German bookstores and publish the appeal at the same time. Wagner told him to consult with Nietzsche since he had "a very special confidence in him—in him particularly."

Before penning the *Exhortation to the Germans,* Nietzsche wrote to Mannheim:

"My dear Herr Heckel, what you are asking of me shall be done. Your plan concerning the bookdealers strikes me as excellent; indeed, the entire plan is once more a credit to its originator. . . . If my health at all permits, I shall come to Bayreuth on the thirtieth of this month. Printed copies will be made of my draft; it will be easier to read and, if necessary, revise."

Nietzsche was not just recruiting for an enterprise; he was focusing his irritated sights on the indifferent, to whom Wagner's art meant little or nothing. The meeting of the donors resolved, however, that the premature consent for Nietzsche's text had best be rescinded. They formally turned it down, using a gentler appeal from another pen, namely that of a Dr. Adolf Stern. Wagner, for his part, fully approved Nietzsche's version. He supposedly was irate at the delegates' rejection. They, on the other hand, felt that while Nietzsche was certainly speaking from the bottom of his and every friend's heart, the exhortation would scarcely bring around the hostile or the indifferent.

In a letter to Gersdorff, Nietzsche reports:

"Well, I was on the road from Wednesday evening until Monday morning, I went alone, and came back with Heckel. In Bayreuth, about a dozen people had assembled, all of them delegates of associations, and I the only patron per se. After the inspection in filth, fog, and darkness, came the main session in the town hall, where my *Exhortation* was politely but firmly rejected by the delegates; I myself protested against any revamping and I recommended Professor Stern for a rapid manufacture of a new model. On the other hand, Heckel's excellent motion about putting up collection booths at all German bookstores was passed."

Both appeals, Dr. Stern's and Nietzsche's, were sent by Wagner to the king for his approval, with the composer mentioning that his "excellent friend" would thus win "important signatures from all ranks." The request for approbation quickly turned into a plea for the only concrete possibility of help, a financial subsidy from the royal friend, who at first did not comply.

Nietzsche kept finding himself doomed to passivity towards the active Master. It wasn't until summer 1876, in the nick of time for the first Bayreuth Festival, that he managed to find a way of becoming active again for the Master's cause—by publishing his fourth *Untimely Reflection: Richard Wagner in Bayreuth.*

Nietzsche greatly admired Wagner's faith that the venture was assured—for the moment, at least, the machines and decorations. Malwida von Meysenbug, who had fled to Italy from the harsh climate of Bayreuth, expressed her own worries about the project to Nietzsche, scarcely aware that her sympathy affected the young scholar in various ways. "Ah! Our hopes were too great!" This outcry of Nietzsche's in his answer did not just refer to material things. He planned to elucidate the shakiness of the undertaking in a subsequent letter to the old lady. He justifiably omitted doing so when Malwida was already frowning at Nietzsche's heresy.

Through spring and summer of 1874, after his critical historical remarks in the second *Untimely Reflection,* Nietzsche was working on the third one, *Schopenhauer as Educator.* In it, he planned to present a powerful, self-contained thinker as a model, although he no longer shared Schopenhauer's principles—a situation corresponding to the state of his Wagner worship. What attracted Nietzsche about Schopenhauer and what he sought in Wagner was the conception of an ideal philosopher, who had to be honest, serene, and steadfast if he were to set an intellectual direction for young men. Waving off the naiveté of a David Friedrich Strauss, Nietzsche preferred Schopenhauer's composure as that of critical self-knowledge.

Like Schopenhauer, the courageous organizer of Bayreuth had features of this wishful image, and Nietzsche sounds as if he were defining his opinion of Wagner: "The heroic man despises his well-being or ill-being, his virtues and vices, and any measurement of things by his standard."

Yet precisely such heroism of practice as evinced by Wagner aroused Nietzsche's secret envy, and soon he could barely conceal it. Respect and admiration for Wagner conflicted with his own inability to knuckle under and with his tendency to be the initiator in relations with others, particularly his friendships. But rivalries were a way for him to probe himself more effectively and gain a more independent view of things. Almost imperceptibly at first, his dreamy-eyed veneration of Wagner was evolving into a love-hate by a man who was misunderstood and perhaps a frustrated musician.

Of course, the serious crisis in the friendship was still ahead, notwithstanding all the present brittleness. The *Reflection* praises Schopenhauer as the educator who takes upon himself the voluntary suffering of truthfulness. Nietzsche singles out Wagner, among artists, as the most powerful exemplar of the fact that "the genius must not fear the most antagonistic conflict with existing forms and orders if he wants to bring to light the higher order and truth dwelling within him." These words proclaim a revolutionary stance which, influenced by Heine, summons others beyond the breaking of the chains between men to the new station of the thinker and creative artist. No exception is made for the relationship with Wagner.

On August 8, 1874, after concerted efforts by friends, the first edition of Nietzsche's treatise on Schopenhauer came out. Gersdorff had temporarily taken over the correspondence with Bayreuth, thereby receiving Wagner's first gratitude and expression of delight for the book.

Meanwhile, Nietzsche felt sufficiently restored to exploit his eyes for lengthier letters. One of the first and longest, unfortunately destroyed in Bayreuth, was addressed to Wagner, who promptly responded:

"Dear friend! That was a lovely surprise, your handwriting once again! And yet at seeing it, I felt mostly anxiety, just as you generally are now causing me more anxiety than joy—and that is saying a great deal, for no one can feel as much joy over you as I. Thus today, all I can communicate is this prevailing anxiety, and so I begin: Has your doctor really permitted you to write such cramped letters? I, for my part, in replying to you, am at least making an effort to write broadly, in opposition to my usual habit, to excuse myself, as it were, for writing to you at all. I have omitted writing for such a long time, sadly and deliberately because—while assuming Gersdorff's intervention—I was vain enough to assume that you would want to read a letter from me by yourself, which must be very bad for you. Well, now I am doing it, although I do not trust your doctor's concessions; for in my own physician, I once again see how much these fellows are worth, since he always keeps assuring me that I am indestructibly healthy, whereas I drag about night and day in a miserable state, which he laughingly describes as the quite usual sufferings of 'genius.' Well, may God grant that your medico be a less enthusiastic creature and be right! As for you, let me repeat the idea that I just recently expressed to my near and dear: namely, that I can foresee the time in which I will have to defend your book against yourself.—I have been rereading it, and I swear by God that I consider you the only person in the world who knows what I am after! On October 31 (Feast of Reformation)—may you see again splendidly, and all sorts of things as well."

Meanwhile, in Bayreuth, there were more and more worries about whether the *Festspiel* idea would come true. The appeal by the surrogate author Stern had no effect, and Ludwig II had cut off subsidies, Wagner was seriously thinking of sending a circular letter to the patrons and participants that his venture had failed. This was impeded by Emil Heckel, who dashed to Bayreuth and wouldn't hear of Wagner's defeatism: "It's out of the question!"

Heckel begged the Grand Duke of Baden to see whether the Kaiser in Berlin would be willing to donate the necessary funds for staging the *Nibelungenring* in Bayreuth for the fifth anniversary of the peace treaty, in 1877. One hundred thousand thalers, mostly from private sources, had already been eaten up, and there were many debts. Another hundred thousand thalers were needed for preparations and constructions. But the Grand Duke declined, suspecting that Wagner's wishes would find little enthusiasm in Berlin.

After they had nervously scraped along for a bit, the king of Bavaria finally came to the rescue. His annoyance and original refusal were explained: The writer Felix Dahn[1] had written a hymn and sent it to the Bavarian residence. Ludwig had had it dispatched to Wagner with no personal note, hoping he would set it to music. The composer, not realizing that this was a modestly tacit personal wish of the king's, had turned it down, thereby offending Ludwig. A friendly courtier cleared up the misunderstanding, and now cash was advanced from the royal treasury. Nietzsche shook his head, wondering how "Wagner will ever repay the money."

Ludwig's letter to Wagner of January 24, 1874, utters the almost shattering anguish of the admirer of Wagner: "No! No, and no again! It shall not end like that; you must be helped! Our plan must not fail!" And Wagner flattered him in return: "Oh, my gracious King! Just glance about at all the German rulers and you will see that you are the only one upon whom the German spirit can look with hope." A contract for the loan was drawn up between Wagner's administrative board and the Court Secretary.

The anxieties of the past four months had not kept Wagner from working; his melancholy was never permitted to gain the upper hand. Cosima, in the brief pauses between corresponding and negotiating, found time to study Nietzsche's essay *On the Uses and Disadvantages of History for Life,* his second *Untimely Reflection.* An opinion that Cosima voiced to her friend Marie von Schleinitz can scarcely be explained with just personal distaste and lack of knowledge:

"The beginning is somewhat difficult, and the reader must be informed about changes in the German university system in order to follow easily. Moreover, the form is not wholly free of affectation of Classicism (Roman and Greek), but it is very remarkable, I think, for its ardor, its wit, and its acute perception of the weaknesses of an age in which, as Schopenhauer puts it, philosophy sprouts forth from apothecaries and clinics, and the soul is thought of as having its seat in the brain!"

Nietzsche, unconcerned about his future, had broken with the university hierarchy, and Cosima compared him to Wagner—wrongly, since the composer's disgust at the "lofty and swollen-headed fraternities of scholars" was actually an expression of wounded vanity.

Wagner, at first just like Cosima, seems to have extolled the essay with his old heartiness. Nietzsche generally found his letter to be well-wishing, as he told Gersdorff: "Wonderful letter from Bayreuth!" But then, at Easter 1874, he learned from the publisher Fritzsch that Wagner had made cool and even derogatory comments about the book.

With the triumph of his project, the Master demanded that all his friends put their own affairs aside and devote themselves exclusively to his cause. They were to suffer when he suffered and to perk up whenever handicaps were disposed of. Nietzsche did make an effort to go along with this; but he also wrote books that had nothing to do with Bayreuth. As Ritschl once pointed out, Nietzsche was less than useless for partisan struggles; but Bayreuth was demanding more and more of a partisan commitment and forcing him into the warfare of political groups. However,

Wagner's fear that "Nietzsche goes his own ways, one has to take him as he is," did come true.

Wagner's thank-you note for the book still sounds cordial:

"Dear friend! A whole week ago we obtained your new work from the bookdealer, devoting three well-considered evenings to its perusal. I kept meaning to write to you in between, but the problem is that excitement always makes one talk and talk; and in the end, whole dissertations lie before one, scarcely proper for a letter.—In all terseness, I would have had one thing to call to you, namely that I feel a fine pride at having nothing more to say and being able to leave everything else up to you. Everything 'else'? Why, that might make one apprehensive, of course! But it is always a comfort to know that a thing has been tackled at the right point.—You aren't expecting praise from me, are you? A fine thing if I were to praise your fire, your wit!—My wife always hits upon the right way to do such a thing—just like a woman. And she will not be caught wanting.—Now may God bless us all! He won't have much to do, for there are so awfully few of us!— My great cause will come through in order. Things will probably start in 1876. Full rehearsals next year, the freest use of time is indispensable.—Our house will be done in May: Your room will then be ready. I hope that you'll be relaxing here, the environs are mountainous enough!"

Later, Nietzsche, in a letter to Rohde, described how he had helped himself tide over the alarming news of the possible collapse of the Bayreuth adventure:

"It was a dismal condition, since New Year's, from which I managed to rescue myself in a most peculiar fashion: with the greatest coolness of observation I started investigating why the enterprise had failed. In so doing, I learned a great deal, and I believe that now I understand Wagner much better than before."

The notes in this connection were apparently intended for a book, though not for immediate publication. The chapter headings and a few additional aphorisms already bear the title of the fourth *Untimely Reflection: Richard Wagner in Bayreuth.*

The following outline occurs in the jottings:

1. Reasons for failure, especially the alienating factors. Lack of sympathy for Wagner. Difficult, complicated. 2. Wagner's double nature. 3. Affect, ecstasy, perils. 4. Music and drama. The juxtapo-

sition. 5. The presumptuous. 6. Late adulthood. Gradual development. 7. Wagner as writer. 8. Friends (arouse my misgivings). 9. Foes (arouse no respect, no interest for the object of feuding). 10. Alienation explained: perhaps removed? Wagner attempts the renovation of art from the only extant basis, the theater: Here, after all, a crowd is still excited and doesn't deceive itself as in museums and concerts. Of course, it's still a very raw mass, and it has not yet proven possible to regain control of the theocracy. Problem: Shall art always be sectarian and isolated? Is it possible to restore its dominion? Here lies Wagner's significance, he attempts *tyrannis* with the aid of the theater masses. There is probably no doubt that had Wagner been Italian he would have reached his goal. The German has no notion of opera and always regards it as imported and un-German. He doesn't even take theater as a whole seriously.—There's something comical about that: Wagner is unable to coax the Germans into taking theater seriously. They remain cold and aloof. He strains himself as if the salvation of the Germans depended on it. Now at any rate the Germans feel they have more serious things to do, and it strikes them as humorous and wildly fanciful that someone can so lugubriously occupy himself with art.—Not reformer Wagner. For until now everything is still the same. In Germany every person takes himself seriously: people laugh at the man who claims seriousness for himself alone. Effect of the financial crises.—General insecurity in the political situation. Doubts in the prudent steering of German destiny. Era of artistic excitement (Liszt, et al) is past. . . . An earnest nation will not let a few frivolities wither away, and the Germans not in the theatrical arts.—Main thing: The importance of art such as Wagner's does not fit into our social and working conditions. Hence, instinctive aversion to the unsuitable.—Wagner's first problem: Why does the impact fail if *I* can feel it? This makes him criticize the public, the state, the society. He (quite naively) places the subject-object relationship between the artist and the audience.—One characteristic of Wagner's: Boisterousness, unrestraint, he mounts to the very last rung of his energy and feeling. The other characteristic is a grand talent for acting, which is shifted, which forges ahead on other paths than the one nearest at hand: for this he lacks physique, voice, and the necessary modesty. —Wagner is a born actor, but like Goethe virtually a painter with a painter's hands, his talent seeks and finds other possibilities.— Now just imagine these frustrated instincts working together.— Wagner appreciates dramatic simplicity because the effect is strongest. He gathers all effective elements in an age that requires extremely brutal and strong expedients against its obtuseness. The splendid, the intoxicating, the confusing, the grandiose, the terrifying, the ugly, the noisy, the ecstatic, the nervous—everything is all right for him. Huge dimensions, huge means.—The irregular, the overladen brilliance and adornment seem rich and lush. He knows what our people react to: yet he has always idealized 'our people' and highly esteemed them.—As an actor, he wanted to imitate man only at his most effective and his most real: in the highest affect. For in all other conditions, his extreme nature saw weakness and untruth. The danger of depicting affect is enormous for the artist. Intoxication, sensuality, ecstasy, abruptness, poignancy at any cost—dreadful tendencies.—Wagner's art gathers everything together that is still attractive to modern Germans —character, knowledge, everything comes together. An enormous attempt at asserting himself and dominating—in an antiartistic age. Fighting fire with fire. All over-exaggerations are polemically directed against great antiartistic powers. Religious and philosophical elements are involved. Yearning for the idyllic, everything, everything.—Not to be forgotten: This is a theatrical language that Wagner's art is speaking, it doesn't belong in a room, a *camera*. It is a national parlance, unthinkable without a great coarsening of even the noblest aspects. It is meant to keep working far into the distance and patch the national chaos together. For instance the Imperial March.—Wagner has a legislative nature: he overlooks many things and is no stickler for details, he arranges everything on a large scale and cannot be judged in terms of isolated particulars.—Music, drama, poetry, state, art, etc. —The music isn't worth much, nor is the poetry, the theatrical art is often mere rhetoric—but as a whole everything is of a piece and on one level.—He has a feeling for *unity* in *diversity*.—That is why I regard him as a bearer of culture.

This analysis, stamped equally with pity, admiration, and disgust, is quoted in its entirety and not just for the light it sheds on Wagner. It also shows Nietzsche's preview of the artistic state of ensuing generations. A determining factor, no doubt, is a despairing anxiety that Wagner might not bring his plans to fruition. Thus Nietzsche all the more readily looked upon it as a "miracle" when the good news reached him. He wrote to Rohde: "If the miracle is real, it still doesn't upset the result of my meditations. But let us be happy and celebrate if it is real!"

Nevertheless, a feeling of doleful melancholy remained whenever he thought of this essay. Who knows the history of his countless secret rebellions?

A commitment to propagating the Master's significance was no longer Nietzsche's point of orientation. On the contrary, he regarded his previous recruitment for Wagner's music as confining and the circle he had hitherto addressed as too limited. His view of higher things became clearer and clearer. Waving off Gersdorff's praise, he owned up to his discouragement.

Wagner presumably at first shared Cosima's enthusiasm for the essay *On the Use and Disadvantage of History for Life.* Yet the beauteous words in Cosima's letter struck Nietzsche more as blossoms covering a harsh put-down. For the Master, this piece must have been "inaccessible." And Nietzsche, as on earlier occasions, could only smirk at Cosima's critique of his style. In conversation, he often made fun of her as the native Frenchwoman, who, in regard to German style, would do much better applying her editorial zeal to Wagner's own writings.

Nietzsche, feeling unfree, rebelled. But at the same time, he was afraid of frittering away his energies in the struggle for inner liberty: "One achieves freedom and is as worn out as an ephemera in the evening." Thoughtlessly, he may have penned such depressed statements in letters to Bayreuth. Wagner would have loved to bring Nietzsche there without further ado.

For the moment, the Wagners had to put off courting Nietzsche. Although distracted by the construction of the Festival Theater and his private villa, Wagner, during that year, orchestrated *Götterdämmerung* and penned the *Parsifal* libretto. Wahnfried, a majestic mansion even for those days, was finished by spring 1874. From the Master's study, one could look down into the garden; the windows of the gigantic room opened in a semi-circle on to a perron; and the walls were covered with book-lined shelves. One could reach the study through a rectangular hallway paved with marble. To its right and left were the parlor and the dining room; the bedrooms and the nursery were one flight up. Carved into three plates on the façade of the house stand the words:

Hier wo mein Wähnen Frieden fand,
Wahnfried sei dieses Haus von mir benannt.
[Here where my illusions found peace,
Illusive Peace be the name of this house.]

The pompous furnishings were in keeping with contemporary notions of sumptuousness. Wagner's pathological love of satin and damask draperies dominated the scene. The inventory, admired and unchanged until 1939, was evacuated during World War II, only to be destroyed by a bomb just a few days before the end. Anyone who visited the old Wahnfried usually never tires of carrying on about its uniqueness and the imposing presence of Cosima, an old lady with princely airs, going about in her world of the past, although mentally mobile and interested in everything around her.

Early in the summer of 1874, the Wagners sent Nietzsche a pointedly friendly invitation to come and view their estate. Once again Nietzsche declined, traveling instead to an Alpine hamlet, where he completed his Schopenhauer essay. Gersdorff's efforts at getting Nietzsche to accept the invitation were unavailing: Why, for no good reason, stir up a mistrust to which Wagner by nature leaned? "Bear in mind," replied Nietzsche, "that I have duties towards myself, which are hard to fulfill considering my very frail health. Really, no one ought to force me into anything."

Trustingly, Nietzsche opened up to Fräulein von Meysenbug: "Even hostile counter-effects now turn into useful and happy things, for they often enlighten me more rapidly than friendly cooperativeness; and there is nothing I would desire more than to be enlightened about the entire dreadfully complex system of antagonisms of which the 'modern world' consists. Fortunately, I lack all political and social ambitions so that on this point I need have no fears of any perils, any distractions, any compulsion for transactions and considerations; in short, I am *permitted* to say what I think, and I would like to test the extent to which our fellow men, who are proud of freedom of thought, actually endure free thought. I do not demand too much from life and nothing excessive. On the other hand, the next few years will bring us things for which both the past and posterity will envy us. At any rate, I have been blessed with excellent friends, certainly more than I merit; and now, speaking confidentially, I would soon wish for a good wife; then, I think, my life's desires will be fulfilled."

But the future would show how hopelessly theoretical Nietzsche's marriage wishes became. During that summer, his mother and his sister, protective and jealous at once, wanted him under their wing. The Wagner family also had matrimonial plans for the professor: They apparently wanted to channel the reveries of the "pathologically" sensitive Nietzsche; and since he was always far away, they wanted to tie him to the Bayreuth venture. Cosima, Wagner, and Gersdorff held a powwow in Bayreuth to determine how they might help Nietzsche. The subject of their deliberations articulated his amusements in a letter to Gersdorff:

"How really childish is the thought of your sitting down with the Bayreuthers as a Commission for Pondering Matrimony! Yes buuuut! My sentiments exactly! Especially when the upshot of the whole thing is to advise me that there are many women and that finding the right one is my task. Shall I then, like a knight, go on a crusade through the world to reach your praised and promised land? Or do you imagine that women will come to me to be inspected so that I can see if any of them is the right one? I find this theme a bit impossible. Or else, prove the contrary, and make use of it for yourself."

In August 1874, to the satisfaction of the Wagners, Friedrich and Elisabeth finally did come to Bayreuth. But this time, the guest was a man of few words. The brother and sister lodged at the *Sonne.* The very first evening, Nietzsche sent a message to Wahnfried that he wasn't feeling well. Wagner straightway hurried over to the hotel, brought Nietzsche to his villa, and spent an interesting evening with him after Nietzsche's speedy recovery.

"But what he reports about the university people is horrifying. As usual he can talk about the articles in the *Neue Freie Presse* and such things, and he also speaks of Dubois-Reymond, who, in a *Speech on the German Language* played Lessing against Goethe, whom he described as detrimental to the German nation." Thus wrote a dismayed Cosima in her diary.

The next day, Nietzsche was sick of the impersonal conversations and seemed intent on provoking Wagner. During June of the previous year, Nietzsche, upon hearing Brahms conduct his *Song of Triumph* for chorus and orchestra at the Cathedral of Basel, had procured himself a piano version. The score in his baggage was just the thing to annoy Wagner, who, he knew, had a great distaste for Brahms's highly traditional music. He deposited the keyboard reduction on the grand piano in the large drawing room of Wahnfried, so that the red thing sneered up at the Master. Wagner did not hold back for long: "I could see that Nietzsche was trying to say: Just look, here's someone who can also do good things. —Well, one evening I burst out, and *how* I burst out!" Nietzsche did not reply, but merely turned crimson as usual and gaped at the herald of future music. Wagner subsequently remarked: "I would give a hundred marks on the spot just to have such fine behavior as Nietzsche, always noble, always dignified." And, with a martyrial pose, he added: "This sort of thing can be a lot of use in this world." Whereas Wagner's outburst quickly subsided, Nietzsche bore him a grudge for this "insult" for a good long time. He refused to visit the composer until July 1876 during the final rehearsals of the *Ring*—two years of abstinence for his still loving devotion.

Nietzsche never depicted the scene of the Brahms score; he was evidently more embarrassed than Wagner assumed. If anyone mentioned it to Nietzsche, he would say: "It wasn't very big of Wagner." The incident acquires a particular shade of meaning if one remembers that by then, Nietzsche's passion for Brahms's music had already cooled off. He had toppled Robert Schumann, the musical idol of his youth, upon finding a new idol under the Italian sun. Yet this boyhood love for Schumann still maintained an urgency for him. Schumann gave way to Brahms, whom Nietzsche likewise loved and revered for the poetry of his music. Nietzsche greeted Brahms with open arms, like all who suffered from a conflict over Wagner. The philosopher found Brahms therapeutic and actually more German than Wagner, which meant a number of things and not just positive ones. For he soon harbored a suspicion that Germany's "solid mediocrity" felt a kinship with Brahms's music. This composer struck Nietzsche as the spokesman of the North German soul—"no event, no exception, no break in the chain before Wagner, but rather *one more* link. If we disregard what he occasionally offered up to a virtually hospitable genius of foreign ways and people (including sacrifices of pious devotion to greater teachers, old and new), then he is *the* musician having, until now, a sole claim to the designation 'the North German musician.'" Nietzsche also coined a phrase for him, "Melancholy of incapacity," later taken up by Hugo Wolf in a review. Brahms struck Nietzsche as thirsting for fullness rather than creating it; a misunderstanding possibly going back to Nietzsche's jealousy as a musician *manqué*.

Returning to Bayreuth in August 1874, he once again overhauled part of his *Schopenhauer as Educator.* Sadly, the first draft no longer exists, which makes it hard to distinguish what and how much was modified out of love for Wagner. On September 24, Nietzsche wrote to Gersdorff:

"The inevitable physical exhaustion and spiritual shock inflicted on me by such brooding and pondering in the depths very nearly felled me, and even now I haven't fully recovered from that childbed fever. Nonetheless, something really good has been brought into the world, and I am delighted to think that you will be delighted at it."

In Bayreuth, Nietzsche announced the speedy arrival of the book, as can be seen from a letter draft, the final version having then been destroyed in Bayreuth:

"The summer is now completely over, and so is my autumn liberty; the coming together of my friends, which I had proposed for this time, has either come to naught or else turned into something else—Gersdorff was expected almost any day and then showed up right in the middle of my school time, Rohde had even worse luck when he moved in here for three weeks. All of us were unbearably overworked and could scarcely devote ourselves to our friend. . . . The next few days, I think, will be bringing you my number 3, which I heartily recommend to your sympathetic favor. Other readers will think I'm talking about the man in the moon."

Wagner promptly cabled back: "Telegraphic—deep and grand. Newest and most daring the depiction of Kant. Truly intelligible only to the obsessed!"

It cannot be maintained that the "obsessed" reader Wagner spared any pains for his friendship with Nietzsche. He heaped lofty praises on *Schopenhauer as Educator,* although the Bayreuthers naturally raised their eyebrows at the following lines: "I want to make an effort at achieving freedom, says the young soul; and should it be prevented simply because two nations happen to hate, and are warring with, one another?"

But this book is largely stamped by Nietzsche's love of Wagner. Like Schopenhauer, Wagner was an experience for young Nietzsche, comparable to Goethe's enthusiasm for Herder, including the later revulsion. It was Wagner who first fulfilled for Nietzsche what Schopenhauer, already silent, could no longer engender.

The philosopher Schopenhauer and the musician Wagner melted, for Nietzsche, into *one* person; and if Wagner initially appeared to embody what Schopenhauer calls a genius, then in *Schopenhauer as Educator* (and not just there) the philosopher becomes a synonym for Wagner, a disguise for Nietzsche's gratitude and devotion to Wagner. Nietzsche may have been seeking the man rather than the doctrine, the thinker rather than the ideology, the teacher rather than the legacy. What he at first believed he had found in Wagner was the venerable man, the timeless man he so desired.

Meanwhile, however, Nietzsche's ideas were germinating for the fourth *Untimely Reflection, Richard Wagner in Bayreuth*, which originally did not promise to be an encomium. As though trying to wrench himself away from planning this book, Nietzsche started on a manuscript *We Classicists*, which got no further than summing up earlier thoughts about education modeled on the Greek ideal. But he was no longer really interested in the topic, and so the piece remained unfinished. The year was uncertain and crisis-ridden for him. A more intense association with his Basel colleagues helped only for a time.

And yet Nietzsche sensed that things were advancing even if the thick air of scholarship "was eclipsing the sun." Of the thirteen *Untimely Reflections* haunting his mind, three were finished and the fourth was drafted. But teaching in Basel was making him miserable. He was stupefied by having to prepare for the following terms, and felt hampered from pursuing what he viewed as his real "obligation." These included his rapport with the few like-minded people, whose existence always reminded him of necessary things. For Wagner was not the only one who had had to realize how greatly Nietzsche now required isolation for creating.

In 1874, on the second day of Christmas, Wagner wrote to Basel, and his letter attests to unchanged feelings as well as apprehensions about the friendship. Anxieties were aired, but the (justified) fear of vexing the addressee, were Wagner to reveal what all the world was saying about Nietzsche, remained. But Wagner also tried to give comfort by pointing out that he himself was not granted the association of other men such as Nietzsche enjoyed every evening in Basel. "I believe you ought to marry or

compose an opera; either would be as good or as bad for you as
the other. But I consider marriage better."

Wagner was luring Nietzsche with the prospect of living together, an idea that already sounded old-fashioned: He and
Cosima had agreed to arrange the house in such a way that there
would be a place "for you too." Doleful (and forgetful), Wagner
reminisces that he was never offered anything of the sort even
when down and out. He had already misjudged Nietzsche's contrary needs when hoping that the friend would lodge with him all
summer. And he had certainly not been mistaken in seeing Nietzsche's refusal as precautionary against an invitation to Bayreuth.

"We can be something to you; why do you scorn this so fervently? Gersdorff and the whole Basilicum can spare your time
here. . . . I don't want to talk about you anymore, it doesn't help
at all! For goodness' sakes! Marry a rich woman! Just why did
Gersdorff have to be a male! Then marry; compose your opera,
which will probably be bloody hard to perform.—What the devil
made you a pedagogue anyway?"

An opera? What can Wagner mean? A ten-day vacation at home
in Naumburg lay behind Nietzsche, and he felt revitalized, chiefly
because all his 'thinking and pondering' had suddenly refocused
on music. He was jotting down thousands of notes, and at least
one opus was complete, the *Hymn to Friendship*, which he had
started the previous year, after the awkward sojourn in Bayreuth,
while spending a solitary Easter in Nuremberg on the way back
to Basel.

He expounded on the form of the *Hymn* to Malwida von Meysenbug. It could be played by two hands or four:

> *Prelude of the friends to the temple of friendship*
> *Hymn, 1st strophe.*
> *Interlude—as in bitter-sweet remembrance*
> *Hymn, 2nd strophe*
> *Interlude, as a foretelling of the future*
> *A view into the farthest distance*
> *In departure: Chorus of friends, 3rd strophe and finale.*

Was he content with the result since he had finally undertaken
to express something about his relationship to Wagner at least in

notes? Ah, if only those fifteen minutes of music could please someone else as much as their creator! To forget time, capture the ideality of man! "Moreover, I have revised my youthful compositions and put them in order. I never cease to be amazed at how the unchangeability of character is revealed in music; whatever a stripling says in music is so markedly the utterance of the basic essence of his *entire* nature that the man would not change anything in it. Except, of course, the imperfection of the technique, etc."

But that was the rub—the technique. That was the thorn of remaining behind the great man who, going beyond his beginnings as a verbal artist, had managed to become a true composer. Nor did any desperate reference to a possibly inherited talent help in any way:

"If, according to Schopenhauer, the will is inherited from the father and the intellect from the mother, then it seems to me that music as the expression of the will might also be the father's legacy. Just look closely at your experience: my experience confirms that statement."

As late as 1886, Cosima explained in a letter to Felix Mottl that the *Hymn to Friendship* had brought about the rupture—a fact that made her "very sad." But Cosima also voiced a derogatory comment about Nietzsche's musical diction.

Soon Nietzsche followed up with a *Hymn to Solitude*, which he talked about to Rohde:

"I work in the most infrequent moments now, ten minutes every few weeks, on a hymn to solitude. I want to capture it [solitude] in all its dreadful beauty."

The manuscript was lost. Peter Gast had a recollection of the piece: "My memory particularly retains his *Hymn to Solitude*, a piece full of harsh greatness and relentlessness, mixed with fascinating *dolce* passages that are siren-like and yet promptly and defiantly rejected."

En route from Naumburg to Basel, through deep snow and biting cold, Nietzsche read a letter from Gersdorff, telling how they were all looking forward to the Bayreuth rehearsals. Cosima had inserted a note, asking Nietzsche's sister to drop by in Bayreuth and "stay as a mother to my children," while the Wagners traveled to Vienna and Budapest. In weighing his answer, Nietzsche, in his compartment corner, welcomed the thought of obligating his friends without really having to commit his own person.

In March 1875, Nietzsche's sister did indeed visit Bayreuth, "in a kind of higher school," as the brother somewhat mockingly put it. He was happy that Elisabeth had made up her mind. As we can tell from earlier letters, Wagner planned to stipulate Nietzsche as Siegfried's guardian in his will. Hence Nietzsche felt it was important for his sister to familiarize herself with conditions in Wahnfried. For he was very serious about the "manifold obligations" he might someday have towards Wagner's family.

The Wagners received Elisabeth very cordially at Wahnfried. Cosima made thirty-two calls with her, as the sister later so proudly counted up, so that she might be acquainted with just about everything concerning the house. Wagner showed himself to be a good *pater familias*. In the midst of his work he would unexpectedly come to the children to play horse-and-wagon with them and spread good cheer. But then again, if outsiders got on his nerves, especially with pleas to look over their compositions, he could turn very impatient. One day, an unusually thick package arrived, and Wagner amusedly related that it contained an opera by a bank director. Elisabeth, shaken, blurted out that this was the bank where she kept her stocks. Wagner raised his finger in warning: "My child! Sell those stocks! A bank director who writes operas is neglecting his bank." As a matter of fact, the institution did go bankrupt, and the young lady forfeited several thousand marks for not heeding Wagner's advice.

Cosima and Elisabeth assumed a sisterly *"Du,"* the German familiar form, as indicated in Cosima's letters to Malwida. Elisabeth felt that Cosima was too lanky and skinny for a woman and her mouth and nose were too big. But she also portrayed her as the "embodiment of the will and the yearning for power in the noblest sense." During Wagner's lifetime, Cosima exercised this power through him. After his decease, she revealed her eminent gift as ruler over the entire Bayreuth enterprise.

Nietzsche was interested to hear details from Bayreuth, which Elisabeth told him in letters and then personally. He realized the Wagners felt as friendly towards him as ever. He learned the same thing from Gersdorff, who visited Nietzsche in Basel for several weeks and whom Wagner evidently considered the only person to whom he could impart his thoughts on Nietzsche. In May 1875, Wagner wrote to Gersdorff: "How often . . . is a close encounter with another person merely a disturbing impact! That certainly doesn't hold true for our beloved Nietzsche, whom I cannot imagine as being happier without knowing me. Yet he met me in a field of life that easily becomes a quagmire for us if we cannot fly away at times." And a postscript adds: "In six days, we are celebrating the sixth anniversary of Nietzsche's first stay at Tribschen!!!"

When it came to festive occasions, the creators of the *Festspiele* were true virtuosi. May and December were the months of the big birthdays: Siegfried's and the father's were commemorated in spring; and at the year's end Cosima celebrated Christmas with religious flatulence. All in all, the festivities, whether pagan or Christian, served the Wahnfried cult. Live tableaux were set up and picture postcards of family happiness dispatched to the four corners of the earth. Thus dwelt the Wagners, in high spirits, with an aviary in the garden, and pomp and circumstance for visiting prominence.

Returning to Basel, Nietzsche wrote to Erwin Rohde:

"In Bayreuth, too, I was asked for news of you. You know, and yet scarcely know full well, *how* warmly and heartily they think of you there and worry about you. At present, my sister is in Bayreuth and plans to stay for several weeks. I also want to pass on that Frau Wagner asks you to petition the burgomaster of Bayreuth speedily and stormily for lodgings this summer; it will be difficult finding quarters for all the guests, and the burgomaster is supposedly being nagged to death because the whole housing matter is in a bad way. You certainly wouldn't want to request 'a modest apartment.' My sister is doing her best to find something for herself and me, so far without success." But meanwhile, the semester was still in full swing: three weeks to go at the university and five at the Paedagogium.

Basel was in a turmoil, for the new constitution of the city was being discussed in the Council. All parties were up in arms, and the populace was supposed to decide the matter in spring. A passage from *Schopenhauer as Educator* was used in the political combat (it criticized the omnipotence of the State). And Nietzsche was all the more delighted because he usually felt "as if I had turned into a lord of a manor—my way of life has become so sheltered and inwardly independent. Number 4 will be ready at Easter."

He now began the essay *Richard Wagner in Bayreuth* with the sincere intention of doing something for Wagner's cause. For he had once again had a surge of genuine enthusiasm at Easter 1875 upon acquiring the newly published piano score of *The Twilight of the Gods.* His judgment: "This is heaven on earth." Meanwhile, parts of the *Ring* were heard at a joint Wagner/Liszt recital in Budapest. Liszt conducted his own *Bells of Strasbourg* and played Beethoven's Concerto in E flat Major under Hans Richter. This was followed by fragments of the *Ring* with Wagner at the podium. The receipts of these concerts in Vienna and Pest went to cover the costs of try-outs, which were starting on July 1, in Bayreuth, under Richter's direction. The *Festspiele* were definitively scheduled for summer 1876, a year later.

At Wagner's birthday, Nietzsche wrote him that he so greatly admired the Master's sprightly resistance during these past few years, in the chaos of tasks, pressures, annoyances, and fatigue. Wagner's life always seemed so dramatic to Nietzsche, "as though you were such an inveterate dramatist that you yourself can only live in this form and, at any rate, die no earlier than at the close of Act V. Where everything rushes and dashes towards one goal, chance drops back—apparently fearful. Everything becomes necessary, an iron law, amid utter agitation, such as I find in your expression on the medallion that I was recently given..." Apparently bitter, Nietzsche adds: "We other human beings flicker somewhat, and thus there is nothing steady even about health." And he evinced tragic clear-sightedness in enclosing a Hölderlin poem[2] that contained the lines:

> *"Du land der Liebe! bin ich der deine schon,*
> *Oft zürnt ich weinend, dass du immer*
> *Blöde die eigene Seele leugnest.*
>
> * * *
>
> *Noch säumst und schweigst du, sinnest ein freudig Werk,*
> *Das von dir zeuge, sinnest ein neu Gebild,*
> *Das einzig, wie du selber, das aus*
> *Liebe geboren und gut, wie du, sei."*

You land of love! Though now I am yours,
I often cursed and wept that you always
Foolishly deny your very own soul.

* * *

You tarry still in silence, pondering a joyous Work
That attests to you, pondering a new creation
That, like yourself, is born out of love,
And that, like yourself, is good.

Nietzsche's failing health wrecked his plans of going to Bayreuth; a bad time was at hand for him. "My stomach was fully out of control, despite a laughably rigid diet; headaches lasting for days on end and recurring every few days; vomiting for hours, without having eaten anything; in short, the machine seemed about to go to pieces, and I cannot deny that there were moments I wished it would. Great listlessness, difficulties in walking out of doors, strong sensitivity to light." The physician, Professor Hermann Immerman, warned him not to travel to Bayreuth. "I won't say anything, you can imagine how I feel" (to Gersdorff).

Under these circumstances, he had no choice but to make sure of his sister's presence. After the summer holidays, the two of them moved into a new apartment near the old one, to find "an extremely precise way of living. . . . Wagner will be quite angry, and so am I."

First, he was to take the waters in Steinabad, a tiny spa in the Black Forest, especially recommended for gastric diseases. But before leaving with his sister, Nietzsche was very intent on discussing Bayreuth once more with Gersdorff. The friend, who scarcely had any time for himself, lost his temper at Nietzsche's "arrogant hankering," for he simply couldn't come to Basel. Meanwhile, Nietzsche roamed about the woods, lost in hopeful reveries about the future. His diet and headaches notwithstanding, he felt better at the thought of the work ahead.

He rashly imagined the household arranged by his sister as "a new, solid skin, a snail's house, in which he could picture himself. Most of his thoughts, however, wandered towards Bayreuth; his letters implored Gersdorff and Rohde to describe the rehearsals. Nietzsche knew whole stretches of the music by heart, and as he went on his lonesome walks, he would hum and conduct it to himself. But mostly, he was bedridden with headaches and vomited all night. The illness, diagnosed as expansion of the stomach, appeared to require a rigorous treatment. To Rohde, he complained:

"Distress and crossness torment me most of all when I see that a man is totally useless and is forced to let things take their course no matter how merciless they may be. And then there are times when I feel I'm something of a lucky devil and that I've been spared the harshest attacks of suffering." What happened was that Rohde was caught in an unhappy love affair. Nietzsche would have been more than pleased to "give you some good fortune," thereby hinting that his absence from Bayreuth didn't necessarily make him miserable and could just as easily be interpreted as a kind of escape from the menacing experience. Other friends were likewise badly off, and Nietzsche asked Rohde in amazement: "Desperation everywhere! And yet not with me! And I'm not even in Bayreuth. And yet I'm there in spirit more than eighteen hours a day and hover about Bayreuth like a ghost. . . ."

The music Nietzsche hummed on his strolls now strained forth to the hammering of the pianos in the rehearsal rooms and on the stage at Bayreuth. Only a brief time ago, Wagner had ended the gigantic task of instrumenting the *Ring*. On the very last page, he noted: "Completed in Wahnfried, that is all I have to say." The entire score was preceded by the words: "Begun with confidence in the German Spirit and completed for the glory of its sublime benefactor, Ludwig II of Bavaria." This sentence mirrored the tempestuous story of the opus through fifteen years. The snide remarks against the philanthropist and the recipient can still be heard today. But one may counter with the question: Could any patronage have been more worthwhile than Ludwig's? We can certainly understand the excitement of the financial authorities in Munich. But without the king's "squandering," the world would be several masterpieces poorer. And the thalers that might have been saved—what good would they do today?

Wagner drew up a schedule for the coming years. The impatient man showed sudden patience, realizing that success could only come without rash haste. The totally new arrangement of a "rehearsal year" was to be maintained in Bayreuth for decades and only given up during World War II. Every other year (as Wagner prescribed), the singers were to gather in Bayreuth for

July and August "to study their roles thoroughly, one month with the piano, but in the second month on the stage, already furnished with the most important decorations." In the Festival year, Wagner wanted to start dress rehearsals right away, after working with the orchestra, the machinery, and the lights for two months without the singers. The entire four-part *Ring* was to be mounted three times in the course of twelve evenings.

Every detail of the plan was ready in 1874, and even today, the Festival (marvelously and astonishingly) adheres to the particulars that Wagner thus defined to King Ludwig:

"Every performance shall begin at four in the afternoon; the second act follows at six o'clock, the third at eight, so that a significant intermission shall take place between every two successive acts, permitting the audience to stroll through the park surrounding the theater and have refreshments out in the open in a charming environment, so that at the peal of the trumpets from the top of the theater the spectators, fully refreshed, may gather in the auditorium with the same receptivity as at the first act. I think that the sunset before the last act will then provide a particularly hallowed atmosphere."

Since, in Wagner's eyes, it was an honor for any singer to be permitted to appear in Bayreuth, they would have to generously forego "any gain or compensation for guest performances and the like." The vocalists he had engaged during the past few years offered him such a wonderful choice of voices and dramatic talents that he could "look at their physiques as well." His "gods, giants, and heroes are all of an excellent stature, so that whenever one of these giants arrived at the railroad station, people instantly said: 'Here comes another Nibelung.' "

The preparations went according to Wagner's specifications. Anything but nervous or authoritarian, he was more like a comrade to his performers. The rehearsals proceeded merrily. At the last piano run-throughs, in the Hotel Sonne, the sixty-two-year-old composer became so exuberant he stood on his head. Demanding unheard-of things from his singers without material compensation, he kept his temper, and stressed the collective nature of the work and the great goal that all of them wanted to attain.

On June 7, Hans Richter began the stage rehearsals in the

Festspielhaus. We can only guess how much technical care and work had gone on ahead, here in the provincial town of Bayreuth, to achieve grand theater with facilities so primitive as to evoke merely a smile today. Wagner's obsessive nature overcame all difficulties. He was a poet, composer, director, theater manager, and conductor in a single person. Once, a bad tooth made his face swell up, and after a few pain-wracked, sleepless nights, he could barely see. But the moment *Valkyrie* went into rehearsal, he forgot his complaint. His cheek bandaged with cotton and a thick cloth, he sprang over the rocks, rearranged any number of things, and discarded old concepts. Sieglinde, crooning: "Fight not the kiss of the accursed woman," was supposed to fling her ardent arms around Siegmund. The vocalist's arms were not ardent enough for Wagner, so he showed her how to do it. And the little man threw himself with such force upon the giant singer Niemann that the latter nearly toppled over. Wagner sang, tore Niemann around, and gave directions for a different position. Right after that, he was up in the mountainous hills, "commanding" Sieg-mund's battle with Hunding. Niemann quaked in his boots and moaned: "Merciful God, if only he'd come down. If he falls, then everything's down the drain!" But Wagner didn't fall. He sprang into the dale like a mountain goat. Hurrying by, he called out to young assistants who had settled behind a rocky wall with their piano scores: "Are you still holding on to those clumsy things? Don't you know them by heart yet?"

When friends wrote him excited letters from Bayreuth in 1875, Nietzsche was seized with his old admiration, forgetting any criti-cism for a while. In his notebook, he jotted down the following aphorism:

"I wouldn't know in what way I could ever have partaken of the *purest* sun-bright happiness except through Wagner's music: and this, even though his music by no means always speaks about happiness, but about the dreadful and uncanny subterranean forces of human action, the sorrows in all happiness and the finite nature of our happiness; hence, the happiness which that music radiates must lie in the manner in which it speaks." Nietzsche was evoking the sixteen years of happiness that Wagner's art had brought him since his fifteenth year, and he recalled those hours of friendship in Tribschen.

Thus he began writing his fourth *Untimely Reflection: Richard Wagner in Bayreuth.* The theme had originally been meant for the fifth *Reflection* and now replaced *We Classical Philologists.* The preliminary studies contain a sentence that Ernst Bertram, in his *Nietzsche,*[3] emphasized as vital to a picture of the philosopher: "I could conceive of a *forward-looking* art, which seeks its images in the future. Why is there no such thing? Art attaches itself to *reverence.*"

Wagner's disciple, who was still imbued with hope, and for whom his Master's art was as yet the only music of the future, was no iconoclast. His polemics against decadence did not exclude deep respect for the achievements of spiritual forebears. The glorifier of the moment simultaneously preached the lasting nature of sublime feeling. And his disquiet and rebelliousness were to give rise to that creative tension that could produce a new and permanent culture.

Elisabeth Nietzsche sensed her brother's inner struggles for and against Wagner when, during fall 1875, in the midst of working on his Wagner essay, he put the uncompleted manuscript aside. He had read her the first eight parts, and she was asking for the rest: "Now when I once ventured to inquire about it (something I never did because my brother generally didn't care to talk about unfinished works), he said very sadly: 'Ah, Lisbeth, if only I could.' " This means: Nietzsche must have realized his own incapacity in regard to the Wagner phenomenon at the "most difficult point," although he did end the essay the following spring and sent it to the printer in July 1876. "However, I lagged far behind what I demand of myself; and so this work only has the value, for me, of reorientation beyond the most difficult point of our experiences hitherto. I do not stand above it, and I realize I have not fully succeeded in this orientation—much less that I could help others!" (to Rohde).

At New Year's 1875, Nietzsche felt so poorly that he relinquished some of his official duties and finally went to Lake Geneva with Gersdorff for a long rest. He came back reinvigorated. Now, confronted with endless discussions about the Bayreuth Festival, he felt he could no longer remain silent about this anxiously awaited event: Gratitude for many things that Wagner had aroused in him impelled him to complete the manuscript.

A man defending a cause for its own sake often learns during the struggle that the opponent's interest really lies elsewhere; he is actually being led by personal motives. Wagner had repeatedly spoken of this experience. And indeed, the attacks based on vanity and impure motives were often more against his person than his art. His counter-attacks, for outsiders, were unedifying or puzzling. Nietzsche, in contrast, was spared any personal enemies and could thus defend ideas for their own sake. When he himself was the aggressor he battled against a type rather than a person. In the *Birth of Tragedy,* Socrates embodied theoretical optimism for him. And when he resolved to "get the lay of the land in Bayreuth," he viewed David Friedrich Strauss, author of the "pothouse gospel" of the "old and new faith," as the prototype of the educational philistine. "Culture is, more than anything, a unity of artistic style in all the life utterances of a nation." Nietzsche knew how remote his age was from such a culture.

Of the great men, few were as devoted as Nietzsche in taking up Goethe's challenge to regard the cause of humanity as one's own cause. If we call idealism the striving to make ideas come true individually and socially, then the idealist is first and foremost the man who sees his task as thoroughly renovating cultural life.

Nietzsche worshiped Schopenhauer and Wagner as models in this sense. Whereas the yawning gap between idea and reality led Schopenhauer to negate life per se, Nietzsche merely rejected the shallow optimism that contents itself with the achievements of given circumstances in life, but he did not reject the will to life. The withdrawal from Schopenhauer was unavoidable, though it did not necessarily entail a withdrawal from Wagner. For the composer, as an artist, affirmed life so obviously. But one may ask: Was Nietzsche's reverence for Wagner compatible with his high esteem for Antiquity and its "healthy doctrine of life"? Did Wagner's oeuvre truly unite the Dionysian and the Apollonian as ancient tragedy had done? Or wasn't he really rooted, perhaps unconsciously, in middle-class Christian soil? Antiquity and Christianity, Renaissance and Reformation, affirmation of life as intensification of life, negation of life for spiritual salvation—for Nietzsche, such opposites were mutually exclusive and demanded a choice from the confessor of faith. Nietzsche was convinced that Wagner's art could set the Germans against "stale Christianity," and lead German mythology to an experience of the world in terms of Antiquity and heathendom. But it wasn't the pseudo-Christian tendencies in the late Wagner that decided Nietzsche's estrangement. This had already come about earlier, and mainly in the area of aesthetics. The crucial question was: Art in the sense of ancient tragedy, or modern theater obeying the demands of the day? Apollonian vision out of the Dionysian spirit of music or naturalistic staging with music subordinate? Would the scenic action of the future be an utterance of inner processes, such as Beethoven's symphonies strove for; or would the mounting and the singing determine the character of the music?

Wagner saw the inclusion of the chorus in Beethoven's Ninth as surpassing the limits of absolute music, and he hailed it as the redemption towards comprehensive art. But Nietzsche called this attitude an "enormous aesthetic superstition," for the symphonic composer had reached, not for the declaimed word, but for the "more pleasant and more joyous" sound. This subjective pronouncement shows that Nietzsche, even during his warmest adoration of Wagner, did *not* consider theater the unification of arts enjoying an equal status, a goal overriding the value of absolute music. In Wagner, the words still had a vital effect on the music. Nietzsche regarded this as simply an old tendency in opera and described the demand for a dramatic singer outdoing the music as a "monstrosity." The true character of Nietzsche's viewpoint is evinced in his marked antipathy towards anything theatrical. Hence, for us, the question is not: How could Nietzsche become an opponent of Bayreuth? But rather: Why wasn't he aware of his opposition to Wagner from the very outset?

One could argue that he was one with Wagner in venerating Schopenhauer. The composer, like Nietzsche, despised what educated Germans called *Kultur* and what Wagner dubbed "war civilization." Nietzsche was thrilled by *Tristan* (of all of Wagner's works the most untheatrical); he had been overwhelmed by the piano arrangement, by a musical absolute, as it were, before hearing Bülow conduct it in Munich. And finally, his love for Wagner created the image of a genius in whom to have faith when he declared Bayreuth the setting for the triumph of a new art form that seemed to promise the ultimate victory over all theatrics.

How did Nietzsche imagine this art form to be? He wrongly surmised that Wagner was unconsciously aspiring to the "greatest symphony of all," which would overcome the basic ill of opera and in which the chief instruments would intone a singing that the action would sensualize. Nietzsche more and more clearly realized how antithetical his viewpoint was to Wagner's. He was now faced with either converting to Wagner's goal or owning up: Here our paths diverge. That the latter could be his only alternative is obvious when we note his zeal in stressing "the repulsive sight of the singer," and rebelling against the "falseness" of the very concept of "dramatic music." Likewise, he attributed a symptomatic importance to the resistance that Wagner ubiquitously provoked. Not lack of understanding—but a deeper revulsion.

Insight and reverence had long been in conflict by the time Nietzsche became aware of it. His mind was set on battling to regenerate the essence of art, while remaining Wagner's loving friend but preserving his own independence of judgment. The composer was far more experienced in life, and thus, earlier than Nietzsche, he sensed the dangers in subconscious incompatibilities. More and more differences occurred. Most biographers, however, wave them off as minor disturbances. Elisabeth Förster-Nietzsche, for instance, blames everything on Wagner's suspicious ways. But today we can sense how Nietzsche became more and more aware of the contrast to his own character. The posthumous works show that in 1874, two years before the first Festival, Nietzsche admitted to himself all that he found alien about Wagner.

For Nietzsche, one of the few positive features in the Bayreuth stage presentation was, strangely enough, the sunken orchestra pit, even though this afforded a greater concentration on the scenic action, something he absolutely refused to accept. Nietzsche's friends Rohde, Overbeck, and Gersdorff similarly admired this innovation, and they said as much at a garden party which was given in Wahnfried for one hundred and forty guests at the close of the rehearsal period.

On August 30, 1875, the conductor Hermann Levi, a daily visitor in Wagner's home during rehearsals, reports to his father, the chief rabbi of Giessen: "I was in Bayreuth from the 9th to the 13th and attended the rehearsals of *Siegfried* and *Götterdämmerung*.

. . . I'm old enough not to deceive myself any longer—and I tell you that the event taking place next year in Bayreuth will cause a radical upheaval in our artistic life."

Nietzsche's introspective retreat from Bayreuth also gave him detachment from his previous esteem of the possibilities of art in influencing culture. His response to the question of the task of modern art was: "All it can convey is obtuseness or intoxication." He is already speaking for the coming century, as when he ascertains that the "soul of today" more or less requires, at least for moments at a time, a silencing of the conscience. Art should not help us back to innocence, it should lead us away from the trauma of guilt. In *Richard Wagner in Bayreuth,* Nietzsche demands that the new man free himself of the modern soul, for only then will he understand and continue the art of the Greeks. Mounting contradictions to Wagner come through treacherously in Nietzsche's words: "The beholder, by seemingly submitting to Wagner's outflowing and overflooding nature, has participated in its strength and has thus become powerful *against* him *thanks to* him, as it were; and any man who examines himself carefully knows that even beholding requires a secret opposition: that of seeing what is opposite one."

Nonetheless, Nietzsche still didn't feel justified in rejecting the dramatist, for first of all Bayreuth had to materialize. At the same time he wondered: To what extent can art become a danger? Nietzsche tried to answer: When the enjoyer takes art as earnestly as the creator may and can, then the enjoyer is tempted to take life too lightly. Overestimating art increases the yearning for the sublime, but then another instinct joins in: the longing to return to the depth, yearning for the happiness of fellowship: "Friends, remain true to the earth!"

In *Richard Wagner in Bayreuth,* Nietzsche primarily turns against the Wagnerites' overemphasis on enjoyment in the Wagner cult. The disciples should not be concerned with art alone, for it is not a narcotic or specific to relieve one's misery. Schopenhauer spoke of a kind of redemption and spiritual surge that only art can transmit, a bliss for the moment. This now included the transformation that Nietzsche demanded of art and had already affirmed in his youth. Art is capable of preparing and creating new forms of being, of collectivities. After the Mannheim concert and the

Siegfried Idyll, Nietzsche had told Rohde about his conception of a monasticism of art, a sodality sworn to save the art of the future, a hundred chosen men of the spirit. And this thought recurs in the afterword to *Richard Wagner in Bayreuth*, when Nietzsche, in the encounter of Wagner's and Schopenhauer's worlds, indicates that culture will soon survive only in the form of cloisterly sects, necessarily rejecting the surrounding world.

Wagner himself vainly (and contrary to his nature), resisted any kind of art that had an air of luxury. Yet opus after opus in the series of his music dramas mainly served to satisfy the world's bogus needs. Could this art help to prepare for a new life? For Nietzsche, this question encompassed the significance of Bayreuth and of art in general. Full of faith and doubt, hope and fear, Nietzsche defended and promoted Bayreuth, enthusiastic and eloquent. By the same token, he prescribed a "five-year Pythagorean silence" for his misgivings as to whether art could really be regenerated from the theater.

At New Year's 1876, Fräulein von Meysenbug offered him her hospitality in Italy for a year that would be free of all work. Nietzsche mysteriously hinted that this invitation had come in the nick of time, but he couldn't have meant only his health, since his letters emphasize a temporary improvement. Prompted mainly by his recent doubts about Wagner and his art, Nietzsche readily accepted the offer. He was so anxious to visit Malwida because he hoped she would help him find his old sentiments for Wagner— he could rest assured that she would only say the most loving and laudatory things about the composer.

The necessary correspondence with Malwida about the planned junket in Italy was taken over by Elisabeth at her brother's request. The Fano project no longer appealed to Malwida after her inspection, and so it was replaced by Castella Mare or Sorrento. The final decision was put off. But whatever it would be, Malwida and Friedrich were resolved to spend an entire year in Italy. The university had granted him a twelve-month sabbatical, from October 1876 to October 1877, on full salary, provided he found and paid someone to take over his six weekly hours of Greek at the Paedagogium. Everything was arranged; and in high spirits at the prospect of a year of liberty Nietzsche once again looked into his fragment *Richard Wagner in Bayreuth*. Peter Gast, who, for Nietzsche's sake was spending his second semester in Basel, copied out the first eight parts of the manuscript in May 1876. His admiration for the piece was coupled with Nietzsche's wish not to remain silent for the Bayreuth Festival in August 1876. And so the author, who had originally intended this manuscript as Wagner's birthday present, had it printed. Hence, on May 22, Wagner only received a letter by way of congratulation. It is one of the few documents from Nietzsche's pen that escaped destruction in Wahnfried:

"On such a day as your birthday, highly esteemed man, only the most personal utterance has any right; for each of us has experienced something through you that concerns him alone in his heart of hearts. Such experiences cannot be added up, and the best wishes of many would today be less than the modest word of one. It is almost exactly seven years since I paid my first visit to you in Tribschen, and all I can say to your birthday is that from that day forward, I have been celebrating my spiritual birthday every May. For, since then, you have been living in me and working incessantly as a totally new drop of blood that I certainly did not have previously. This element, originating in you, drives me, shames me, heartens me, eggs me on, and has left me no peace, so that I might almost desire to be angry at you for this disquiet, if I did not most definitely feel that this restlessness incessantly impels me to become freer and better. Hence, to him who aroused it, I owe the most profound feelings of gratitude; and my finest hopes for the events of this summer are that *many* people shall be moved to such disquiet by you and your labor and thereby have a share in the greatness of your being and your life. For this to occur is my only happy wish for you today (what other happiness could I wish you?). Accept this amicably from the lips of your truly faithful Friedrich Nietzsche."

Wagner replied that Nietzsche's sickliness had caused terrible hardship during the seven years of friendship. Still, he adds:

"Unfortunately, I too have reached the point of coping with the morass of days only with good and bad jokes! Yesterday (on May 22), there was an impromptu banquet in the newly completed artist's restaurant by the theater: one man toasted the enormous spread of my fame through the Festival. I retorted that I had found a hair in this fame and was glad to relinquish my fame, hide and hair and all, to the clever restaurateur Albert!—I yelled at my coachman for not congratulating me!—Otherwise, everything was very lovely because it passed by. The enterprise has brought me its share of troubles: everyone fears me like the devil!''

Wagner's letter was conspicuously long; he usually sent telegrams.

Two handwritten copies of the new and incomplete essay *Richard Wagner in Bayreuth* were dispatched to the composer. Nietzsche's insecurity can be read between the lines in a draft of the accompanying letter to Wagner:

"It's as though I had once again put myself at stake. I urgently beg you: Let be what has happened, and grant your pity and silence to one who has not spared himself. Read this piece as if it were not about you and as if it were not by me. Actually, the living should not discuss my piece, it is something for the underworld. . . . When I look back at a thoroughly tormented year, it seems to me as if I had devoted all its good hours to conceiving and working out this piece; today it is my pride to have plucked a fruit even from this length of time. Perhaps, despite all good will, it would not have been possible, had I not been carrying with me since my fourteenth year the things of which I have now dared to talk. . . ."

Nietzsche's anxiety that Wagner might take the confessions in his latest work amiss turned out to be unfounded. The composer, totally absorbed in the final *Ring* rehearsals, failed (like the enthusiastic Malwida von Meysenbug) to perceive both Nietzsche's change of outlook and the explicit criticism. Otherwise Wagner would not have replied: "Friend, your book is tremendous!—Just how have you come to know me so well?—Please come soon and let the rehearsals accustom you to the impressions."

Towards mid-June 1876, when *Richard Wagner in Bayreuth* was about to be run off the press, Nietzsche made up his mind to add several concluding chapters, which he sketched on June 17 and 18, in Badenweiler. By the end of the month, printed copies were ready, so that the piece appeared in time for the *Festspiele*. King Ludwig read the book in Hohenschwangau Castle, where Wagner had sent it. The sovereign wired his friend, assuring him that the piece was "exceptionally fascinating."

9

THE FIRST FESTIVAL

I n late July 1876, Nietzsche undertook a pilgrimage to Bayreuth. He shouldn't have done it. He still viewed Bayreuth with the hope that Wagner and his art would be presented there in a new way. Nietzsche was thrilled by the vision of a festival at which both performers and spectators would be extraordinary and admirable, united in feelings raised to an enormous pitch. Later, however, he noted:

"My mistake was to come to Bayreuth with an ideal. I was forced to experience the bitterest disappointment. The excess of ugliness, distortion, and overexcitement repulsed me vehemently."

When the Bayreuth pilgrim Nietzsche sat drinking milk in Malwida's garden, he did not reveal any of his mental convulsions to his hostess; after all, the house was nearly always filled with company. Malwida's foster daughter Olga Monod, together with her husband, her sister, and her little boy, stayed there for the entire length of the *Festspiele*. They were joined almost daily by Edouard Schuré,[1] from Paris, and a few of Nietzsche's fellow professors from Basel, so that Wagner, dropping by one day from Wahnfried, jested, "Goodness! You've got a professor coming out from behind every bush here."

Nietzsche, in the fourth *Untimely Reflection*, describes what he had expected for himself and like-minded people.

"In the picture of that tragic artwork of Bayreuth, we see the struggle of individuals with all the things that confront them as seemingly invincible necessities, the struggle with power, law, convention, contract, and entire hierarchies of things. Individuals cannot lead a finer life than when they make themselves ripe for death and sacrifice themselves in the struggle for justice and love. The gaze with which the mysterious eye of tragedy beholds us is not an enervating or paralyzing spell. Although it does demand calm as long as it stares at us; —for art does not exist for the struggle itself, but for the intervals of calm prior to and during the struggle, for those minutes in which one retrospectively and presagingly comprehends the symbolic, and in which a refreshing dream draws near to us with the feeling of a faint weariness. The day and the struggle dawn together, the holy shadows drift away, and art once again is aloof from us; but its solace lies upon men since the early hour."

Such an aesthetics is a far cry from the area of agitation and propaganda, which art, especially in the case of Wagner, has always been striving to touch.

It cannot be denied: The cornerstone ceremony at Bayreuth in 1872 had raised hopes for gathering people of the same convictions at the *Festspiele*. But then, of course, the masses came and not the "chosen few." These masses left a decisive stamp on the events, both at the Festival Hill and at Wahnfried. The illusory nature of Wagner's "ideal" became clear to Nietzsche when he observed the people he met at Wahnfried. Above all, he had to acknowledge that this ideal wasn't the cardinal factor even for the people most closely involved. Amorous, bored, unmusical patrons and patronesses mingled with the wealthy do-nothings of Europe as though Bayreuth were the scene of a sporting event. In Nietzsche's eyes, they had merely lit upon a further pretext for idleness along with all the old excuses. And Wagner's music, with its secret and persuasive sexuality, struck Nietzsche as a device for binding together a society in which everyone was merely out for pleasure. The people who mattered all but vanished amid the elegant toilettes and diamonds.

Wagner had to hold mass audiences because the throng of personal visitors in Wahnfried was much too big. On the first day of the Festival, over five hundred calling-cards were left at Wahnfried. Committed Wagnerites could be seen gathering every evening at Angermann's beer hall, pounding their fists on the table, menacingly raising their steins, and ready to take arms at the slightest deviation from the strict Wagnerian code. To Nietzsche, these people were a parody. What a pity that Rohde and Gersdorff seemed absorbed in their love affairs!

Nietzsche, as a result, closed off his feelings from the outer world. He didn't like hearing about his latest work, and said, "Ah! People ought to forget about those old stories!"

If someone countered that this work had only appeared five weeks ago, he would retort, "It seems like five years!"

Later, comparing his *Schopenhauer as Educator* with *Richard Wagner in Bayreuth,* he saw that the third *Untimely Reflection* had been his first step towards liberation:

"The Schopenhauerean man drove me to skepticism towards anything and anyone that had ever been venerated, adulated, defended (even the Greeks, Schopenhauer, Wagner), genius, saints, pessimism, or knowledge. By taking this roundabout path, I reach the height with the freshest wind. —The piece on Bayreuth was merely an intermission, a sinking back, but not a rest. It was here that I realized Bayreuth's superfluousness (for me)."

Nietzsche did not find the Festival he had been hoping for and idealizing, and in which only "untimely" people could participate. Wagner, with an eye to the financial plight, had also opened the gates of the house to the curious and the malevolent. And these were the people who, in Nietzsche's eyes, gave the Festival its flavor. Wagner also suffered from this, as revealed in his letter to Emil Heckel before the *Festspiele:*

"The enterprise originally projected is thus actually a complete failure."

Nor did Nietzsche find the "greatest symphony of all," but, instead, "grand opera." He observed the vehemence of its effect on the nerves. The intoxicating influence of that music—an effect that was appreciated as fateful—did not live up to the moderation that Nietzsche reckoned as an essential element of human nature. He shuddered at the naturalism of acting and singing. "A realm of goodness will blossom here," he had rashly announced. This expectation was thwarted.

Just a few days after his arrival, he had moaned in a letter to his sister:

"I wish I were somewhere else . . . I shudder at the thought of every one of these lengthy evenings of art. . . . I'm sick of it all."

The fat matrons from Marienbad were a macabre parody of what was written in his Festival piece: "In Bayreuth, the spectators are themselves a spectacle!"

Nietzsche's malaise wasn't just limited to the aesthetics; his health had declined again. Before the first dress rehearsal even got underway, he escaped to Klingenbrunn in the Bavarian Forest. Nothing can be more revealing about his inner aloofness from all the hustle and bustle around Wagner than the sketches that he began here to *Human, All Too Human.*

While in Klingenbrunn, he wrote to his sister on August 6, 1876:

"Dearest sister, I hope you're in Bayreuth and are finding good people to take care of you after my disappearance from there.— I know perfectly well that I can *not* stand it there; in fact, we should have realized it beforehand! Just think how cautiously I have had to live these past few years. I am so worn out and drained from that brief sojourn there that I simply can't quite pull myself together. Had a *bad* day here, lay in bed; but *constant* headaches, as at certain times in Basel. The place is very good, deep woods and mountain air, as in the Jura. I want to stay here, ten days perhaps, but not return via Bayreuth; for I won't have the money.— . . . The way things happen! I have to gather all my strength just to endure the boundless disappointment of this summer. Nor will I see my friends; everything is poison and destruction for me now.—I'm glad to know you're with Fräulein Meysenbug and her family. They're such fine people; thank them with all your heart on my behalf."

The separation he desired from Wagner and Elisabeth did not come. At her urging, Nietzsche came back to Bayreuth ten days later to attend the public opening of the *Rheingold.* He did manage to get through the rest of the Festival; but he gave the tickets for the other performances to relatives. "So much for Bayreuth," he said with tears in his eyes before departing.

Let us mix into the Festival throngs for a moment.

On the night of August 6, King Ludwig arrived at Bayreuth in his special train. His presence was not to be revealed anywhere. Extremely shy and anti-social, he avoided any contact with the crowd. Even a drive through the streets of the decorated town was unbearable. Wagner welcomed his former friend at the railroad station. Deeply moved, he uttered his gratitude to the king for his willingness to attend the dress rehearsals for the sake of the Project. Alone with the illustrious guest, he drove up the old Promenade, past *Rollwenzelei* (once the refuge of Jean-Paul Richter, the German novelist), and on to the *Eremitage.* Here, in the pleasure palace of the Markgravine of Bayreuth, the king took up his abode, far enough from the town, in the middle of a park that was easy to "close off." The king, accustomed to working by night and sleeping by day, kept Wagner for a private conversation until morning.

The next potentate arrived one week later, on August 13, together with the flood of Festival visitors: Kaiser Wilhelm I. Although anything but close to Wagner's art, the old gentleman considered it his duty to attend the opening of the *Festspiele*. Ludwig, the ruler of Bavaria, could not get himself to receive the German Emperor. He left Bayreuth right after the rehearsals as secretly as he had arrived.

At 4:00 P.M. on the dot, on the thirteenth of August 1876, the curtain rose on *Rheingold*. What everyone, except for a handful of devotees, had considered absurd five years earlier, Wagner's own theater away from the world, was now a reality—with certain qualifications. The political triumph seemed greater than expected. People were bowing to Wagner's achievement. In the past, princes had certainly had artists come to them; but never had princes gone on a pilgrimage to an artist and his work in a provincial nest. For all the criticism of certain artistic defects, most of the visitors admired the courage and persistance with which Wagner had driven his project to its goal. Wagner's disappointment was due in part to a suspicion that this admiration for his energy rather than his artistic deed per se was the real reason for the universal interest.

The public was surprised that King Ludwig popped up in Bayreuth again for *Siegfried*, the third of the four *Ring* evenings, and that Wagner once more, as at the *Meistersinger* premiere in Munich, sat next to the king during the performance. When the *Ring* terminated with *The Twilight of the Gods*, Ludwig retreated into isolation the very same night.

Much about this Festival was merely a tentative start. No one was more aware of this than Wagner. He was filled with gratitude towards his artists. Thus he acknowledged:

"Everything was a beautiful, deeply inspired will here, and it created an artistic obedience that someone else might not so easily ever encounter again. . . . A wonderful magic made all of us good."

Nonetheless, Wagner had to put up with the fact that nearly all the singers were not yet capable of the delivery that he was aiming for and that ultimately became known as the "Bayreuth style." The settings seemed both grotesquely overdone and touchingly primitive although unmistakably ahead of what was usually seen on opera stages. The dragon in *Siegfried,* taken terribly seriously in the music, provoked laughter from the audience—which Eduard Hanslick[2] of the Viennese Brahms party naturally registered with great contentment. Nietzsche laconically voiced his impression of the dress rehearsal: The dragon lost a great deal when visible. With disgust he turned away from the Nibelungen clan, "wild animals with seizures of sublimated tenderness and profundity."

The sunken orchestra proved its mettle. The auditorium, ascending like an amphitheater, made a sensation—and even more so the darkness during performance—a revolutionary innovation. The spectators were taken aback at having to sit in the dark —and not be seen. They were amazed that there was no applause while the curtain was up and that the singers didn't bow after every "aria" (a thing which didn't exist anyway). At the end, no "curtains" were counted up; the onlookers went away in lugubrious silence.

The organization of facilities generally mired down. The city had done its best, but it simply wasn't prepared for so many and such spoiled visitors. There was a dearth of hotels. A free-for-all broke out over every ham sandwich during intermissions. The fanatic "Wagnerites" with their slouched hats and long hair added a comical touch. All this met with vicious criticism.

Wagner himself, forestalling the bad reactions of the press, had gone on stage after the initial *Ring* production and spoken to the audience, but his words were misconstrued:

"You owe this deed to your graciousness and to the unlimited efforts of the participants, my artists. What I still have to say to you could be summed up in a few words, an axiom. You have seen what we can do: it is now up to you to will it. And if you will, then we shall have an art!"

A cue for his antagonists to accuse him of megalomania. What Ludwig Speidel[3] wrote in his *Critical Conclusion* basically overlapped with Nietzsche's attitude: "When the Bayreuth Festival was still developing, when the active enthusiasm of the adepts swept cooler minds along with them, one might have thought that the German nation had something to do with the whole thing. But no, and no again! The German nation has nothing in common with this crying shame! And if it were to find any delight in the fool's gold of the *Nibelungenring*, it would thereby cross itself out of the roster of civilized nations of the West."

Nevertheless, the first Bayreuth *Festspiele* ended in good cheer. A huge banquet once again united the circle of friends who had stayed till the finish, and Wagner gave a speech. The next speaker was Liszt, whom Wagner had touchingly extolled as one of the noblest spiritual and material supporters of his work. Liszt gracefully uttered a few words: As he bowed to Dante and Michelangelo, thus must he bow to the genius whose achievement they had just experienced.

During the next few performances, the expected throng did not come. Empty rows of seats demonstrated the effects of nasty press accounts and exorbitant prices of admission. Wagner had to resign himself to the fact that the improvements in later performances went unnoticed; but for months the newspapers had turned a harsh light on all the difficulties and foretold a catastrophe. Wagner was also dissatisfied with Carl Brandt's technical performance and with the musical delivery. Cosima's diary claims that "Richter was not sure of *a single* tempo," that "Richard [was] very depressed, he says he would like to die." Furthermore the catastrophic deficit rose by hundreds of thousands of marks per annum. In December of that year, 1876, Wagner made plans to put everything up for sale and leave Bayreuth for the Royal Theater in Munich.

When the supposed conquering hero took his family for a vacation in Italy after the close of the *Festspiele*, more and more dismal tidings arrived about the financial failure of the summer. A repeat was out of the question. As in 1874, the undertaking was on the verge of collapse. A call to the "patrons" went unheeded. Wagner covered part of the deficit by very reluctantly allowing the *Ring* to be produced outside of Bayreuth. Vienna, Munich, and Leipzig obtained permission.

Nietzsche's sojourn in Bayreuth had been bad for his weak eyes. He had to strain them greatly just to recognize the stage, and reading the score in the penumbra taxed his vision. Since the doctor now had to forbid all reading and writing, Nietzsche's friend Rée read aloud to him, and Peter Gast, taking his dictation, wrote down those sentences that Nietzsche had first sketched in Klingenbrunn and that eventually went into the book *Human, All Too Human.*

This book was the first open skirmish that ultimately led to the onslaught against Wagnerism per se. In the foreword to the *Genealogy of Morals* (1887), Nietzsche describes the months up to spring 1877 as the time that brought him a first overview of the "vast and dangerous domain" that he had already traversed. The values and intellectual conclusions which had offered him a solid ground for so many years now collapsed. But it was difficult for him to break away from Wagner, as shown, in part, by his going back to Bayreuth for the premiere of the *Ring* cycle. The mountings nourished his doubts afresh. He was also shocked by the Jew-baiting so candidly mouthed at Wahnfried, and his repugnance hastened the break. After his sister's marriage in 1885 to Dr. Bernhard Förster,[4] one of the most vociferous members of the anti-Semitic movement, Nietzsche wrote to her: "Your alliance with an anti-Semitic boss expresses an alienation to my entire way of being, an alienation that keeps filling me again and again with resentment or melancholy."

After the summer holidays and the Festival torment, Nietzsche spent a short time in 1876 with friends in Basel, since his sister had gone from Bayreuth to their mother in Naumburg. On September 27, overcoming his reluctance, he wrote a letter to Wagner:

"I now have time to think about the past, both distant and recent, for I spend a great deal of time sitting in a dark room for an atropine treatment of my eyes, which was deemed necessary after my return home. The autumn, after this summer, is, for me, and most likely not just for me, more of an autumn than any earlier one. Behind the grand event lies a streak of blackest melancholy, which one certainly cannot escape rapidly enough in Italy, or in work, or both."

If Wagner sensed the meaning of these words, he gave no sign of it when, a few weeks later, he came to Sorrento with his family and met Malwida and (for one last time) Nietzsche.

Wagner had another source of bitterness. On November 30,

while in Rome, he wrote to the singer Albert Niemann, whom he thanked particularly for his accomplishment as Siegmund:

"Do you believe that I have found relaxation or recreation for even one day? These things have never been granted to me. Everything that ever tormented me still pursues me, the eternal distress in regard to insufficiency. Even when I do not think of the material worries about my enterprise, then you of all people will understand me when I tell you this: After all the enormous heart-felt zeal that brought these performances into being, I can only acknowledge the product of our labors as almost a frittering of energy with no purpose or use."

Still in Rome, Wagner unsuspectingly wrote to Nietzsche, asking him to order some linen for him from a Basel firm. This letter delighted his suffering herald because such an informal contact reminded him of the Tribschen days. Wagner in Italy! It was here, Nietzsche recalled, that his friend had gotten the inspiration for the *Rheingold* prelude with its endless E-flat major chord. And so Nietzsche wrote back:

"May it always remain the land of beginnings for you! You can thus be rid of the Germans for a while, and this seems to be necessary every now and again if you want to do something decent for them. —You may know that I am going to Italy too next month, not, I think, to a land of beginnings, but to a land of the end of my sufferings. These sufferings are at a peak again; it's really about time: the authorities know what they're doing when they give me a year's sabbatical, although such a sacrifice is disproportionately enormous for such a small community; they would of course lose me in one way or another if they didn't allow me this possibility; during the past few years, thanks to my enduring temperament, I have swallowed pains upon pains, as though I had been born for no other purpose. I have paid a heavy tribute indeed to the philosophy that teaches such endurance. This neuralgia works so thoroughly, so scientifically, it literally probes the extent to which I can endure the pain, and it always spends thirty hours on this investigation. I have to reckon with a repetition of this study every four to eight days: You can see, it is a scholar's disease; —but now I'm fed up with it, and I shall either live in health or not live at all. Complete quiet, mild air, strolls, dark rooms—those are the things I expect of Italy; my skin crawls at the thought of having to see or hear anything there. Don't think I'm morose; only people, not illnesses, can put me in a bad mood."

Many authors have tried to track down the causes and dynamics of Nietzsche's diseases. The results strongly diverge from one another. Karl Jaspers, in his Nietzsche biography,[5] cautiously summed up a few of the most important conclusions. He pointed out how many questions still remain moot. The generally accepted paralysis of Nietzsche's collapse has been ascribed to an early syphilitic infection; but Paul Deussen's account of this matter does not definitively prove that such was indeed the cause of the mental illness. Likewise, the misuse of medicaments and poisons has been seen as crucial. Some people have claimed, along with Cosima, that as of 1873, Nietzsche showed signs of a psychoneurotic development connected with his inner break from Wagner. There is probably more reason to maintain the opposite: Nietzsche's crisis-ridden health contributed to the rift, since the sickness increased his hypersensitivity and irritability, making him prone to abrupt reactions. We can most likely assume that the habits and responses of a man exposed since earliest youth to all kinds of sufferings are in part affected by disease.

Luckily, he was surrounded by friends; helpful, considerate friends. First, after his return from Bayreuth, the ethical philosopher Dr. Paul Rée; then, the musician Heinrich Köselitz, who had taken the pen name Peter Gast. When Gast was studying counterpoint and composition in Leipzig from 1872 to 1874, his friend Wiedemann called his attention to Nietzsche's *Birth of Tragedy*. Gast felt that the "most secret impulses of culture" had been unveiled to him. Nietzsche saw the Apollonian and Dionysian forces of art as ultimately destroyed by the both utilitarian and rationalistic tendency, such as expressed by Socrates. And now Gast perceived why a blossoming of art was impossible under the dominion of a culture shaped by knowledge and reason. In 1874, Gast met Nietzsche's friend Franz Overbeck, from whom he found out more about the man he so venerated. What interested him most was the relationship to Wagner, which had already been indicated in the preface to *The Birth of Tragedy*.

Hoping to meet Nietzsche, Wiedemann and Gast set out for Basel in 1875. With recommendations from Nietzsche's publisher

Schmeitzner in their pockets, they traveled via Bayreuth, reaching Basel in mid-October. During that semester, Nietzsche invited them several times, usually for an evening, to his home on Spalentorweg 48, in a quiet neighborhood, where he lived with his sister. At such times, he would play the piano. Gast, as already mentioned, particularly remembered the *Hymn to Solitude,* which he described as a work full of grandeur and relentlessness.

Nietzsche seemed to take an instant liking to young Köselitz, alias Gast, for he asked him over at Christmas and even surprised him with presents. A closer friendship, however, only began in late April 1876, when he told Gast that he had an abortive *Untimely Reflection* on Richard Wagner. Nietzsche noticed how eagerly Gast wanted to read the fragment and so he let him borrow it. When Gast returned these pages, he did not conceal his regret that such a work should remain a mere torso. At the time, Nietzsche considered it too personal for publication. A few days later, it struck him that Wagner might enjoy it as a birthday gift, so he had Gast do a clean copy. This so aroused Nietzsche's interest in his piece that, as mentioned, instead of sending the copy to Bayreuth, he actually decided to let Schmeitzner print it, adding the three missing final chapters in June, so that the book came out as a *Festschrift.* Gast now had constant opportunity to make his veneration of practical use to the genius Nietzsche. In his lovely, legible penmanship, he took Nietzsche's dictation and prepared final drafts for publication. Meritoriously, he cut down more and more on his own creative activities, winning the unqualified trust of his friend. It was he who, in September, wrote Wagner the dictated message that *Richard Wagner in Bayreuth* was about to be printed in French. Marie Baumgartner,[6] the mother of a pupil of Nietzsche's, had done the translation. Louise Ott,[7] a married woman living in Paris, was also informed about the translation. This could lead one to infer that she was a further reason for Nietzsche's premature departure from Bayreuth. They had met while strolling during an intermission; and Nietzsche's amorous mood was darkened when the lady went back to Paris with her little boy. "It was as if someone had taken away my light. I had to come to my senses again."

Nietzsche appears to have felt how greatly his progressive illness made him dependent on a few friends and their sacrifices.

And he was well aware that his condition wasn't just temporary, he would require constant care. This was probably the only reason why Nietzsche's sister was able to enter his life more and more and even take over many of his important matters. As of August 1875, the brother and sister shared a home in Basel. But their mother still lived in Naumburg, and since Elisabeth also had to attend to her, she could help Nietzsche only for short periods of time.

Nietzsche's existence became one of continual disquiet, a quest for what was salutary to mind and body. Always on the road between Basel and many places in Germany, Italy, and Switzerland, visiting friends and resorts, he fled from unbearable pains, which, however, were only aggravated by the many changes of climate.

Now he wanted to solve the problem of his need for help by following Wagner's advice: he toyed with the idea of marriage. Rashly and with no real interest, he proposed to a young lady named Mathilde Ramperdach at Lake Geneva, in spring 1876; she turned him down. But then, in June 1877, he wrote: "Marriage, though greatly desirable—is really utterly improbable. I know this very clearly!"

10
FINAL MEETING

Nietzsche spent winter 1876–77 in Sorrento, with no improvement of his health. No one noticed anything: he looked tanned and powerful, acted cheerful and witty. When the sirocco began blowing in Italy, he escaped to Switzerland, staying in Lucerne for two weeks. Here, he was overcome by a confidence about the future, as reflected in his notes:

"I feel as though I had recovered from an illness; I think with ineffable sweetness about Mozart's Requiem. Simple dishes taste good again.—The 'Song to Joy' (May 22, 1872) one of my loftiest moods. It's only now that I feel I'm on *this* path. —Freely as His suns are soaring, Brothers, Brothers, change your path! —What a false and dejected Festival that was in 1876! —But subsequently, my eyes were opened to the *thousand* wellsprings in the desert. That period very useful against premature precociousness. —*Now* Antiquity and Goethe's insight into great art dawned on me: and only *now* could I acquire a *plain* view of genuine human life: I had an *antidote,* so that no corrupt pessimism would come of it."

Wagner and Nietzsche, as mentioned above, met in this autumn of 1876 for the last time. Twelve years later, in *Nietzsche vs. Wagner,* the philosopher summed up:

"I already bade farewell to Wagner as early as summer 1876, in the midst of the first Festival. I cannot put up with any ambivalence; ever since Wagner has been in Germany, he has lowered himself step by step to everything I despise—even anti-Semitism. . . . It was really high time to say farewell; I soon obtained evidence for it. Richard Wagner, seemingly at the height of triumph, in reality a rotting, despairing *décadent,* suddenly prostrated himself, helpless and broken, before the Christian cross. . . ."

Together with Rée and the student Albert Brenner, Nietzsche spent the entire winter with Malwida von Meysenbug in Sorrento. It was merely a coincidence that the Wagners likewise spent their holidays in Sorrento from October 5 to November 5, 1876. They lived in the Hotel Victoria, just a few steps from Malwida's domicile, the Villa Rubinacci. Wagner rapturously perused *The History of the Italian Republics* by the Swiss historian Sismondi. He often called over Cosima and Malwida to read passages aloud to them. Later, in Rome, he recommended one such episode to the Italian writer Cossa, telling him to work it into a play; but the adaptation never materialized. The Wagners often invited the four neighbors to their rooms. Malwida noticed a forced naturalness and cheerfulness in Nietzsche—things otherwise alien to his behavior. But since he didn't voice any objections to spending time with the Wagners, it never occurred to her that his attitude might have changed.

The paradise of Sorrento had its difficulties. Nietzsche had at first been dismayed by the news that the Wagners were coming; but then he looked forward to it, hoping for a heart-to-heart talk with the composer. In Bayreuth, he hadn't fully freed himself from the Master; the conflicts between loyalty to his friend and his own conviction were still unresolved. Now he was sincerely glad to see him again, and Malwida subsequently claimed "they hurried towards one another" each day. However, Nietzsche himself never spoke about such frequent contact. Nevertheless, the possibility was there, since Wagner had brought along the latest *Untimely Reflection,* which he had apparently admired in Bayreuth. But the Master refused to indulge in any conversation about the *Festspiele.* Letters from the Bayreuth board of directors about the enormous deficit put him in a plaintive mood, and Malwida begged Nietzsche to keep the conversation away from Bayreuth.

One of the last days in Sorrento, Wagner, strolling with his friend, told him about his work on *Parsifal.* They walked up the coast to the rise with its sweeping view of islands, ocean, and bays. The lovely autumn day with its touch of winter caused Wagner to exclaim: "A mood of departure!" All at once, and for the first time, he began talking about *Parsifal.* But rather than expanding on the artistic intention, he got deeply involved in describing a

Christian experience he had had. Did this man who always liked to put himself in the limelight feel he had to change the lighting? After all, this *Bühnenweihfestspiel*, this "Consecrated Theatrical Festival," was conceived by an out-and-out atheist, who, until the early 1870s, had always made the most disparaging remarks about Christianity. But now he avowed new inward experiences, regrets over his atheism, a sympathy with Christian dogmas, and he told about the pleasure he derived from Holy Communion.

Nietzsche already knew the *Parsifal* text, for Cosima had read him a prose sketch at Christmas 1869, and she had mentioned his "awesome impression," a deliberately ambivalent wording. Nietzsche considered it impossible for Wagner, who had declared himself an atheist to the bitter end, to ever return to a naive faith. The philosopher thus regarded Wagner's transformation as an attempt to white-wash himself for success. Hadn't Wagner jeered in regard to the bad box offices at the *Festspiele:* "The Germans have no interest in heathen Gods and heroes, they want to see something Christian."

Here in Sorrento, Nietzsche used all kinds of excuses to explain his embarrassed silence. He didn't discuss this dismal stroll until later. He would certainly have understood and concurred if Wagner had spoken about the artistic impulses he received from the intense religious feelings of the Christian Middle Ages, from the challenge of musically shaping such a sense of life. Nietzsche was also irritated by his derogatory comments about Nietzsche's friend Dr. Paul Rée, the radical Jew. Wagner suspected that Rée's influence on Nietzsche was unfavorable to the composer; and chronologically, Nietzsche's break with Wagner overlapped with the friendship with Rée, which had begun in 1874.

The influence of the skeptic Rée was all the stronger since Nietzsche's new opus *Human, All Too Human* expresses the very opposite of his earlier glorification of genius—hence, Wagner too, though with no direct reference. Looking back, Nietzsche commented on his anti-Wagner treatise as follows:

"In this book, I freed myself of the things that didn't belong to my nature, such as idealism. The title says: Where you see ideals, I see things that are human, alas, all too human. One error after another is quietly put in cold storage, ideals are not refuted, they freeze, genius freezes here, at the next corner the saint, the hero freezes under a thick icicle, in the end faith freezes, so-called conviction, and even pity cools off significantly."

Could they really then see eye to eye on *Parsifal?*

How had *Parsifal,* this final stumbling block between the friends, come about? Frustrated by the public failure of his *Festspiele,* the productive composer had sought refuge in the new work. In late January 1876, he said to Cosima: "I'm beginning *Parsifal,* and I won't leave it until it's done." Twenty years had passed since Wagner first found the subject. At the time, he had been working on Act III of the "Ur"-*Tristan.* The *Parsifal* inspiration had come at his Zurich haven *Zum grünen Hügel,* during his love affair with Mathilde Wesendonk:

"On Good Friday, I awoke in this house for the first time, in bright sunshine; the little garden had turned green, the birds were singing, and at last I could sit on the pinnacle of the cottage to delight in the yearned-for stillness that was heavy with promise. Imbued with all this, I suddenly recalled that it was Good Friday, and it struck me how significantly this reminder had once loomed up to me in Wolfram's *Parzival.* Ever since that sojourn in Marienbad, where I had conceived the *Meistersinger* and *Lohengrin,* I had not gone back to that poem; but now its ideal content came to me in an overwhelming form, and under the Good Friday spell, I quickly conceived a whole drama, which I divided into three acts and rapidly and roughly sketched."

For years on end, the manuscript lay as good as forgotten at the bottom of trunks during his constant travels. Eight years after the first plan, he did a second draft for King Ludwig, who was very excited by the story of the "pure fool." This second sketch was likewise put aside. For another twelve years, the *Meistersinger* and the *Ring* prevented any further work on this opus, certainly to its advantage, and, in a higher sense, according to design.

Now, during that autumn stroll in Sorrento in 1876, he explained to Nietzsche what the name "Parzival" signified (or Parsifal, with an "s," as he spelled it since 1873). The name is Arabic: *parsi* means "pure" and *fal* means "foolish." Wagner spoke about the religion of compassion, which, he said, was crystallizing more and more clearly in him with age, and which he now intended to proclaim in an opus late in life. Before even working on the material, he had written to Mathilde Wesendonk: "I recognize

compassion within myself as the strongest trait of my moral being, and it is most likely the source of my art." But then he
instantly and surprisingly qualified the concept: "It is not so
much what the other man suffers, but what I suffer when I know
that he is suffering. . . ." The faculty for a redemption of the world
through human compassion is such a poorly developed thing, in
Wagner's eyes, that "it makes man so repulsive and weakens my
compassion for him to the point of a total lack of feeling about
his misery." Was it, hence, compassion with himself?

Wagner, fifty years ahead of Spengler's *Decline of the West*, felt
he could foresee the fall of historical mankind. But he clung to
the possibility of a renewal and a rebirth of Western man. To be
sure, not through the church, in which regard Nietzsche misconstrued *Parsifal.* "When religion becomes artificial," proclaimed
Wagner in the *Bayreuther Blätter*, "it is the province of art to save
the crux of religion. Compassion, rooted in the deepest nature of
human will, is to be shown as the only true foundation of all
ethics." That was how he expounded the theme of *Parsifal* to
Nietzsche. It would not be "opera," which Wagner had never
planned to create and certainly wasn't intending now; nor was it
a "musical drama," as the early art evenings were called. *Bühnenweihfestspiel* was the high-faluting term, literally a "consecrated
festal play for the stage." And the only place of performance
forever was to be the Bayreuth Festival House (though his wishes
ultimately were not followed).

During that Sorrento stroll, the Master was lively, chatty, and
imaginative, just as his friend had once admired him. But now
Nietzsche's response was one of defensive silence. He immediately excused himself and walked away through the twilight. The
two men never saw one another again. The old magician failed
to realize that now the greatest gift of friendship in his life was
gone. The unpleasant sequel, publicly confirming the tacit break,
didn't come for another two years.

11

THE APOSTASY

I n spring 1877, Nietzsche, seeking a wedding gift for Rohde, decided to part with his Wagner bust, which had been gathering dust on his closet for some time now: ". . . I can't seem to hit on anything else, my *stupidity* is awful." His sister had to take care of sending it. An invitation came from Frankfurt to give a speech on Wagner, but he begged off. Nevertheless, while in Rosenlauibad, he had Malwida von Meysenbug convey his regards and best wishes to the tireless people of Bayreuth, whose courage he "admired three times a day." In London, fragments of the *Ring* had been performed to great acclaim but without the expected receipts. Wagner's mood hit rock bottom. In mid-June, he wrote to his friend Feustel, the banker: "I have reached the extreme now and am ready to literally go off the deep end at any moment. All I can probably do now is fret about covering the deficit and getting rid of the theater." The heroic struggle against the creditors lasted all summer long, a predicament Wagner was long familiar with.

There was no hope of continuing the *Festspiele* until spring 1878, when Ludwig once again came to the rescue. He presented a large advance to satisfy the chief creditors, although this time not as an outright gift: *Parsifal* was "pawned" to Munich's *Hoftheater,* and Wagner renounced part of his royalties from the performances.

However, the wave of failures did not terminate. Wagner intended to realize his old plan of establishing an academy for the study of dramatic and musical performance. The institute, projected for Bayreuth, was to train singers, musicians, and conductors not only for the "new style," but for all German opera houses. Wagner issued a dramatic appeal to all German artists before the opening day of January 1, 1878; the result: one single vocalist applied.

This academic effort generated the *Bayreuth Blätter,* initially meant as a mouthpiece for the institute. Despite dissuasive voices from Nietzsche's circle of friends, the negotiations finally led to the periodical being started in 1878. Cosima, at Wagner's behest, asked Nietzsche's publisher Schmeitzner to print it. The union of patrons financed the journal, in which Wagner published everything he deemed necessary to voice. Characteristically, the editor he appointed was one of the most doctrinaire of the Wagnerians: Hans von Wolzogen,[1] a well-to-do Berliner. He was to replace the "traitor" Nietzsche, which was somewhat beyond him, no matter how sedulously Wagner tried to explain to the inquiring king that Wolzogen had also studied Classics. In reality, it was Cosima who ran the paper and determined its profile. Her accurate estimation of Wolzogen's abilities was aired in a letter she wrote to Hermann Levi after two years of editorial efforts: "Wolzogen certainly cannot now measure up to Nietzsche as a stylist. But I do hope that he can train himself to be a writer; I agree with you that he's not a *born* writer. Wolzogen is one of the most peculiar people I have ever encountered, a life so totally absorbed in the ideal would seem beyond belief if one didn't experience it personally." And such traits were highly desired in Bayreuth, so that Wolzogen's participation was held on to.

In January 1877, Nietzsche still had every intention of writing for the periodical, since in Sorrento, Richard and Cosima had promised him a free range for his opinions. Peter Gast suggested Jacob Burckhardt as a "backup" for Nietzsche; but Burckhardt had already given up all journalistic activities. As it turned out, however, Nietzsche did not take part either.

Nietzsche spent that summer in Rosenlauibad. From there, he developed an exciting correspondence with Carl Fuchs,[2] a pianist, organist, and writer on music. The letters show that Nietzsche was studying Wagner's compositional technique as intensively as ever. Fuchs tried to probe the meaning of the most diverse compositions by rhythmically counting the measures. This reminded Nietzsche that in 1870 he had been "in quest of five- and seven-measure periods." And now, by industriously counting through the *Meistersinger* and *Tristan,* he gained insight into Wagner's rhythms. He noted a distaste for rigorous mathematics and symmetry, "as shown on a small scale in the use of triplets, I mean even an excessive use." Wagner's aversion seemed apparent in the way he tended to draw out four-measure periods into five-measure ones, and six-measure periods into seven-measure ones. "In the *Meistersinger,* Act III, there is a waltz: just look if the number seven doesn't dominate." Nietzsche likened this to a mannerism of Bernini's.[3] The sculptor, regarding an undecorated column as too plain, would adorn it with volutes from top to bottom in order to liven it up. "Of Wagner's dangerous effects, the most dangerous I think is his desire to 'liven up at any price': for it quickly turns into a mannerism, a gimmick." Nietzsche hoped that a specially competent person would some day figure out exactly how Wagner did it; and he considered the theoretician Fuchs to be such a person. "The others writing about Wagner basically just say that they had a great pleasure and that they're very thankful; the reader learns nothing. Wolzogen doesn't strike me as being enough of a musician; and as a writer he's ludicrous with his confusions of artistic and psychological parlance." Wagner's term *"Motiv"* for the mnemonic musical quotations was, for Nietzsche, unclearly formulated, and he pled for the word "symbol." "That's all it is, after all." Nietzsche wanted a personal dialogue with Carl Fuchs, who was not uncritical of Wagner; the philosopher hoped for confirmation of his qualms about the aesthetic impressions at Bayreuth.

It wasn't just in regard to musical theory that Nietzsche's mind was preoccupied with Wagner. The "motherly" friend Malwida had invited Nietzsche to her Swiss resort but he liked Rosenlauibad so much that he decided to remain there, even though he missed Malwida and would have liked to discuss "certain things" with her. He wrote to her that he was longing to converse with Frau Wagner once more: "It's always been one of my greatest delights, and I've had to do without it for years now." Nietzsche was reluctant to own that Cosima had shorn her Samson's locks, and that his estrangement from Wagner could not be helped by way of his one-time friendship with Cosima.

Nietzsche's "hunt for health" in the mountain air did not bring the desired success. He shuddered at the thought of his academic drudgery that winter. He felt that a man who has little time every day for his own crucial matters and is forced to devote nearly all his time and energy to duties that someone else could attend to equally well, is out of harmony, lives in a dichotomy with himself, and must eventually fall ill. "If I have any influence on young people, then it is due to my writings, and these in turn are due to my stolen hours, nay, to the interims between vocation and vocation—intervals that are conquered with the help of illness."

On August 10, 1877, Malwida reported to Nietzsche about the Wagners: "Cosima has finally sent me news from Bayreuth. They all seem to be well and are enjoying their home." The couple had just returned from England, where Wagner together with Hans Richter had conducted eight concerts at London's Albert Hall. He had also met Robert Browning.[4] In addition, Queen Victoria received him at Windsor Castle, where he read the entire text of *Parsifal* to a select group. After further travels, in Switzerland and southwestern Germany, he went home and started composing *Parsifal*. Cosima, on August 1, heard the first few bits of it from his study.

In October 1877, Wagner caused a grave incident, for he took the liberty of informing Nietzsche's physician Dr. Otto Eiser of Frankfurt, that the young man's sufferings were basically due to excessive masturbation. He absolutely ought to go and take the waters.

Nietzsche was beside himself. Wagner's biographers usually see a loving concern in this correspondence between the composer and Dr. Eiser. Nietzsche himself construed the incident as a vicious and destructive nastiness, and it was this he mostly referred to in subsequent letters when he spoke about Wagner's perfidious doings and a "mortal offense."

By winter, Nietzsche felt quite well physically. But after Christmas, his eye pains and headaches came back violently. So in March, he decided to take the waters in Baden-Baden, and the visit seemed to help. Malwida von Meysenbug was jubilant and praised Wagner, who submitted over and over again to even the most arduous of such treatments: "Wagner was right once again, he always maintained a sensible course of waters was just the right thing for your brother" (to Elisabeth Nietzsche).

Disappointed in love and forced to train his sights on a goal,

Nietzsche exclaimed in January 1878: "When I walked on alone, I trembled; shortly thereafter, I was sick, more than sick, I was *tired*—tired because of my irresistible disappointment at everything that remains to inspire us modern men, at the ubiquitously squandered energy, labor, hope, youth, love; I was tired because of my disgust at all the idealistic lying and mollycoddling of the conscience—things that have once again carried the day over one of the bravest of men."

Not suspecting anything, Wagner had sent Nietzsche a copy of the *Weihefestspiel* libretto in January 1878. Nietzsche informed his friend Reinhard von Seydlitz:

"Yesterday, Parsifal, sent by Wagner, came into my house. Impression after the first reading: more Liszt than Wagner, spirit of the Counter-Reformation; for me, since I'm much too accustomed to Hellenism and the human universal, everything is too Christian, temporally limited; nothing but fantastic psychology; no flesh and much too much blood (the Communion in particular gets too full-blooded); and then I don't care for hysterical females; many things that are bearable to the inner eye will be unendurable in performance: just imagine our actors praying, quivering, and with throats stretching in ecstasy. Likewise, the interior of the Grail Mountain *can*not work on stage, any more than the wounded swan. All these lovely concoctions belong in an epic and, as I said, to the inner eye. The language sounds like a translation from a foreign tongue. But the situations and their sequence—aren't they sublime poetry? Aren't they an ultimate challenge to the music? . . ."

Nietzsche said nothing to Wagner. In the midst of ending his new book *Human, All Too Human*, Nietzsche was greatly excited by *Parsifal.* He regarded the arrival of the lovely copy at this time as a "miracle of significance in chance." The inscription read: "To his dear friend Friedrich Nietzsche/Richard Wagner, Councilor of the Church." Another one of those meaningful strokes of fate! Nietzsche could just about hear swords being crossed.

More clearly then before, Nietzsche sensed how lastingly his book would shock the Wagner party. So he decided to have *Human, All Too Human* come out anonymously. He hit upon a false name and a fitting explanation as to why the work was being published by Schmeitzner. Wagner, however, was not to be left in the dark. Nietzsche's notes include the drafts of a letter seeking to reconcile the composer with the content of the book:

"In sending you the enclosed book, I place my secret trustingly into your hands and the hands of your noble spouse, and I assume that from now on it will be your secret too. This book is by me: in it, I have brought to light my innermost feelings about people and things and, for the first time, encircled the periphery of my own thinking. In times that were full of paroxysms and torments, this book was a means of solace which never failed when all other means failed. Perhaps I am alive today because I was capable of writing it.—A pseudonym had to be chosen, first of all, because I did not want to interfere with the effect of my earlier writings; and then, because the public and private defilement of my personal dignity was thereby to be prevented (my health no longer can endure such things); finally and especially, because I wished to make an *objective* discussion possible, one in which also my so intelligent friends of all kinds could participate without any delicacy of feelings getting in the way as earlier. No one cares to speak or write against my name. But I know that none of them has the opinions of *this* book, still I am very curious about the counter-arguments to be offered.—My mood is like that of an officer who has stormed a bulwark. Albeit wounded—he is *on the top* and is now unfurling his banner. More good fortune, much more than sorrow, as dreadful as the surrounding scene may be. —Although, as I have said, I know no one of the same cast of mind as myself now, I do have the vanity of having thought as a collective rather than an individual. The most peculiar feeling of loneliness and manyness,—A hurrying harbinger, a herald, who does not quite know whether the corps of knights are coming up behind or whether they even still exist."

But now the publisher could not be talked into letting *Human, All Too Human* appear anonymously. He refused to forgo the name of Nietzsche, and he had no objections to a bit of scandal. So the author went through the entire manuscript again to blue-pencil anything that Wagner might take personally. Nietzsche clung to the hope that a rupture between them was still avoidable and that Wagner would permit him the freedom of his own convictions in their friendship.

After Easter 1878, Nietzsche, revitalized by Baden-Baden,

came home to Basel to resume his lectures. He gave up having a household of his own since it had been shown that steady changes of climate did him the most good. He rented a room in Basel. His intention of fully giving up his teaching job had now yielded to a resolution to try it once again. Nietzsche wanted to live in the mountains as much as possible and come into town only for his lectures. Despite all the terrible problems he had been having with his health in winter 1877–78, he managed, with Peter Gast's help, to prepare his opus for the printer: the first volume of aphorisms, *Human, All Too Human—A Book for Free Spirits.* Since it came out shortly before the centennial of Voltaire's death (May 30, 1878),[5] Nietzsche dedicated it to the memory of that free spirit. In regard to this memorial day, he wrote to Malwida in June: "The destiny of the man about whom there are still only partisan judgments after a hundred years, struck me as a fearful symbol. Human beings are most unreconcilable in hating and most unjust in loving the liberators of the mind." It is unclear who sent Nietzsche a bust of Voltaire on May 30, with the lines: "L'âme de Voltaire fait ses compliments à Frédéric Nietzsche." (The soul of Voltaire offers its compliments to Friedrich Nietzsche.)

When Nietzsche sent *Human, All Too Human* to Richard and Cosima Wagner, he added a whimsical dedication to pretend that many things in the book could be taken humorously. With a hammering heart and vague expectations, he put the package in the mails. The first page of the book contained the lines that had been sketched as follows:

> *To the Master and the Mistress*
> *a cheerful greeting*
> *from Friedrich Freemind in Basel,*
> *blessed with a new child.*
> *He desires that they with moved hearts*
> *examine the child to see*
> *whether it takes after the father,*
> *who knows?—even with a moustache.*
> *And whether on all twos or fours*
> *it will romp about the earthly precincts.*
> *In mountains, it would slip towards light*

and hop and spring like new-born kids.
Whatever its fate in its earthly wandering,
it wants to be liked;
not by many; fifteen at most;
for others it will be mockery and torment.
But before we send it out in the world,
may the Master's faithful eye gaze on it and bless it,
and may the wise grace of the Mistress
follow it for evermore. "

The barely concealed attacks, throughout the book, against Wagner, merely apostrophized as "The Artist," were bound to offend the Bayreuth friends. For the moment, Gast, Rée, and Burckhardt were the only ones to nod assent to the new work. Rohde did not withhold his "painful feelings." The Wagners shrouded themselves in silence, and it was only in an article *Public and Popularity,* in the August issue of *Bayreuther Blätter,* that Wagner uttered sarcasm and criticism about Nietzsche's views, although allusively and with a self-control that was quite out of character. The article, drawing a bead on "conditions of art in Germany today," explained that nothing could be worthwhile if it was meant to be a presentation for the public. Goodness could only appear "in the guise of mediocrity." And he kicked out against "the professors," to get back at Nietzsche for his attacks.

Wagner wrote to Overbeck: "I maintained my friendship for him by not reading the book, and all I could hope and wish for is that he thank me for this favor."

Nevertheless, Nietzsche was hurt by Wagner's polemics. He was too bruised by hateful letters from other people, and dumbstruck by their unreasonable comments. Wagner's scorn was the crowning blow among such "All Too Human" things.

On May 31, Nietzsche admitted to Gast: "If, along with you, I include the two men who have really delighted in my book, Rée and Burckhardt (who has repeatedly called it the 'sovereign book') then I have a clue to what people would have to be like if my book were to have a quick impact. But it *will* not and *cannot*, as much as I regret it for the sake of our marvelous Schmeitzner. In Bayreuth, it has been placed on a kind of Index: and in fact, the great Excommunication seems to have been spoken upon its author. However, they are trying to hold on to my *friends* while losing me—and thus I keep finding out from others what is happening and being planned behind my back. Wagner has *forgone* the grand opportunity of showing grandeur of character. It must not dissuade me from my opinion of him or of myself."

The publication of the book in 1878 was followed by two addenda: *Various Opinions and Statements* (1879) and *The Wanderer and His Shadow* (1880), later designated by Nietzsche as the second volume. Wherever he traveled during these years, he must have been incessantly absorbed in writing to fill the some six hundred pages in the complete edition. The subtitle *A Book for Free Spirits* helps to understand Nietzsche's attempt at revealing his road back to his own essence, away from outer influences. The discoverer of a new insight into life and the formulator of a new, aphoristic style is blazing a trail for himself. The French *moralistes* and Rée's book *Psychological Observations* may have suggested the polish and the skeptical tone of Nietzsche's new diction. But what belongs to the mature Nietzsche alone is his way of dealing sharply with the ensnarements of metaphysics and Wagner's aesthetic opinions—which involved his liberation from Schopenhauer, whom he had venerated for so long. Nietzsche had to become independent, he had to forward new things against the moral philosophy and epistemology of earlier times.

The most interesting point here, of course, is his challenge to the leading role of art—a prophecy that, in the end, was fully justified. His title for the fourth section was: *From the Souls of the Artists and Writers.*

In revising the Dionysian concept, Nietzsche bade farewell to Wagner, whom he calls "Artist" and consigns to the area of the "Sunset of Art":

"The artist will soon be seen as a splendid vestige and be paid honors, like a marvelous stranger on whose energy and beauty the fortune of earlier times depended, and these honors will be the kind that we do not easily accord our peers. The best things about us are probably inherited from the feelings of earlier times, which we now can scarcely reach by a direct route; the sun has already set, but the sky of our lives is still glowing and shining even though we no longer see the sun."

The sunset of art, according to Nietzsche, will be followed by a sunrise of philosophy whose aim must be to reevaluate all values. The variations on these new themes in the addenda making up the second volume, especially the thoughts on a future without Christianity and on the vices of the Germans, were just the thing to finalize the break with Wagner.

The radical change documented in *Human, All Too Human* perplexed contemporaries and later generations. Of course, the solution ought not to be sought in personal matters alone. The object of Nietzsche's thoughts now seems like a preview of what shapes our world today: the loss of art for lack of self-renewing cultic rites, which are the only possibilities for new artistic forms.

Nietzsche's presumed confidence in his views, his wide travels, which he loved to describe, do not camouflage the strains on his constant poor health or the additional vicissitude of the rupture with Wagner. On June 11, 1877, Nietzsche wrote to Reinhard von Seydlitz:

"I hope and wish that one of my friends would be good and friendly to Wagner; for I am less and less able to give him any pleasure (the way he simply is—an *old* man who won't change). His and my aspirations now diverge completely. This is painful enough—but in the service of Truth, one must be prepared for any sacrifice. If he knew, a propos, the way I feel about his art and his aims, he would regard me as one of his worst enemies—which, as everyone knows, I am not."

The "old man who won't change" kept feeling more and more strongly that the end was nigh. Working tooth and nail on the score of *Parsifal*, Wagner realized that this giant opus was the only thing he could wrest away from his "repulsive" fate, and that it was bound to be his "last victory over life." On December 29, 1877, he wrote to King Ludwig: "I have no hope for the 'German spirit,' which I felt I could announce in the dedication of my Nibelungen work: I've had my experiences—and I shall hold my tongue. I have no hope for Pommerania or Brandenburg or any other province of this peculiar German Empire: I do not even have any hopes for the Markgraviate of Bayreuth. But—I conclude a peace with the world, and my first clause is: 'May the world leave me alone!' "

In October 1878, Wagner finished the second act of *Parsifal.* King Ludwig, who was once again closer to Wagner, was the first to get the news: "I have flung myself into purgatory and re-emerged safe and sane. I know—this labor too is worthy of Us." The letter is signed: "His immortal own for this world, Richard Wagner."

The new wave of bombastic friendliness aroused Cosima's jealousy, just as Nietzsche's estrangement—for all her solicitude—basically caused her relief. She confided her misery about King Ludwig to her journal: "A rather strange feeling, something indescribable, takes hold of me when I read, at the conclusion, that his soul belongs to him forever. It is like a serpent's tooth in my heart, and I don't know what I would like. I wouldn't want these words to be rhetoric, and I wouldn't want them to be the truth; if it were in my power, I would not let these words be unwritten. For whatever he does is right. But I suffer and I vanish, in order to conceal my sorrows."

Taking breaks from his scoring, Wagner delighted in tracking down lost compositions of his youth. Zealous and shrewd, Cosima helped in his investigations. Friends in Dresden lit upon a trunk containing some instrumental works (the *Polonia* and *Columbus* overtures, plus the *Symphony in C-Major*).

Wagner had a new score copied out of the extant orchestral voices, and from week to week he was surprised by a new symphonic movement, a music which had been written forty years earlier and premiered in Leipzig.

He wrote to the king: "Its fate is bizarre. In the year 1835, that is to say, forty-three years ago, I wanted to give it to Mendelssohn (in Leipzig then) to have him look through it; rather than pressuring him, and in order to give him all the time he needed, I asked him to keep my manuscript! Later on, I saw him many times, but he never said a word about this symphony. He died—and I went on.—In Tribschen, I told my wife about it. She didn't have a moment's peace after that. Our young friend Nietzsche got to know Mendelssohn's son; through him, an investigation had to be undertaken: not a trace. When this son died in turn, old heirs were questioned:—in vain, the manuscript was—and to all appearances—is gone."

From a present viewpoint of the piece, Mendelssohn's indolent behavior seems understandable. The younger Mendelssohn, shortly before his death, had invited Nietzsche for a tour of Italy and Greece. How eagerly Nietzsche would have accepted! But he begged off, worried that the distrustful Master might take it amiss if "his Nietzsche" were to go traveling with the son of the dead but still hated Felix Mendelssohn-Bartholdy.

Wagner spent the winter of 1878–79 quietly working on the third act of *Parsifal.* There was no mention of further Festivals. The building on the "lovely hill" waited in desolation. In February 1879, Wagner quite unusually opened up his heart to his royal friend when he wrote:

"I and what I create do not endure any haste now. I have produced much too fast, much too much, and much too early for our age; all the performances (except for the only one which I witnessed at the side of my sublime ruler) were botched and bungled. The worst thing about it is that I cannot even lament them anymore! There just is not any mishap, any lost opportunity that I can complain about, for I can see that there is nothing to improve in the entire condition of the present; it is thoroughly bad, and only badness can thrive in it. A man to whom this is bleakly clear and obvious cannot give in to any more deception. . . . But where all hope remains silent, there the demon speaks, or—genius? I feel happier than ever: my work is the source of my life, which surrounds me, friendly and soothing, in more and more spiritual images."

The much younger man in Basel displays a none too different frame of mind when he writes to Malwida on June 11, 1879:

"I want to go my way quietly and renounce everything that might hinder me. The *crisis* of life is here. If I did not have the sense of the superlative fruitfulness of my new philosophy, I would most likely feel terrifyingly alone."

A number of Nietzsche's friends, especially those committed to Wagner, felt they had to confront him about his latest book. They demanded that he follow his public attack with a personal justification.

To Wagner's old friend Mathilde Maier,[6] Nietzsche confessed he had helped himself out of his misery by articulating his thoughts. He had branded Wagner's art as a foggy veiling of all that is true and simple, as a struggle with reason against reason, as a "Baroque art of grandiloquence and glamorized excess." This stigmatization was meant to help Nietzsche overcome the disease and get beyond the alienation towards his own talent and temperament. (Nietzsche's estimation of Wagner's work was precisely reflected in the distorting mirror of Fascism.) Scarcely anyone, he wrote, could be capable of feeling in what lofty mountain air, but also in what a mild mood toward humanity he was now living, "resolved more than ever to devote myself to all that is good and right, a hundred paces closer to the Greeks than before: . . . even in the tiniest detail, I am now striving towards Wisdom, whereas earlier I merely honored and adulated the wise."

In fall 1878 or in spring of the following year, Nietzsche's sister made an ill-starred attempt to intervene in Bayreuth. Cosima's answer left nothing to wish for in pedantry and dogmatism. Nevertheless, Elisabeth was apparently still a *persona grata* at Wahnfried. Cosima also stayed in contact with her.

Wagner, for his part, coped with the gloomy situation by devising a pun attacking Paul Rée's supposedly corrupting influence on Nietzsche: *Reékleckse* (a portmanteau word containing *Kleckse*, "splotches, smudges," and rhyming with *Reflexe*, "reflexes, reflections"). Since, suddenly, all the earlier praises from Nietzsche's pen could no longer be true, but were merely waved off as reflections, Wagner felt impelled to remark: "It's no great honor for me to be praised by that man." And if ever he was depressed and Cosima worriedly asked: "Are you unsatisfied with your life?" he would retort: "Not with *my* life, but *with* life."

Those days of autumn 1878 also saw Wagner's great destruction of Nietzsche's letters in Bayreuth. Nietzsche's sorrow over the parting of ways was much too deep for any rancour or malice. A man intending vengeance and dominated by a sense of grievance would hardly be capable of writing, as Nietzsche did to Peter Gast in 1880: "There was never an angry word between us, only many encouraging and cheerful words, and I probably haven't laughed so much with anybody."

A wrathful Cosima, however, never concealed from Elisabeth Nietzsche what she felt about her brother. The breach of faith by a friend could only be an act of mental derangement. But Cosima dropped her mask when she wrote: "Many things contributed to the dismal book! Last but not least, Israel in the guise of Doctor Rée!"

The Cosima in whom Nietzsche saw a reincarnation of Ariadne

failed to sense anything of the psychological background to the Dionysus tragedy first documented in *Human, All Too Human*. Nor did she realize that, even after the apostasy from Wagner, Nietzsche still regarded her as "the most likable woman I have met in all my life" (to Malwida, on January 14, 1888).

During the genesis of the book, Nietzsche's pains and illnesses never let up. Over and over again, he had to be excused from his teaching duties, which had become a drudgery. Marriage plans, virtually taken out of thin air, came to naught, and all that remained was a possibility he had frequently considered: to give up his professorship at Basel. Outer circumstances were also forcing him towards this decision. His sister went back to their mother in Naumburg for good; she dissolved the household in Basel. Headaches, eye pains and constant vomiting afflicted Nietzsche with a tormenting regularity. So finally, on May 2, 1879, he addressed his letter of resignation to the Basel Board of Education. With great regret, the officials released him from his duties six weeks later. For all the disruptions, the university appreciated his accomplishments. Nietzsche, though he had continually been oppressed by his academic work, suffered terribly at his departure, and he was very thankful to have his friend Marie Baumgartner nearby. He told her: "I am leaving Basel for ever and ever."

A brief sojourn in the mountain air of the Bremgarten spa near Berne put him back on his feet again, so that he could travel to St. Moritz alone. "To think that I could live to see this!" he wrote gratefully. "I did not realize the earth showed such things, and I thought the good painters had invented it." Later, he used to say: "Engadin restored me to life!"

When Nietzsche spent winter 1879–80 in Naumburg, his headaches continued relentlessly. As a result, he made up his mind to go south in February 1880, first to Riva, and then on to Venice. Here he began the notes to his new work *Morgenröte (Sunrise)*, which developed further in Marienbad, Naumburg, and Stresa that summer and fall, and was concluded in Genoa in 1881. When the year was over, Nietzsche described himself to Marie Baumgartner as half dead from pains and exhaustion.

In Bayreuth, Wagner terminated the year on December 25, with a private concert of the Meininger Court Orchestra in the hall of Wahnfried. Once again, it took place as a surprise for

Cosima at seven in the morning. The program featured the prelude to *Parsifal*, with a concert finale that Wagner had added for this purpose. The evening brought a recital, with the *Siegfried Idyll* and individual movements from Beethoven symphonies.

At the end of that year, Germany, after the victorious war, was in a state of growing prosperity. A powerful contrast to this was Nietzsche's bitterness toward his Fatherland. His mood in many ways paralleled Wagner's fear that Germany as a nation was doomed. This estimation was, of course, due to Wagner's private disgust at his incessant financial difficulties. He certainly didn't mean the Germany that was waxing into a world power with considerable colonial possessions. "My lack of hope for Germany and her conditions is thorough and complete," wrote Wagner in March 1881, from Italy, to the banker Feustel in Bayreuth, "and that is saying something, for once, when I started out with total awareness in my own decisive direction, I wrote on my banner: Stand and fall with Germany!" He was so deeply convinced that Europe, and especially Germany, was steadily deteriorating, that for the sake of keeping the intensity of his work, he seriously thought of pulling up stakes and settling in America.

By fall 1880, Wagner apparently regretted giving the king *Parsifal* in exchange for covering the Festival debts, and he stepped back from the agreement:

"How can a drama openly presenting the most sublime mysteries of the Christian faith be performed in theaters such as ours next to an opera repertory and in front of an audience such as ours? I would really not take it amiss if our church authorities were to raise highly justified objections to the exposure of the hallowed mysteries on the same boards on which frivolity makes itself comfortable yesterday and tomorrow, and to a public that only feels attracted to frivolity."

Dictatorially, as though he had never "mortgaged" *Parsifal* to the king, Wagner demanded: "*Parsifal* may be performed for all time only in Bayreuth and nowhere else. Never shall *Parsifal* be offered as an amusement to the public in any other theatre, and my making sure of this is the only thing now occupying me and making me determine how and by what means I can assure the destiny of my work. I feel daily as if I were writing my last will and testament!"

A few days later, the king indulgently gave in and retracted all earlier agreements about the performance of *Parsifal.* He also took over the sole protection of the *Festspiele* when Wagnerites, particularly Wolzogen, rashly began circulating a plan to have several German rulers as patrons of Bayreuth. Thus ended the right that the king had acquired in 1876 to premiere *Parsifal* in Munich.

In winter 1880, Wagner has several strokes with convulsions. Doctors recommended a lengthy sojourn in the south, and so the family and the servants moved to Naples for eight months. The scoring of Act III of *Parsifal* advanced there very slowly. Wagner, previously driven and harried, now took time to devote himself to his family, primarily Siegfried, and enjoy the ease of Southern life. His thoughts focused more and more on spiritual things; he was preoccupied with the beliefs of Christianity and the intermediary role of the church. The following religious epistle went off to Wolzogen:

"I almost fear it may be difficult for us to reach some agreement as to what an incomparably and sublimely simple Savior signifies and is for all time in the historically tangible guise of Jesus of Nazareth, truly acknowledged, and cleansed and redeemed from all the Alexandrian, Judaean, Roman, and despotic distortions. Nevertheless, by ruthlessly abandoning the Church, and Christianity, nay, the whole phenomenon of Christianity in history, we want our friends to know forever that we have done so on behalf of that Christ whom we wish to preserve in his full purity for the sake of his absolute incomparableness and childlikeness, in order to take him along into those dreadful times that must needs follow upon the necessary decline of all that now exists."

In summer 1880, Wagner had finished his essay *Religion and Art,* which submits that Socialism might be worthwhile in connection with vegetarianism, protection of animals, and temperance.

Nietzsche, who thundered against Christianity eight years later in the *Anti-Christ,* was involved, at the same time as Wagner, in similar theological speculations. To be sure, his ideas, expressed in aphoristic terseness, are more convincing than Wagner's hazy remarks. "It is wrong to the point of absurdity," writes Nietzsche, "to see the sign of the Christian in a 'faith,' nay, in faith in redemption through Christ: all that is Christian is Christian *prac-*

tice, a life such as He *lived,* the man who died on the cross.
. . ." Nietzsche's immoralism, to the very end, remained in radical
opposition to the Christian religion. This fact must be borne in
mind if one prefers to view the exalted conclusion of the *Anti-
Christ* as dictated by the starting degeneration.

For Nietzsche, too, death seemed near. His sojourn with his
mother and his sister in Naumburg was inconceivably bad for
him. Life was a dreadful torture, so that he craved the end. He
also believed he had terminated his life's work, "to be sure, like
someone who was not given any time." Malwida von Meysenbug
was his last link to the Wagners, for she could inquire how things
were in Naples:

"Have you had any good news from the Wagners? I haven't
heard from them for three years: *they* left me after all, and I had
already known long since that as soon as Wagner noticed the gap
between our aspirations he would no longer stick with me. I have
been told he is writing things against me. Let him continue: Truth
must come to light in every way! I think of him with everlasting
gratitude for it is Wagner to whom I owe some of the most
powerful impulses towards spiritual and intellectual independence . . . But I am quite useless for any association with him, or
any resumption, It is too late."

On October 20, 1879, a man came to Wahnfried, seeking a new
tie between Wagner and Nietzsche, whom he so venerated: Heinrich von Stein, a writer and philosopher, born in Coburg in 1857,
was hired as Siegfried's tutor. At last, another young man who
could be taken into the family! The baron, from an ancient Franconian dynasty,[7] a slender giant with blond hair, a small moustache, big blue eyes, who looked more like a soldier than a
philosopher, charmed everyone and was instantly claimed by the
Master for himself. This lovely hope was similar to Nietzsche in
many ways: equally young, equally modest, equally quick to blush
at off-color jokes, and passionate for all his stiffness. Von Stein
also took part in the festive life of the family in Naples. Malwida
was there, and told about how the Russian painter Paul Joukowsky,[8] a friend of Henry James,[9] was engaged as set designer
for the Bayreuth *Parsifal,* and how they had taken on Engelbert
Humperdinck,[10] particularly to copy the orchestra parts at Bayreuth. Malwida also attended a home production of the Grail

scene in Act I of *Parsifal,* with Humperdinck and the composer Martin Plüddemann performing.

In spring 1880, Nietzsche traveled south, going to Venice for the first time, together with Peter Gast, and his health improved there. His special love for Venice began at this point, just as the city was to fascinate Wagner a short time later. Nietzsche spent July and August in Marienbad, where he zealously dug in his "moral mine." There he discussed Wagner with a high church-official and showed interest in his work on Palestrina,[11] which had inspired the priest to cultivate old Church music in Regensburg. Wagner, while laboring on his *Parsifal,* studied old Italian church music. One result of these studies was the version of Palestrina's *Stabat Mater,* which was put out by Kahnt in August 1878. Nietzsche's ecclesiastical interlocutor belonged to the circle around Hebel, the *Kapellmeister* of the Regensburg cathedral, who functioned in the Breitkopf publishing house as the main editor of the Palestrina edition.

These conversations with the priest made Nietzsche realize there could be no substitute for his exciting association with Wagner. He often dreamt about Wagner, always recalling their long-ago intimacy. It made no sense to Nietzsche to be right about certain things, for the lost friendship could not be wiped from his memory. And it wasn't just with Wagner! "These are the heaviest sacrifices that my life and thought have demanded from me—even now, after an hour of friendly conversation with perfect strangers, my entire philosophy is shaking: it strikes me as so foolish to insist on being right at the price of love and *not* to be able to impart one's most valuable possessions in order not to remove the friendly feelings."

In September, Nietzsche again visited his mother and sister in Naumburg. On the way back south, he met Overbeck in Basel, spent a few weeks in a terrible state on Lago Maggiore, and then traveled to Genoa, where he delighted in a "garret solitude," which, however, could scarcely shield him against his miserable health. Without a stove and with constant headaches, "often with paralyzed limbs," he had a hard time during this first Southern winter. Gast wrote him his thoughts about Wagner, and Nietzsche admitted how greatly he needed to hear something "more absolute" about Wagner from time to time. Spring 1881 found him in the small mountain spa of Recoaro by Vicenza. Gast was accompanying him. And then in summer, when he went to Engadin again, his health unexpectedly improved.

For by a fluke he had come upon the tiny market town of Sils-Maria in the valley of the Inn. This setting in one of the most charming of mountain valleys enchanted Nietzsche. He compared the landscape to Mexican plateaus. But, exceptionally that year, the sky was not pure here either, and by early October he was back in Genoa, writing countless letters on a newly invented, monstrous typewriter he had just acquired. His eyesight had gotten so bad that his handwriting was nearly indecipherable. However, that very first summer, Sils gave him the starting point for *Also sprach Zarathustra (Thus Spake Zarathustra)*.

In Genoa, he was once more deeply impressed by Bizet's *Carmen*. The opera seemed to breathe the spirit of Mérimée,[12] and he quickly recalled that Mérimée had indeed written a tale called *Carmen*. The date of Nietzsche's first acquaintance with Bizet's *Carmen* was probably November 27, 1881 in Genoa. As a precaution, in case his friend Gast were to smile at his preference, Nietzsche informed him: "I am not so fully injudicious in my taste." He greatly admired the *Carmen* libretto by Meilhac and Halévy (they had also supplied a great number of operetta texts to Jacques Offenbach,[13] whom Nietzsche so highly esteemed as a master of allegro art). A piano reduction of Bizet's opera, with countless marginal glosses by Nietzsche, reached Gast shortly thereafter. This musical encounter was to have its most important echo in *The Wagner Case*.

In Bayreuth, the *Parsifal* premiere was already casting its shadow, and Nietzsche did not hesitate to send Feustel a note for his sister, which Overbeck was to hand her in lieu of him, so as to ensure a ticket for Elisabeth in time. "With an express declaration on your part, my dear sister, for whichever of the three days of the main performance you have decided on (July 26, 28, 30)," he wrote from Genoa.

Rée happened to be staying with him, and, like many visits, it ended badly. "The first day, a very fine mood; the second I endured with all kinds of tonics; the third, exhaustion, I fainted in the afternoon; an attack at night; the fourth, in bed; on the fifth, I got up again, only to lie down once more in the afternoon; the sixth day, and until now, headaches and weakness."

Yet being with Rée was always refreshing and heartwarming. They also went to the theater, where Sarah Bernhardt[14] happened to be doing *Camille.* At the premiere, she had the misfortune to fall into a dead faint. The audience endured an embarrassed hour of waiting, until she could get on with the show. But in the middle of the same act, she suffered a hemmorrhage right on stage, curtailing the performance. Nevertheless, she performed again the following nights with enormous success. Her appearance and manners reminded Nietzsche of Cosima.

In March 1881, he found out about a letter, in which Edouard Schuré described Nietzsche's new way of thinking, to Wagner, as "heart-breaking nihilism." Gast was careless enough to tell Nietzsche, and the remark went "too deep into my heart . . . but, let's buck up!" (To Gast on March 13, 1881.)

He also had to tell himself this, because, for the sake of his eyes, he had given up reading scores and playing the piano for good and seldom had the chance to hear music.

His last meeting with the Wagners in Sorrento was a thing of the distant past now. Cosima was corresponding with Ludwig Schemann, her father's biographer and a writer for the *Bayreuther Blätter.* The two of them agreed: Nietzsche's "mania for independence" had lost him for Bayreuth. For any man who did not do his research in pure acquiescence and renunciation in the shadow of the Master was doomed to unproductiveness. With some melancholy, Cosima looked back to the time of the *Birth of Tragedy,* when the young initiate had been in harmony with Wagner. Following the "finest example" of Herr von Wolzogen, Schemann, as a further successor of Nietzsche, was to stand at Wagner's side. It was understandable that Nietzsche did not care to be ranged into such a "finely structured army of heroes under the king, the genius," as Cosima described it.

Heinrich von Stein, for example, had done right by Cosima and forsaken the views of his idol Nietzsche, in order to help underpin the ideology of the Festival Hill. But even he wasn't radical enough to "denigrate all that is outside, on the basis of our understanding." Everything (even the universities) was to be scrutinized in terms of Bayreuth. But: "Such a man will not be found; those who concern themselves with this are looking for something on the outside." And it was such a demand for exclusivity that Nietzsche had escaped.

The guests on the Festival Hill had little choice but to worship. For Cosima more and more often confused her husband with the object of the fuzzy Christian faith that the Master was tacking together for home use at the *Festspiele*. Cosima's statement to Schemann was drawn from Wagner's essay *Heroism and Christianity:* "Happily, it is not just a doctrine that is coming from Bayreuth, but an injunction for action, and in nearly all areas. And the Saviour did not know anything else when sacrificing himself so that his disciples would act."

Schemann likewise joined the flock of traveling lecturers who recruited for the Bayreuth cause by holding introductory talks with musical examples. In this area too, he was a kind of pinch-hitter for Nietzsche, who many years earlier had thrown in his fickle straw-fire suggestion, saying he wanted to organize such evenings for Wagner himself. In 1887, a resigned Cosima wrote: "He has apparently lost faith. He never really had any, most likely, but how comforting to know that you are stepping in for him and that a friendly fortune is letting us experience a realization for a defective beginning." Nevertheless, in reference to Schemann's paper on Schopenhauer, the Wagners remembered Nietzsche's "warm, lovely, simple language," which seemed to recur in Schemann's "substantial élan." The Master himself maintained that young Nietzsche had once blossomed and then remained a mere bulb—"really a beastly thing."

Surrounded by family and friends, Wagner, in November 1881, went by way of Munich, Bolzano, and Verona to Naples, and then sailed to Palermo, where he stayed at the Hotel de Palmes. Here he began instrumenting the third act of *Parsifal.* Joseph Rubinstein[15] prepared the piano score of the entire opera, publishing it in April 1882. Tortured by abdominal pains, Wagner had to keep interrupting his work. Chest cramps afflicted him more and more often, but they weren't diagnosed as heart disease. In January, he finished the orchestration.

After overcoming repeated cardiac difficulties, Wagner took Hermann Levi along on an excursion to Messina. The conductor, in a letter to his father on April 13, 1882, writes: "He is the finest and noblest person. It is natural that the world misunderstands and calumniates him; men always blacken anything that shines; Goethe didn't have a better time of it. But posterity will some day acknowledge that Wagner was as great a man as he was an artist, as those now close to him are well aware. Even his struggle against what he calls 'Jewry' in modern music and letters arises from the noblest motives, and the fact that he doesn't have any petty *risches** like, say, a land junker or a Protestant bigot is proven by his behavior towards me and Joseph Rubinstein, and his earlier intimate relationship with Tausig, whom he tenderly loved." Thus writes the Jew Hermann Levi, as dazzled by Wagner as most of the young firebrands who came into contact with him.

In point of fact, the anti-Semitism of the mature Wagner seems to have been mainly stoked by Cosima, who supported the so-called Förster Petition, a new agitation by Elisbeth Nietzsche's husband, the wretched Dr. Förster. Cosima, however, could scarcely sense (or did she divine it in terms of Bayreuth's exclusivity) how greatly she thus imperiled the Berlin plans for staging the *Ring* with the help of the Jewish agent Angelo Neumann. In reply to his inquiry, Wagner declared: "I am completely distant from the present anti-Semitic movement; an article of mine, appearing soon in the *Bayreuth Blätter,* will proclaim this in such a way that it will be impossible for persons of a lofty intellect to connect me with that movement." Since Neumann, a dauntless Wagnerite, joined those "persons of a lofty intellect," the Berlin premiere of the *Ring* was mounted by his company in May 1881.

Levi was supposed to lead the first Bayreuth *Parsifal,* and in April he discussed rehearsal plans with Wagner. He reported to his father from Bayreuth: "I have spent three marvelous days here. The Master was in an excellent mood, we spoke of a number of things for the coming year. . . . It is no longer a secret that I will be conducting the work."

In June, Levi once again dwelt in Wahnfried. Two days after his arrival, Wagner opened an anonymous letter accusing Levi of having an affair with Cosima. The writer challenged Wagner to "keep his work pure," and not let it be conducted by a Jew. The Master promptly showed Levi the ominous message. Deeply

*A Western-Yiddish word meaning "anti-Semitism" and still in use among German Jews. [Trans.]

offended, the conductor secretly left Bayreuth right after lunch. When Wagner wired him to come back from Bamberg, Levi asked to be relieved of his obligation. In a letter of July 1, Wagner implored: "For goodness' sake, come back immediately and get to know us properly. Lose nothing of your faith, but acquire a strong courage along with it! Perhaps—there will be a great change in your life—but come what may—you are my *Parsifal* conductor!" Astonishingly, the incident was closed thanks to this vague appeal.

Nietzsche took up contact with Hermann Levi in 1882, but his efforts at having Peter Gast's compositions performed came to naught. He had no better luck with Bülow, whose critical attitude towards Gast's opera *Scherz, List und Rache (Fun, Cunning, and Revenge)* rather piqued Nietzsche. Bülow opened his reply about the manuscript as follows: "Wagner is a phenomenon!—Phenomenons do not create a school!" The conductor, scanning the first few pages, scarcely glanced at the rest of the composition. He regarded Gast as a pure Wagner epigone, which prompted Nietzsche to tell Gast: "Herr von Bülow has the poor manners of Prussian officers, but he's an honest fellow;—his refusal to deal any further with German operatic music has all kinds of secret reasons."

These reasons were not just tied to Bülow's separation from Cosima. He rejected Wagner's new music and was now close to the group around Johannes Brahms. Despite this, Nietzsche advised Gast to visit Bayreuth in summer 1882, because the opera celebrities of Germany would be coming together there, and Hermann Levi would also be present. In addition, he suspected that all his friends and his sister would likewise attend. But Gast resolved not to go—to Nietzsche's great disappointment, for the philosopher felt it was a major omission for a composer not to get to know Wagner's orchestra and his instrumental innovations.

At Gast's recommendation, Nietzsche heard Rossini's *Barber of Seville.* He found the performance exemplary, but was disappointed by the music, which didn't seem to be speaking about the Seville he loved. "The tremendous agility is even embarrassing, like the sight of a clown." In Bellini's *La Sonnambula,* the title role was sung by a Miss Nevada, who delighted Nietzsche.

Finally, he kept enjoying Bizet's *Carmen,* this time with Galli-

Marie as the heroine, "une personne très jolie, très chic." She had done the part at the Paris première on March 3, 1875. At her wish, Bizet had added the *Habañera,* in lieu of a less effective number. As we know, the Parisians turned their backs on the opera, forgetting it after Bizet's death. A few years later, Galli-Marié succeeded in making a great hit with it in Southern France and Italy. And she managed to get the opera mounted again in Paris, bringing triumph at last to herself and the name of Bizet.

The musical antipode to Wagner, whom Nietzsche had chosen years earlier, this Georges Bizet with his *Carmen,* did not cease to provide themes for the philosopher's aesthetic and cultural reflections. Not only did Nietzsche attend *Carmen* some twenty times in the course of those years, he also gathered material to play this music off polemically against Wagner's in his pamphlet *The Wagner Case,* 1888.

In Genoa, Nietzsche divulged in a letter to Malwida: "Though all the world may leave me alone now, I am not complaining—I actually find it, first of all, useful, and, secondly, natural. That's how it is and that's how it always was as a *rule.* Wagner's behavior towards me too is part of the banality of the *rule.* Moreover, he is the man of his party; and the happenstance of his life has given him such a random and incomplete education that he can comprehend neither the gravity nor the necessity of my passion. The notion that Wagner could have once believed I shared his opinions makes me blush now. Ultimately, if I do not fully deceive myself about my future, the best part of Wagner's effect will survive in the effect I have—and that's just about the funniest aspect of the whole thing . . ."

By way of precaution, Nietzsche asked Peter Gast in February 1882 whether the Wagners were already back from Palermo, since he was thinking of traveling to Sicily and feared the possibility of an unpleasant encounter.

First, Rée came to Rome on March 13, and he met young Lou von Salomé at the home of Malwida von Meysenbug. On March 29, Nietzsche, having boarded a Sicilian sailing freighter in Genoa, arrived in Messina, where he remained until April 20. He had deliberately chosen the most adventurous kind of passage. Using a romantic pretext, he managed to convince the captain of the freighter to take him along as the only passenger. In Rome,

Malwida and Rée inevitably invited him over and introduced him to the charming and highly intelligent Russian woman. Like Rée, Nietzsche fell in love with her. The three of them, the two friends and the girl, went to Tribschen to renew their memories. The only photograph of the three together was taken at that time. Their joint travels didn't last, for Nietzsche visited Professor Overbeck in Basel and then on May 23, he went off again, passing through Naumburg on the way to Berlin. But he didn't stay for long; the Grunewald apparently didn't live up to his expectations for his health. He went back to Naumburg and, with the aid of a scribe, began preparing *The Cheerful Knowledge* for publication. But then, as a substitute for the Grunewald, for the sake of his eyes, and in order to meet Lou, he took off for the Tautenburg Woods.

There, in Tautenburg, Nietzsche felt that he had at last come upon a person who could give his life some coherence. He toyed with the idea of marrying her and asked Rée to intercede. But Lou's affection for Nietzsche did not involve any lifelong plans; her creative participation in his thoughts actually made her shy away from the fetters of matrimony. Nietzsche was too inhibited to speak his mind to her plainly, and this brought about a situation that can only be called tragic. If Rée likewise had no success with his own proposal, then the friend had turned into a rival, and one with intimate knowledge at that. No matter how much Lou assured Nietzsche she wanted to remain friends, it didn't help. The situation became all the more complicated in July, when Nietzsche's friends, his sister, and Lou came together in Bayreuth for the premiere of *Parsifal*.

On this occasion, Elisabeth Nietzsche asked Wagner if she could talk to him at Wahnfried. Departing, she heard the Master murmur: "Tell your brother, ever since he went away from me, I've been alone." These words, if they were really uttered, were spoken about six months before Wagner's death, in the time of his greatest renown, when he was surrounded by reverence and admiration. Nietzsche, of course, found out about this message, which affected him so deeply that he instantly sat down to compose the aphorism *Astral Friendship*,[16] in which he confessed:

"We were friends and became *alien*. But that is proper, and we shall not conceal or obscure it as though we ought to be ashamed.

We are two ships, each with its goal and its course; we may cross paths and celebrate with one another, as we did—and then the fine ships lay so calmly in one harbor and under one sun that it seemed as though they had reached their goals and had one and the same goal. But then the all-powerful force of our tasks drove us asunder, into different seas and climes, and perhaps we shall never see one another again—perhaps we *shall* meet once again but not recognize one another: the different seas and suns will have altered us! Our mutual alienation is the law *above* us: that is the very reason we should become more venerable to one another! That is the very reason why the thought of our former friendship should become more sacred! There probably exists an enormous invisible curve and astral path, in which our so disparate courses and goals may be *included* as tiny stretches of the way —let us raise ourselves to this thought! But our lives are too short and our eyesight too trivial for us to be more than friends in terms of that sublime possibility.—And so, let us believe in our astral friendship, even if we have to become earthly enemies."

Nevertheless, Nietzsche missed the Festival; he remained in Tautenburg. He wouldn't dream of coming anywhere near Bayreuth again. He had talked Elisabeth and Lou into visiting him after the *Festspiele*. But first, on July 23, he quickly went to Naumburg to prepare his sister for *Parsifal*. The wounds he had inflicted upon himself in Bayreuth showed no sign of healing. His voluntary self-exclusion from the circle of Wagner disciples was more than painful to him.

As he was playing the *Parsifal* keyboard version for his sister, he was overcome with a peculiar sense of identity: He suddenly realized that he himself, as a boy, had also written such music— when his *Oratorio* was taking shape. Nietzsche, in his writing, liked to date back presages, and thus, in his final notes, we come across the following remark:

"In my boyhood, I was a pessimist, as ludicrous as this sounds, a few lines of music from my twelfth and thirteenth year are at bottom the blackest and most decisive example of everything I know of jet-black music. I have thus far found no thoughts or words in any writer or philosopher that derive so deeply from the ultimate abyss of negation."

During this same period, there was a backward view describing the break with Wagner as having been presaged rather early: "In my boyhood, I loved Handel and Beethoven: but, when I was fifteen, *Tristan and Isolde* was added as a world I could understand. Whereas I felt *Tannhäuser* and *Lohengrin* to be 'below my taste'—In matters of taste, boys are insolently proud."

In a letter to Peter Gast, Nietzsche excitedly wrote:

"Finally, I said: 'Sister dear, when I was a boy this was *exactly the kind of music* I composed, brought forth, and then played after a long interim: the *identity* of *mood* and *expression* was like a fairy tale! Why, a few passages, e.g., *The Death of the Kings*, struck us two as more poignant than anything we had played in Parsifal, and yet totally Parsifalesque! I must confess: I once again realized with a true dread how *closely akin* I really am to Wagner."

Of course, he planned to get Gast's verdict as a final appeal; he did not care to pass a definitive musical judgment. He also added: "You do understand, dear friend, that this is not meant as a *praise* of Parsifal!—What sudden *décadence!* And what Cagliostrism!" In a letter to Lou, Nietzsche expressed his contentment at not having to be in Bayreuth. "And yet, if I could be near you ghost-like, whispering things into your ear, then I could even endure the *Parsifal* music."

Wagner didn't finish orchestrating *Parsifal* until January 13th of that same year, 1882, when he said to Cosima: "Everything out of love for you. . . . No God could have made me instrument *Parsifal.*" All the same, Wagner's mind was relieved of the greatest worries about the Festival budget since the king, in his edict *Towards Promoting the Great Goals of the Maestro Richard Wagner,* had decreed that the orchestra and chorus of Munich's *Hoftheater* were to be put at the disposal of the Bayreuth project for two months every year as of 1882.

The sensation caused by the new opening promised financial security. With unbelievable energy, the almost seventy-year-old composer concentrated his strength on mounting *Parsifal.* Rehearsals had begun on July 2. Wagner was always present; he sang and played through every role for the others. If the knights of the grail strode at the wrong pace, he would tear upon the stage, grab the shrine, and walk at their head. If a member of the chorus dared to laugh, he would yell: "Get off the stage this instant! A man who can laugh now is not a good person and has no business being here!"

At first, King Ludwig announced he would attend the premiere. But three weeks before the opening, his regrets came unexpectedly. Deeply hurt, Wagner wrote to the king:

"Who inspired me to this highest and ultimate upsurge of all my spiritual energy? With a constant eye on Whom did I execute all this, daring to look forward to success? The now assured success will become the greatest failure in my life: what good is it all if I cannot gladden His heart with it? And—it is the last thing I shall create. The terrible fatigue, which allows me only just enough strength today for these few lines, tells me what point I have reached with my strength."

The European musical world flowed to the production on the Green Hill on July 26. Only the first two performances were reserved for the "Patrons." The next fourteen were open to the public because of the astonishing demand. To enable people with less money to attend, Wagner suggested creating scholarship funds, an idea that was soon realized.

No one was as disturbed as Nietzsche by the verbose ramblings of this late work, the lack of harmonious ensembles for the solo voices, the endless monologues. The audience was fascinated and left the theater in a hush.

At the last performance, something unexpected happened. Before the entr'acte music for the last tableau, Wagner declared he wanted to conduct the remainder of the act himself, something he had never done before. Levi withdrew from the desk, handing him the baton. But he and his assistant stayed in the orchestra pit to give the musicians any necessary auxiliary signs. The spectators didn't notice the change. The enraptured musicians followed Wagner's directions. Theodor Reichmann, singing Amfortas, moaned after the final curtain: "That's something you can go through just once! Only the Master can force you to use so much breath and so much vocal strength!" This remark implies extremely slow tempi and a great volume.

When Wagner put down the baton, his actual musical experience was over.

Full of impressions and not yet driven apart by jealousy, Elisabeth and Lou came to Tautenburg. Nietzsche instantly resumed the philosophical dialogues with Lou, who understood and encouraged him. He was particularly delighted by her poem *Prayer to Life*,[17] which he soon set to music because of the affinity he felt with it. When Peter Gast read the poem, he mistakenly assumed his friend had written it himself.

Though Nietzsche's feelings for Lou were unchanged, she saw their relationship as merely a spiritual friendship nourished by deep respect. At the end of August, Lou left Tautenburg in the middle of the day: Nietzsche's sister had turned into her deadly enemy. Full of moral indignation, and jealous of a supposed rival, Elisabeth now started claiming that she was the only one who knew what Nietzsche's philosophy was all about. Writing to their mother, she said she was terrified by his new attitudes which had come to life in Tautenburg: He loved evil now, under Lou's influence, but she [Elisabeth] loved good. Nietzsche was confronted with the Naumburg "virtue;" there was a real break with the family. His mother got so angry at him one day that she said things that made him pack his suitcase and take off for Leipzig at the crack of dawn.

From there, writing to Franz Overbeck in October 1882, he summed up the two events of that year that he declared as "miracles":

"Whereas Lou is prepared more than anyone else in the world for that part of my philosophy that has hitherto been just about concealed, Köselitz is the musical justification for my completely new practice and rebirth—just to speak egotistically for once. This is a new *Mozart*—I have no other sensation: beauty, sincerity, serenity, fullness, excess of invention, and the ease of contrapunctal mastery—these things have never been combined in such a way; I already cannot listen to any other music. How poor, artificial, and theatrical all that Wagnerian stuff now sounds to me!"

His only solace in the falling-out with his family was the correspondence with Peter Gast. This musician, whose works seemed to be fortifying Nietzsche's belief in a Dionysian future of art, signified a promise, which, however, was not fulfilled. Just as Gast came to feel Nietzsche's writings "more strongly and uncomfortably than anyone else, so must I feel everything coming from you as balmier than others could; this is quite a civil relationship between us! Perhaps it is like a relationship between comic and tragic poets (I think I once told you that Wagner saw a disguised tragic poet in me): what's certain is that in general I get off as more epicurean than you; and thus it is the 'law of things': the comic poet is the higher genre and *must* please more than the other, whether he wishes to or not" (to Gast on September 3, 1883).

Nietzsche's praises scarcely concerned Gast's music, which passed into oblivion. Its value and greatness are limited to its significance for Nietzsche. The philosopher's attitude to Gast's music has to be understood in terms of his personal relationship to the composer of *The Lion of Venice*.[18] Nietzsche was always thankful for an unselfish devotion. The lonely man made Gast's cause his own. After all, Gast, in his music, was striving for some kind of liberation from the German spirit of gravity, which is why Nietzsche set such great hopes on him. Not that the music appeared to fulfill his wish for a new Classicism; but he applied all his persuasive powers to encouraging the musician Gast to pursue his course.

Time has left Gast's *oeuvre* behind. Memories in letters and writings of Nietzsche's are all that remain. Nietzsche's frequently expressed enthusiasm for his friend's productions has induced some musicians to question his musical judgment altogether, especially in regard to Wagner. The error about Gast allegedly spoke against his musical sense of values. But anyone who knows how to read Nietzsche and subtract the tribute of gratitude from his pronouncements realizes that Gast merely provided a pretext for drafting and repeatedly exhibiting the ideal prototype of a musician.

Gast was a typical promising beginner who remains a hope, ultimately lacking the fire and passion for his own achievements. Nietzsche's praise pertained not so much to Gast's music as to that ideal type he had demonstrated in Wagner in the *Untimely Reflections*. We witness an anguishing situation: The isolated philosopher, whom no sign of love had reached for so long, inventing the friends, disciples, and love he so terribly needed. He made up the music he yearned for. Thus, he outrageously embroidered and exaggerated his impression of Gast's music. In 1886, he wrote to Rohde: "A man grows old, a man grows nostalgic; already, like King Saul, I *need* music—and heaven has fortunately granted me a kind of David. . . . Actually I ought only to be surrounded by people of the same qualities as this music that I love . . . but not everyone who wishes to find can seek."

In his search, Nietzsche at times weighed the notion of again giving (free) lectures. It is one of the great ironies that the University of Leipzig, which had once voluntarily given Nietzsche a doctorate, could not offer him a position when many people already acknowledged his significance, and he asked for a teaching job there.

In the long run, it was impossible for Nietzsche to ignore his sister's chatter about Lou. When he met with Lou and Rée for the last time, in Leipzig, he annoyed Lou with disparaging remarks about Rée, which made it easier for his sister to interfere. The result of her constant intrigues was that by fall Nietzsche's friendship with Lou, and thereby with Rée, was over. There isn't space here to go into the awkward correspondence that went on into the following year. Nietzsche probably sensed his own unfairness and tried to make up for it later. But he remained more solitary than ever. His outward reconciliation with his sister did not restore her brother's trust. Elisabeth presented a totally different picture, and the exposé, mainly by Karl Schlechta,[19] of all her forgeries and falsified "Nietzsche letters," didn't come until after her death (1935).

In Leipzig, the scene of his great disappointment with Lou, Nietzsche also sought out Arthur Nikisch, the conductor of the *Gewandhaus* concerts, and tried to make a case for Gast's compositions. Then, by way of Basel, he traveled down to Genoa. In order to absorb himself fully in the comforting world of his *Zarathustra*, Nietzsche left the big city, settling in the Albergho della Posta in Rapallo, where he wrote the first part of the book.

At this time, Richard Wagner, in Venice, was reading Nietzsche's earlier work, *The Cheerful Knowledge;* the perusal increased his irritability and lack of self-control. This book had been ended in January 1882, after a creative period of unusual energy. The title was suggested by the Provençal term *gaya scienza,* the "unity of *singer, knight,* and *free-thinker* with which that wonderful early culture of the Provençals stood out against all ambivalent cultures." The book itself describes Wagner as a musician who, more than any other, is capable of "finding music in the realm of suffering, oppressed, tormented souls. . . . No one can hold a candle to him in the colors of late autumn, the ineffably poignant happiness of a final, ultimate, utterly brief enjoyment, he knows a sound for those secret and sinister midnights of the soul, when cause and effect seem out of joint and something might arise from the void at any moment; he draws most happily of all from the lower ground of human happiness and virtually from its beaker, which has been already sipped and where the bitterest and most repulsive drops have blended with the sweetest in the—good and evil—end." The ovation climaxes in the line: "As the Orpheus of all secret misery he is greater than anyone else."

What irritated Nietzsche most at the time of the *Cheerful Knowledge* was the problem of Wagner's play-acting. The author admits: "The problem of the actor disquieted me the most." These words are not autobiographical, as can be gathered from the total lack of anything theatrical in Nietzsche's life, aside from a growing intellectual self-mirroring in his late life. He is not being arch when he continues, in his book: "My melancholy wishes . . . to relax in perfection: for this, I need music. What do I care about drama! What do I care about the convulsions of its ethical ecstasies . . . the whole gestural hocuspocus of the actor! One can divine that I am essentially antitheatrical—but Wagner, on the other hand, was essentially a man of the theater, a player, the most inspired mimomaniac ever, even as a musician!" This can be underscored if we compare Nietzsche's autobiographical and self-analytical remarks, which sound like desperate revelations, with Wagner's memoirs, which delight in mummery and present themselves in a brilliant staging. It was only through Wagner that Nietzsche encountered the problem of acting. He was fascinated by the enigma; and it occupied him until well into his mental decline.

In the winter of 1882–83, Rapallo became a refuge for Nietzsche during the most agonizing time of his life. After a particularly awful insomnia and depression, January and February brought him the euphoria that had already surprised him during the first summer in Sils. The wealth of great ideas marking this condition was joined by his concentration on *Zarathustra,* the first part of which was committed to paper in only ten days.

Wandering about, as usual, for many hours of the day, Nietzsche mulled a problem that had first emerged with Wagner and was still unresolved: How could an entire act in an opera be shaped into a symphonic, organic unit? Along with a number of questions about practice, he felt that a musician ought to avoid mere *leitmotif* structures à la Wagner and create a complete movement as an opera act on the basis of thorough familiarity with the pertinent part of the drama and all the changes and conflicts of the emotions. *"But* not the word! The text itself ought to be written only when the music is done, and in steady conformity to the music: whereas until now, the word was what towed along the music. . . . The other point is that the course of the emotions, the overall construction of the act would have to have something of the scheme of a symphonic movement. Certain *responsios* and the like, that is to say, the poet would, from the very start, have the task of structuring the act *so that* it could become a symphonic *whole* as *music* too" (letter to Gast on January 10, 1883). These thoughts, although having a different basis, resemble *On Music and Words,* a section intended for *The Birth of Tragedy* but omitted out of consideration for Wagner. Nietzsche was much too musical to accord music merely a secondary position in his commentary.

12
DEATH IN VENICE

Nietzsche, like Wagner, suffered from the weather, which was particularly bad even in Italy that year. In a letter to Gast, the philosopher described himself as "the victim of a *disturbance of nature.* The old Europe of the Deluge will destroy me yet, but perhaps some person will come to my aid and drag me to the plateaus of Mexico. The dreadful burden weighing on me because of the weather (even old Etna is starting to spew!) has turned into thoughts and feelings of a terrible *pressure:* and from the sudden *relief* from this burden . . . arose my *Zarathustra,* the most *released* of my creations."

Wagner, too, soon after the final *Parsifal* performance, had gone South again with his family. But catastrophes had already beset them on the way from Germany. The railroad bridge in Ale and the Agide bridge by Verona "collapsed half an hour after we crossed them; no one used the latter bridge after us. This seemed to speak for our destination." For their winter in Venice, the Wagners moved into the Palazzo Vendramin. The princely household looked as regal as ever: children, tutors, and all the personnel had come along from Bayreuth. Wagner initially did not intend to work, for his heart attacks were increasing.

Yet his plans for Bayreuth could not have been more optimistic. The last letter to the king sounded like a testament: "I gradually would like to stage all my works in our *Festspiel* House in such a way that these performances could at least be handed down as models of correctness to my closest posterity." Wagner asked Destiny for only ten more healthy years of life, until fourteen-year-old Siegfried would become a man. But still, his wish for another decade was overshadowed by a foreboding of death.

Cosima's birthday on the first day of Christmas was celebrated with the children. They were joined by Blandine, Bülow's daughter, with her husband, whom she had married the previous August, a Count Gravina, from an old Sicilian dynasty. Cosima's father, Liszt, interrupted his winter holidays in the South to visit Venice, where he composed the piano piece "La lugubre gondola." He and Wagner discussed a new formal concept: single-movement symphonies, which Wagner intended to compose. Siegfried's tutor Heinrich von Stein and Hermann Levi also took part in the celebration.

Cosima forgot her worries about her husband for only hours at a time. During a particularly strong attack (the illness would be recognized today as angina pectoris), Cosima herself was so frightened that she fainted. Losing consciousness, she blissfully felt as if she were dying with her beloved husband. Now, on the evening of her birthday, Wagner had a student orchestra at the Liceo Marcello play his youthful *Symphony in C-Major,* which had been last performed half a century ago in Leipzig's *Schneiderherberge.* In the brilliantly illuminated auditorium, there was no one to be seen except for the family and their closest friends. Liszt once again played the piano in honor of his daughter. While the bells of all churches were pealing Christmas Day out, the gondolas brought the exclusive concert visitors back to the palazzo. "... in a moonlight vapor," writes Cosima, "such as one probably sees only in Venice."

In mid-January, the Festival Committee scheduled the *Festspiele* for that summer. Despite Wagner's hopes, only twelve of the projected twenty *Parsifal* performances could be slated. "I don't get annoyed about anything now, and I have a massage twice daily," he reported to Germany. In the days after Ash Wednesday, he felt no worse than before; his mood was mellow, and he spent many hours alone with Cosima. He presented her with the dedicatory page of *Parsifal,* held her in a long embrace, and begged her forgiveness for many hours of torment. On the evening of February 12, the stage designer Joukowsky was invited to dinner. After the meal, Wagner read aloud from Fouqué's *Undine,* while Joukowsky sketched a portrait of Wagner on a pad that Cosima had handed him. "Richard, reading, February 12, 1883," wrote Cosima below the drawing. Alone with Cosima again, Wagner opened the grand piano and played the *Lament of the Rhine Daughters.* Scanning, he spoke the words to it: "False and cowardly joy above! . . ." And turning to Cosima, he added: "How good that we realized early that only the depths are loyal and true . . . I am so fond of them, these creatures of the depths, these creatures of yearnings." In the morning, he was found unconscious. At two-thirty in the afternoon, his heart stopped beating.

At the very moment Wagner was dying in Venice, Nietzsche in Rapallo was finishing the first part of his *Zarathustra,* a fact he himself emphasizes as fateful and demonic. He added the second part in Sils-Maria that June and July, the third in Nice the following year, and the fourth in Zurich, Mentone, and Nice during 1884–85 (although this part wasn't published until 1892). The "yearning man" in Rapallo assumed that Wagner's death would bring him the most essential relief he could have at such a time. In his first statement, on February 19, to Peter Gast, he was still hiding his shock: "It was hard being an opponent for six years of the man whom one venerated the most, and I am not coarse enough for this. In the end, it was an aging Wagner against whom I had to defend myself; as for the real Wagner, I want to a great extent to be his *heir* (as I have often told Malwida). Last summer, I felt that he had taken from me all the people in Germany whom it makes any sense to affect and that he had started drawing them into the confused and wild hostility of his old age."

But by February 22, different things were erupting from him when he wrote to Franz Overbeck: "*Wagner* was by far the most complete man that I have ever known, and in *this* sense I have suffered a great loss for six years. *But* there is something like a mortal offense between us; and it might have turned out dreadfully if he had lived any longer.—Lou is by far the *most intelligent* person I have ever met. *But*, etc. etc.—My *Zarathustra* is probably being run off the presses. . . . No! *This life!* And I am the advocate of life!!"

Nietzsche wrestled with the thought of writing to Cosima. How could he do it? Gast urged him to let the widow know how deeply moved he was by Wagner's demise, for it was still in his power to offer her some comfort despite everything that had happened. After a few bad days, which Nietzsche spent in bed, he actually did write to her.[1]

The double portrait sketched here remains as such until Nietzsche's death, although it now has to forgo the presence of the older man. Nietzsche's outer biography scarcely reveals any more significant events. He seemed to have found a definitive rhythm of life, even in terms of his travels: He summered in Sils and wintered in Italy, especially in Nice; as of 1888, Turino was one of his favorite places.

His relationship to Peter Gast, whose music he unswervingly sought to promote, cooled temporarily, probably because Gast had taken up secret contact with Elisabeth. Meanwhile, a fight with Rohde had even worse consequences (this was more a sign of declining health, which drove Nietzsche into mental isolation, making him more and more hypersensitive). In the house where Nietzsche usually stayed in Nice, he was surrounded by gossipy people and even received a growing amount of fan mail, which elicited his ironical remark to Overbeck: "It was R. Wagner who brought this kind of admiratory style into German youth; and something I prophesized long ago is beginning: I to a great extent shall become R. W.'s heir."

"Honored Master," commenced a letter from a Herr Paul Lansky, and Nietzsche was overcome with "curious sentiments," thinking back to the days when he had thus addressed Wagner in his own letters.

While *Zarathustra* was taking shape, life brought Nietzsche neither relief nor brightness. His annoyance at others became all the more vehement the longer it took for *Zarathustra* to be printed. His publisher Schmeitzner had no hopes for even a modest success, so that Nietzsche, rather than dance attendance on him, had forty copies of Part IV printed at his own expense.

This book introduces ideas that had never before emerged on Nietzsche's intellectual horizon: the eternal return as a new energy source for intensifying and deepening life. It was in the very year of his farewell to Wagner that Nietzsche's philosophy acquired the significance of an example. Nietzsche realized his impact on his readers and the corresponding increase in responsibility. He felt like a teacher, while realizing how disastrous his philosophy could be to the minds of the unworthy.

In August 1884, he again felt the presence of Wagner's world when Heinrich von Stein visited him in Sils. And for a brief while, it seemed as if he had found in Stein a man devoted to his person and his teachings. Even for the Nietzsche of Tribschen days, obedience was the start of all education. This demand now became personal when he told Malwida: "By a disciple I would mean a man who swore unconditional allegiance to me—and this would require a long trial period and difficult trials."

Stein's relationship to Nietzsche had begun two years earlier, in Leipzig. The young "baron," while teaching at the University of Halle, visited his friend Dr. Paul Rée during the first half of October 1882. Craving to meet Nietzsche and encouraged by Rée, Stein made a pilgrimage to Nietzsche's home on Auenstrasse. But Nietzsche was out of town: A letter had summoned him to Naumburg for one day. It wasn't until after a brief correspondence that they met personally, in the Engadine. Stein's visit was one of the three good things that Nietzsche felt thankful for in this year of *Zarathustra.* Such an encounter always contained a great deal of "consequence" and "fate" for him. Gratefully he sent Stein a poem. Nietzsche could not divine that it was Stein's secret mission to win him back to the Bayreuth cause, that his visitor thereby stood in the opposite camp. In a letter thanking Nietzsche for the poem, Stein expressed a wish that Nietzsche take part, after all, in a lexicon on Wagner's writings and a mythological analysis of his libretti.

In December, an indignant Nietzsche informed his sister about Stein's "opaque" gratitude for the poem. "People have no sense of propriety anymore." Indeed, Stein's letter sorely tried Nietzsche's patience. The request to spend valuable time and worthy effort on a list of Wagner's written works must have struck Nietzsche as incredible. A man familiar with Nietzsche's letters and writings ought to have realized that Wagner had brought the thinker, philosopher, and stylist Nietzsche to despair, and he ought to have understood that Wagner as an epistemologist deserved Nietzsche's rejection. Retrospectively, Nietzsche saw the amateur scholar Wagner as an immodest and awkward intruder in the world of philosophy, and he put down his philosophizing as one of the most unlicensed kinds of dilettantism. "It is so German that no one even thought of laughing, and that is part of the old German cult of murkiness."

Hence the tone of the following letter draft to Stein, which, like countless, multiply pre-formulated writings of Nietzsche's, never reached a final shape:

"While perusing your *very* worthy recent letter, I was so over-come with nastiness that I laughed long and hard at your expense and was in high feather. No, my worthy friend, you are free to love and should not on my account abbreviate your love for Richard Wagner by even an inch. But on the other hand, I crave your indulgence for not confusing me with him—for I am not an actor; why, you may even consider me cold—without angering me."

In a letter to Malwida who was always loyal to Wagner, Nietz-sche jabbed (March 1885): "Poor Stein! He even regards R. Wag-ner as a philosopher!"

The long-distance attempt at getting the philosopher to discuss the Wagner lexicon appears somewhat less incredible if we bear in mind that *The Wagner Case* was still unwritten and that no one could guess the chasms yawning between the opponents. Nothing of Nietzsche's disillusion had reached the public, and his not mentioning it to Stein reveals his delicacy and considerateness, for he shied away from encroaching on another man's veneration, especially Stein whom he so respected as a poet.

Nietzsche had privately hoped that Stein would join him. Stein, however, was further so imprudent as to tell the Bayreuthers how enthusiastic he was about the days in Sils-Maria.

Three years later, Heinrich von Stein died of a stroke. And thus his desire to live at Nietzsche's side (a desire thoroughly shared by Nietzsche) could not be realized. Nietzsche wrote to his sister: "I have so few people in Germany whom I can truly enjoy; most of them I simply endure, like a very patient animal. But with Stein it was different!" To Peter Gast: "I really loved him; I felt as though he were reserved for me for a later age. . . . He was by far the finest species of man among the Wagnerians: at least to the extent that I have gotten to know them."

Nietzsche supposedly told friends that he had known the bliss of feeling *inter pares* only in his youth with Rohde and Wagner and on that August day in Sils-Maria with Heinrich von Stein.

13

AGAINST DECADENCE

෬෴෬

In the winter of 1884–85, Nietzsche resumed his epistolary discussion of musical issues with Carl Fuchs. *Carmen,* he divulged, had aroused "illicit secret thoughts" about all German music. The decay of *melos,* that he felt he could sniff at every contact with German musicians, the increasing propensity for individual emotional gestures, and yet the perfection of rhetorical devices, the convincing "theatrical" shaping of the moment—all these things struck him as not just getting along together but actually determining one another. "Bad enough! Everything good in this world must be paid for at an exorbitant price!" So goes an undated letter to Fuchs. For Nietzsche, Wagner's term "unending melody" symbolized the danger of maintaining a sound conscience while losing one's artistic instinct. "The rhythmical ambivalence which must, and is meant to, keep you from making head or tail of a thing, is without any doubt an artistic device for achieving marvelous effects: *Tristan* is filled with it—but as the symptom of an entire art it is nevertheless a sign of dissolution. The part dominates over the whole, the phrase over the melody, the moment over time (even the tempo), *pathos* over *ethos* (character, style, or however one may term it), and finally *esprit* over 'meaning'. . . . But this is *décadence,* a word that, needless to say between us, is meant to describe and not condemn." Here we can hear the descendant of Heinrich Heine, whose utopian hope for a new human happiness and free human gods influenced Nietzsche as much as his abrupt estrangement from Christianity.

In *Beyond Good and Evil,* that provoking book on which Nietzsche worked all that winter, he mentioned *Parsifal* in this context, although in reference to Wagner's secret kinship with the French

Romantics of the first half of the nineteenth century. "They certainly were tormented by the same *Sturm und Drang* and certainly *sought* in the same way, these last of the seekers! All of them dominated by literature up to their eyes and ears—the first artists educated in world literature—most of them even writers, poets, mediators, and mixers of the arts and the senses (Wagner as a musician belongs among the painters; as a poet, among the musicians; as an artist in general, among the actors); all of them fanatics for *expression* 'at any price.' "

More than Wagner, Nietzsche took from Heine (who, to be sure, was not the only one he meant) the juxtaposition of "Hellenic" and "Nazarene", i.e., Christian attitudes. Nietzsche's book praises "Greek religiosity" and criticizes Christianity as a religion of the mob and of fear. He is borrowing ideas from Heine's piece on Ludwig Börne and thereby moving far, far away from Wagner, who, although constantly drawing thematic material from Heine, always adjusted it to his own momentary philosophy, as, say, in *Tannhäuser.* In his *Anti-Christ,* Nietzsche's chief accusation is that Christianity first brought hypocrisy and sin into the world, and to this continuation of Heine's attacks he joins an onslaught against the rule and cunning of priests. Wagner stops at sin as a natural phenomenon; he can only fight it with the believing savior Parsifal but not abolish it as an invention.

On such a basis, *Parsifal* challenged Nietzsche to his utmost irony. Without a doubt, the *Bühnenweihfestspiel* was the turning point in the relationship of those two minds. In *Nietzsche versus Wagner,* Nietzsche goes so far as to say that one can only laugh at this work, it is an operetta subject par excellence. . . . But what would a serious *Parsifal* be like? Precisely that which Nietzsche's judgment of Wagner was attacked for: "The spawn of an insane hatred of knowledge, mind, and sensuality, a curse upon senses and spirit in one hate and breath, an apostasy and return to Christian-diseased and obscurantist ideals. And in the end, even a self-negation, a self-deletion by an artist who hitherto, with all the might of his will, was after the very opposite, the highest spiritualizing and sensualizing of his art." A secret allusion to his own self, a concealed acknowledgment become manifest, symptomatically characterizing Nietzsche's final train of thought. Thus it comes that he gathers on the head of Wagner, whom he once so adulated, everything characterizing Socrates, Christianity, and

Schopenhauer in his eyes as the most despicable thing of all: decadence.

For Nietzsche, the incorrigible opera fan, this art form had to be conceived anew, in terms of his strong, fine man, but in contradiction to Wagner. Here, one cannot help reproaching him for being too personal, too unobjective, even though such behavior may be part of the picture of this poet-philosopher. His gradual rejection of Wagner had left a palpable hollow in his musical soul until the day the lonely man first heard *Carmen.*

Symptomatically, Nietzsche wasn't the only thinker attracted to this work. He himself calls the brief D-major motif at the close of the prelude "an epigram on passion, the best thing written *sur l'amour* since Stendahl." The latter had already depicted a Carmen figure. "Love is a precious flower, but one must have the courage to pick it at the dreadful edge of an abyss." This remark by the French author was a starting point for Nietzsche's interpretation of the Carmen character, probably the most cogent thing ever written about her: "At last love, love translated back into *nature! Not* the love of a 'sublime virgin'! No Senta sentimentality! But love as fate, as *fatality,* cynical, innocent, cruel—and for that very reason *nature!* Love, in its devices, the war, in its foundation the *mortal hatred* between the sexes!—I know of nothing in which the tragic joke that is the essence of love is so severely expressed, becomes such a dreadful formula, as in Don José's final shriek, which concludes the work: 'Yes! *I* killed her, *I*—my adored Carmen!' "

Nietzsche turns from Wagner to the virtually primitive, the elemental, to "love as fate." This interpretation provided a whole generation of thinkers and artists with philosophical food for thought. The route that Heine marked out, the escape from compassion, from the decadence-feeling of the weak and the sick, and the counterfeiting of salvation—this route was taken by Nietzsche. Something unheard of occurred. Not only did philosophy sing the praises of opera, but an opera of all things influenced a whole series of philosophers. "I kept inditing songs to Dionysus all the while," is how Nietzsche portrays his *Carmen* experience. The high quality of the music was not the crucial factor of this experience; the basic mood virtually affected Nietzsche as a stimulant of life philosophy.

The comments that Nietzsche jotted down for Peter Gast in the piano score of *Carmen* attest to his practical and concrete study of Bizet's music—something he failed to do with the last Wagner opus. His pronouncements reveal his belief in opera as a higher aesthetic creation than drama. Even our most modern dramaturgy does not aspire to anything else or anything more than to have all theater arise from a *single* process of the will.

The years 1886–87 saw new editions of earlier works. Adding thorough introductions, Nietzsche conformed them to his present ways of thinking. The only pieces he left alone were the *Untimely Reflections*. The 1886 edition of *The Birth of Tragedy from the Spirit of Music* was given a foreword: *An Attempt at Self-Criticism*. With critical detachment, to wit, as early as during his work on the aphorisms in *The Re-Evaluation of all Values*, he says: "Today I find this book impossible—it is badly written, clumsy, embarrassing, overladen with a confusion of images, emotionally meager, at times effeminately sugary, uneven in tempo, devoid of any will towards logical tidiness."

Nevertheless, he let the work come out again because he still believed in what it said, even though he now pilloried the esteem for Wagner. Contradictions with his present ideology could not be avoided. Nevertheless, the authorized republication sheds light on how greatly Nietzsche wanted his previous work to be seen as a whole.

In his *Attempt at Self-Criticism* and the preface to the second volume of *Human, All Too Human*, he wanted to put an end to the eternal misunderstandings about his break with Wagner. Nietzsche decided to unambiguously emphasize the chief problem, and he thereby went out on a limb. He wrote to Gast on September 13, 1886: "By the way, I'm simply delighted to look back at this terrible and mortally dangerous turn as something 'behind me.' I might have been destroyed by it in the twinkling of an eye; I am not crude enough to *part* from people I have loved, but it did happen: and I am still alive."

The memory of the cornerstone ceremony at Bayreuth is evoked, and Nietzsche refers to it as a "victory celebration," for he saw Bayreuth as the greatest triumph an artist could possibly achieve. He now saw his triumphal and festal speech *Richard Wagner in Bayreuth* as a tribute secretly addressed to a piece of the past and signifying a release, a farewell. Nietzsche doubted whether Wagner could have really been deceived by it. As long as the younger man said an unqualified yes to everything, such images, seen from afar, could never have been objective. Nietzsche ascribed a secret *opposition* to them, as betrayed by the words "looking opposite," which were used in the speech.

It was only in *Human, All Too Human* that Nietzsche managed to talk about the long years of inner solitude and his deprivation. With the coolness of a psychologist, the "Book for Free Minds" touches the most sensitive spots, which he "retrospectively determines for himself and *pins fast* with a needlepoint as it were: Is it any surprise that sometimes blood flows during such a pointed and ticklish labor, and the psychologist gets blood on his fingers, and not always just on his fingers?"

14

WAHNFRIED
WITHOUT WAGNER

◦◦◦

Nietzsche strove for a cool view of Wahnfried, too, after Wagner's death. Cosima was managing the Festivals. The hush of mourning in the house was deceptive: A busy correspondence was maintained in all directions. Bülow's daughter Daniela, in order to complete the archive at Wahnfried, asked for copies of missing Wagner letters through Malwida's foster daughter Olga Monod. Malvida's inviolable love still belonged to Cosima and could not be swerved. She had been through the conflict with Nietzsche, which still weighed heavily upon Bayreuth; but as the confidante of both friends, she could only witness it sadly. It is safe to say that Cosima likewise suffered from this shadow over the last years of Wagner's life.

For the moment, she was worried about Siegfried, who had recovered from a lengthy illness. An excellent student, he had returned to secondary school and was exhibiting artistic and musical bents. In addition, the mother had to prepare for the new mounting of *Tristan* in 1886.

Cosima urged her father to attend the premiere at Bayreuth, and Liszt agreed, despite his shattered health. Arriving on July 21, in an alarming condition, he had to take to bed immediately. But a fever and fits of coughing did not prevent him from enduring a reception at Wahnfried that evening and letting himself be gaped at as the main attraction. The next day brought him more social obligations. On July 23, he saw *Parsifal* and on July 25, *Tristan,* not without admiring the enormous amount of work that all the participants had to do.

This was the first and only staging publicly credited to Cosima, for her name never appeared on any later playbills, and the people involved were instructed not to mention her as director. The artistic success of *Tristan* was dazzling. Cosima's "discoveries," the conductor Felix Mottl and the Isolde Rosa Suchers, decided the triumph of the evening. In the back of the Wagner box sat Liszt, laboriously breathing, often half asleep, straining with all his might to suppress his cough.

While the *Festspiel* progressed during the next few days, and while Cosima performed all her social duties, Liszt, at the home of Frau von Froehlig, was struggling with death. The physicians diagnosed a severe pneumonia and forbade any visitors whatsoever. Toward midnight of July 31, he passed away in the arms of Cosima, who claims his last words were: "Oh, Tristan!" She directed that his body lie in state in the vast hall of Wahnfried.

A number of Liszt devotees were indignant that the Master's illness and death were concealed with apparent design, so as not to imperil the Festival. The performances kept on; the Wagner family did not fail to attend; and the Mistress of Bayreuth even betook herself to the grand closing celebration in the restaurant *Zum Frohsinn.* Liszt's pupil Göllerich lamented:

"Unhallowed and undignified were Liszt's demise and burial in the Wagner city, which partly owes him its very existence! There was no room for him next to Wagner's sun. Liszt's friends suffered terribly from the situation."

And Princess Wittgenstein was furious as Cosima's enemy: "The father dies, and the daughter lets the show go on!"

But was Bayreuth an entertainment to be shut down because of death? Cosima knew that there could not have been more beautiful obsequies for her father than the performances of *Tristan* and *Parsifal.* "People gave me trouble because of my father. I remained cognizant of not giving in to any selfishness but to a commandment of fate that had been entrusted to me to carry out" (to Countess Schleinitz). The world citizen Franz Liszt was interred in the graveyard of the provincial town—a contradiction with a story of its own.

Voices were raised in Weimar, Rome, and Budapest, declaring that the dead composer belonged to Hungary, his homeland, or to Rome, where his fellow Franciscans claimed him for themselves, or to Weimar, where he had resided for decades. Cosima stated that she would yield the corpse to Weimar only if the

Grand Duke, instead of erecting the projected mausoleum on the Altenburg, agreed to bury Liszt in the princely tomb, next to Goethe and Schiller. She would let Pest have the body only if the Hungarian parliament promised a ceremonious transport and a state funeral. No one would comply with Cosima's conditions. The Grand Duke of Weimar (Carl August was long since gone) was not very intrigued by the thought of tolerating a composer as well as two poets next to his august forebears. And in Hungary, Liszt's foes had spoken out against solemn rites in Pest. The Bayreuth cemetery appeared to offer the musician a place of undisturbed rest. Or did it? There was a recurring rumor in Bayreuth that the bones of Franz von Liszt no longer lay in peace under Professor Seidel's monument; they had at some point been spirited away to Hungary after all.

Nietzsche concurred with the opinion of the Wagner adversaries when he wrote to Malwida von Meysenbug:

"So old Liszt, who knew all about life and death, has now, in the end, been *buried,* as it were, in Wagner's cause and world: as though he belonged, completely inevitable and inseparable. It made my heart bleed for Cosima: it is one more falsification in regard to Wagner, one of those almost insuperable misunderstandings amid which Wagner's renown is growing and running wild. Judging by the Wagnerites I have met so far, all this Wagnerizing strikes me as an unconscious emulation of Rome, which is doing the same thing on the inside that Bismarck is doing on the outside."

Wagner wasn't the only one whom Nietzsche renounced. He was unable to keep up any lasting friendships, except with Peter Gast, the unconditional disciple. Characteristic in this respect is Nietzsche's relationship of twenty years to Erwin Rohde, the third professor among his closest friends (along with Overbeck and Deussen). We can recall the pamphlet that the young philologist Rohde authored against the polemics of Wilamowitz. Rohde did not conceal his qualms about Nietzsche's change of attitude in *Human, All Too Human:*

"But I seriously believe, dear friend, that you have not arrived at the destination of your route. Your development is taking a curving road and may some day even return to its original direction."

Rohde assured him it made no difference to his friendship, for which Nietzsche was all the more grateful since he usually lost a friend upon the publication of each new book. Rohde did not care for *Morgenröte*. He didn't thank the author quickly enough for the book and had to put up with Nietzsche's huffy request not to write him anything about it at all, since he did not wish to force any letters of gratitude.

This notwithstanding, Nietzsche also sent him a copy of *The Cheerful Knowledge*, but adding that since 1876 his work had borne the epigram: *Nihi ipsi scripsi* (I wrote for myself); and that he didn't care what others thought of it.

Rohde's answer was lost. But not his letter to Nietzsche after receiving *Zarathustra:* his reaction was not one of wholehearted approval. Nietzsche appeared to be displeased with the reservations, for he maintained a silence of two years. Nevertheless, scarcely petty and quite devoted, he traveled to Leipzig in 1886 to hear Rohde's inaugural lecture at the university. But once again, his great expectations were not fulfilled. The two men's attitudes only converged in their mutual rejection of *Parsifal.*

Peter Gast too, naturally under Nietzsche's influence, rejected *Parsifal.* It was in Bayreuth that he heard the work, which he had known since 1882 in its keyboard form. His verdict: "Siegfried's conversion to Catholicism." Nietzsche was overjoyed by this confirmation of his "judgments and prejudices," which he ventured from afar. From Sils-Maria he advised Gast to hear the *Nibelungen* cycle in Munich: "Strike this marvelous iron while it's still hot" (August 16, 1886).

Gast actually did have the opportunity, for he was offered the column "Musical Account of Munich" in the *Süddeutsche Presse.* Interested in this paper as the one that had run Richard Wagner's series *German Politics and German Art,* he let his feelings of reverence move him to accept. Nietzsche hailed his decision; he hoped Gast would succeed in presenting as an experience the aesthetic problem they were both so concerned with, and that he would also thereby make his (Gast's) music accessible to a greater readership. For the Germans seemed intrigued only by an artist in whom they could discern the so-called "earnestness of principles": Nietzsche remembered only too well how Wagner had known how to make use of that need.

In fall 1887, Gast surprised his friend (who was terribly deprived of music in Nice) with his own instrumentation of Nietzsche's *Hymn to Life* for a symphony orchestra. The only other version was Nietzsche's setting for a wind orchestra. His publisher Fritzsch was ready to go to press immediately after Nietzsche made some expert corrections. The publisher even added voices without being told to do so. This minor sign of subordination to the music and practically to the musicians delighted Nietzsche; he thus hoped that his music would eventually make it easier for others to comprehend the psychological problem of his musicianship. Johannes Brahms, who had become an interested reader of Nietzsche's books, soon received a score of the *Hymn*, but held his tongue; whereas, upon receiving the dedicatory copy of *The Genealogy of Morals*, he had expressed his (for him) cordial thanks.

From Nice, Nietzsche visited Monte Carlo for the first time in January 1888, and there he attended a "concert classique" of the latest French works. Since a letter to Gast talks about a "wild hunt," the program most likely included the symphonic poem *The Wild Hunter* by César Franck. "Lots of bad Wagner," seemed to strike his ear, which was greedy for a new simplicity. He found the music artificially picturesque with no real idea; formless, and devoid of naiveté and veracity. "Nervous, brutal, unbearable, obtrusive, self-important—and so rouged!! . . . This is decadence!"

He was particularly irritated by an Erinny ballet of Massenet's, which nevertheless harked back to his beloved *Oresteia* of Aeschylus. Otherwise, music at that time gave him unknown sensations. "It releases me from myself, it sobers me up from myself, as though I were overviewing myself, *overfeeling* myself from far, far away; it strengthens me, and after every evening of music (I have heard Bizet's *Carmen* four times) there comes a morning full of resolute insights and ideas. . . . Life without music is simply a mistake, a hardship, an exile" (to Gast on January 15, 1888; similarly to Brandes).

Hermann Levi, who had conducted the first *Parsifal* mountings and had been serving as Munich's Court Conductor for some time now, gave in to Peter Gast's urging and read Nietzsche's books, expressing his enthusiasm about them. In order to help Gast, Nietzsche had taken up contact with the *Kapellmeister*, who greatly impressed him as a highly intelligent musician. And although well aware that his Wagner veneration might offend the philosopher, Levi felt "a kind of rapport" with Nietzsche that he didn't care to lose. The same was true, incidentally, of many Wagnerites around Nietzsche, "albeit I cannot make head or tail of it," as Nietzsche wrote to Gast. "In Munich last fall, I was awaited 'with feverish anxiety,' as Seydlitz (now president of the Wagner Association) announced."

That winter, Nietzsche took off from his second-floor apartment on Rue des Ponchettes in Nice for an outing to Monte Carlo, where he planned to hear the *Parsifal* prelude for the first time. The next time he saw Gast, he wanted to tell him his reactions. His letter of January 21, 1887, which renders his initial response, contains the most cogent statements to be made about this music:

"Aside from all irrelevant issues (what use this music *can* or *should* be), and as a purely aesthetic question: Did Wagner ever do anything *better?* The very highest psychological consciousness and definiteness in regard to what should be said here, expressed, communicated, the shortest and most direct form for it, every shade of feeling reduced to its most epigrammatic; a clarity of music as descriptive art, whereby one thinks of a shield with a relief on it; and finally, a sublime and extraordinary emotional experience, an event of the soul in the basis of music, which is the greatest credit to Wagner, a synthesis of conditions that many people, even 'higher people,' will see as incompatible, a synthesis of judgmental severity, of 'loftiness' in the terrifying sense of the word, of a complicity and comprehension that cuts through a soul as with knives—and full of compassion with what is seen and judged here. The like can only be found in *Dante,* but nowhere else. Has ever a painter depicted such a melancholy gaze of love as Wagner with the final accents of his prelude?"

Here Nietzsche most surely did not mean the finale tacked on for concerts, for the prelude to Act I doesn't have any real conclusion. The concert that Nietzsche attended used the ending with the Faith Motif, identical with that Dresden *Amen* that Mendelssohn also employed in his *Reformation Symphony.* Nietzsche knew of course that Wagner hadn't really devised these notes, and thus he meant the dying measures beforehand.

15

THE SUMMING-UP

⤳᭼⤶

There are many apologists who feel they have to point out a premonition of the end in the last phase of Nietzsche's work, because these late creations sound like a summing-up of all his previous ideas and plans. But these apologists are certainly making a mistake. During 1888, Nietzsche had an unbelievable creative surge, which, however, showed visible signs of his coming insanity. Thus, five years after Wagner's death, he once again confronted the man whom he regarded as his real spiritual opponent. The energy concentrated in *The Wagner Case,* from the Basel period till the months of Nietzsche's collapse, indicates Wagner's crucial significance in his development. It was clearly not just the age difference that made Nietzsche play a much smaller role in Wagner's artistic evolution. There is something painful about the philosopher's comments on *The Wagner Case* at the end of his life.

"To do justice to this piece of writing, one must suffer from the fate of music as from an open wound.—What do I suffer from when I suffer from the fate of music? From the fact that music has been deprived of its world-transfiguring, affirmative character, that it is a music of decadence and no longer the flute of Dionysus. . . ."

This pamphlet, written during Nietzsche's first visit to Turino, has a satirical coloring; yet the note of desperate gravity cannot be missed. At moments during the publication, especially in evening hours, Nietzsche became despondent about this mixture of harshness and madness. But the "madness" is itself mingled with sentences of admiring recognition. For instance, when the author honors Wagner as the greatest "melancholic of music . . . full of gazes, affectionate gestures, and comforting words that no one would have anticipated, the master of the tones of a melancholy and drowsy happiness."

In 1888, the year the pamphlet was penned, Bayreuth, in order to fill the philosophical-propaganda gap caused by Nietzsche's apostasy, was hunting for a new disciple. In the unconditional devotion of the young English philosopher Houston Stewart Chamberlain,[1] Cosima saw just the right man to ward off the dangers that the much more important German seemed to conjure up. To Bayreuth's misfortune, but probably through a fluke, Chamberlain was the first to deliberately connect the world of Wagner's oeuvre (and not just the music as a part of the whole) to the spook of a "national renovation." The Jew-baiting Chamberlain doubtless encouraged Cosima's "idée fixe": her ever latent anti-Semitism, which some biographers have ventured to tie in with the Jewish ancestry of her step-mother Princess Wittgenstein, whom she despised all her life.

In his first addendum to *The Wagner Case*, Nietzsche critically examines Wagner's *My Life*. The autobiographer claims he is the son of Carl Friedrich Wagner, although he admitted being the child of his step-father, the Jewish actor Ludwig Geyer. Nietzsche shuddered at the way the inventor of the super-hero Siegfried recklessly ignored truth. And when Wagner claims "unadorned truthfulness" for his book, Nietzsche counters that these reminiscences are a *"fable convenue,* if not something worse." Nietzsche simply asserted that Wagner was Geyer's son; he was irate about the composer's terror at owning up to his Jewish background. Of course, he overlooked Wagner's precarious situation: When publishing his memoirs, he had already degenerated into one of the most prominent anti-Semites in Europe.

Nietzsche did not just stop at *The Wagner Case*. Towards the end of the year, he compiled all the arguments he had ever forwarded against his declared adversary Wagner, and he gave the title *Nietzsche versus Wagner* to a new manuscript that he completed at Christmas. *Ecce Homo* lunges even further, with the author precisely explaining the change in his musical taste. Wagner gets a rather partisan come-uppance and the image of an abortive genius with unsure taste. The attacks reach the point of diagnosing allegedly pathological aspects; here Nietzsche seems to be projecting: "Wagner's art is diseased. The problems he puts on stage (all of them the problems of hysterics), his convulsive affect, his high-strung sensivitivity, his taste, which always craved hotter and hotter spices, his instability which he disguised as principles, last but not least the choice of his heroes and heroines, observed as physiological types (a gallery of diseases!): Everything together adds up to a etiology that leaves no doubt: *Wagner est une névrose.* [Wagner is a neurosis]."

When Nietzsche visited the composer-conductor Friedrich Hegar in Zurich, with whom he again discussed possible performances of Gast's works, the philosopher and the conductor took a trip to Lake Vierwaldstätt. Lost in thought, Nietzsche sat on a lakeside bench between Lucerne and Tribschen, by the path on which he had so often and so cheerfully peregrinated to Wagner. Incessantly, his cane drew circles and bizarre figures in the sand, All at once, uncontrollable tears gushed from his eyes. He may have thought something that he wrote the following spring to George Brandes, a scholar in Copenhagen who, surprisingly, had begun holding talks on Nietzsche. In this letter, Nietzsche discusses the providence that had brought him together with Burckhardt in Basel. He continues: "An even greater favor: from the very start of my Basel existence I entered into an incredibly close intimacy with Richard and Cosima Wagner. For several years, we had everything great and small in common, there was a boundless trust." It is, however, questionable whether Wagner had even the foggiest notion that he was close to the greatest mind of his age.

Having been sent *The Wagner Case,* Brandes, in his reply, confessed (at the risk of angering Nietzsche) that Wagner's *Tristan* had made an indelible impact on him, as much as he was willing to join in the praises of Bizet's *Carmen.* Brandes suggested that Nietzsche send a copy of the book to Bizet's widow since she had some knowledge of German. August Strindberg likewise received a copy.

Malwida, upon reading the work, was beside herself and wrote Nietzsche a nasty letter, which in turn infuriated him. Malwida just couldn't understand how Nietzsche could publicly express his "error" about Schopenhauer's philosophy and Wagner's music. Nietzsche writes:

"People, at least among my friends, remember that I first set out into this modern world with a few errors and overestimations, and in any case hopeful. I comprehended (who can tell by what personal experiences?) the philosophical pessimism of the nineteenth century as a symptom of a higher power of thought, a more triumphant richness of life than had found expression in the philosophy of Hume, Kant, and Hegel—I took the most *tragic* knowledge as the finest luxury of our culture, as its costliest, noblest, and most dangerous squandering, but nevertheless, on the basis of its over-wealth, as its *permitted* luxury. In the same way, I interpreted Wagner's music according to my own terms, as an expression of a Dionysian power of the soul; I believed that in it I could hear the earthquake in which a primal force of life, pent up since time immemorial, was finally bursting forth, indifferent as to whether all that is known as culture today was starting to tremble. One can see what I failed to grasp, one can see what I presented to Wagner and Schopenhauer: *myself.*"

But that very same year, 1888, he also wrote about his former rapport with Wagner: "When I think back to that time in which the last part of Siegfried came into being! We loved one another then and hoped everything for *one another*—it was really a deep *love,* with no side motives."

Wagner had been petty and malicious about Nietzsche's following other routes. If *The Wagner Case* passionately airs Nietzsche's disillusion, if it uses harsh words, then it is mainly expressing the disappointment of that love. Outsiders could all too easily take over the attitudes of the pamphlet without going through Nietzsche's sufferings.

Until 1872, when Nietzsche began speaking up for Wagner, there was little written about the composer aside from his being the revolutionary of opera. The author of *The Birth of Tragedy* and the *Untimely Reflections* regretted that these works had contributed to such a confusing appreciation. He had set up an idol for the Germans, especially for the younger generation, and the worship of that idol included such German vices as unclarity, bombast, and clumsiness. Yet he didn't want the youth of his country growing up without a knowledge of Wagner; he saw such knowledge as indispensable for any further development. He once wrote to Heinrich von Stein: "I have been told that you, perhaps more than anyone else, have turned to Schopenhauer and Wagner with heart and mind. This is something *invaluable,* assuming that it has its time." Nietzsche judged by a number of signs that the Wagner cult had had its time for exerting a good influence. Now it was time to open minds to new ideals—everything, namely, that he missed in Wagner: "Nimble feet, wit, fire, grace, grand logic, the dance of the stars, exuberant spirituality, the quivering light of the south, the *smooth* sea, perfection." He hated seeing young men who were gloomy, clumsy, and negative about life. Impatience seized him when his voice was not heard in an age in which decadence and flight from the world celebrated orgies. No one with interest and capability could be discovered to understand life with its rising and falling. Terrified, Nietzsche saw decadent ideals being promoted by Wagner's art, and their authority consistently increasing. With Wagner, music struck Nietzsche as having forfeited its world-transfiguring character.

For most readers, the publication of *The Wagner Case* was premature. Wrenched out of the context of an overall attitude, the facile, mocking tone was misleading. From today's perspective, it is easy to see why a true-blue Wagnerite like Malwida von Meysenbug did not understand the book. Nietzsche's wrath at her bitter letter culminates in the pronouncement: "The fact that Wagner succeeded in making people believe him to be (as you put it with such venerable innocence) the 'ultimate expression of creative Nature,' its 'last word' as it were—that indeed requires *genius,* a genius for *lying.* . . . I myself have the honor of being the very opposite—a genius of *Truth.*"

A few days later, this letter was followed by a second, and Nietzsche's notebooks contain very sharp drafts of it. One draft goes:

"Dearest friend, have you really divined *why* I sent you this 'execution of Wagner'? I wanted to hand you one more proof that you have never understood a single word, a single *wish* of mine. The reasons why I turned my back on Wagner ten years ago are presented in this work in a literary form—as measured, as serene as possible, incidentally: for I could have spoken harsh and scornful words. I have kept back all my *major arrows.* . . . That deep lack of instinct, of subtle discrimination between 'true' and 'false' for which I reproach modern men—you yourself are an extreme case of that,—you who all your life have been deceived by nearly everyone, even Wagner, but how much more so in the somewhat more difficult case of *myself!* . . . . Do you understand *nothing* about my mission? What does the 'Re-Evaluation of all Values' mean?"[2]

Nietzsche maintained the continuity of his thinking since *Human, All Too Human* even when raving and ranting in a language that dismayed not just Malwida. As of *The Wagner Case*, Nietzsche alarmingly lost one inhibition after another. An exaggerated self-importance kindled uncontrolled vituperation, as illustrated by the growing clusters of words like "idiot" and "idiotic" in *The Wagner Case*, *The Twilight of the Idols*, and *Nietzsche versus Wagner*, all penned in 1888, the year before his breakdown. *Nietzsche versus Wagner* essentially characterizes an antipodal relationship. Many passages from earlier writings crop up in this more earnest counterpart to *The Wagner Case*. Nietzsche didn't want it to be published; he felt that *Ecce Homo* contained all that was crucial on this theme.

Nietzsche's writings could not affect the ideals of the Bayreuth Wagnerites. The conflicts around Cosima began to disappear, the irony of the journalists turned into admiration, and all who participated in Bayreuth at last formed a unity. Foreign countries acclaimed the works and the performances, and the public success was satisfying. In 1888, every difficulty seemed to be overcome, and a first goal had been reached, thanks to the cooperation of all concerned and first and foremost Cosima's energy. In contrast to her outer equanimity, there was a weight on her mind; she could not forget past happiness, and had to gather all her strength to keep anyone from noticing what was going on inside her. She refused to interpret Nietzsche's departure; she blamed it on his "complaint." Not reading any of his books after the *Untimely Reflections*, she formed no opinion about them. It was like her to evade opinions repugnant to her. The Nietzsche cult, the imitation of his hymnal diction, the arrogance and unclarity of some overzealous devotees seemed to confirm to an aging Cosima, even in our century, something she had refused to see as anything but dilettantish and due to illness.

In 1889, Nietzsche collapsed on the street in Turino. On January 3, he had mailed three totally confused letters from that town. One of these letters announced the completion of the *Dionysus Dithyrambs*, from the years 1884 to 1888, of which he had just finished the last draft. These long poems blend his first sentiments of love and friendship for Cosima with the myth of Ariadne, revealing levels of his condition after the break with the Bayreuth friends. "The Lament of Ariadne" includes these lines:

> *No!*
> *Come back*
> *With all your tortures!*
>
> * * *
>
> *All my brooks of tears are running*
> *Their course to you!*
> *And my final heart-flame—*
> *It glows up to you!*
> *Oh come back,*
> *My unknown god! My torment!*
> *My final—happiness!*

Ecce Homo adds something to these verses: "The reply to such a dithyramb of the solar isolation in light would be Ariadne. . . . Who besides me knows what Ariadne is! . . ."

Did Nietzsche reveal this knowledge in his last letter to Burckhardt, which he wrote when already deranged: "The rest for Frau Cosima . . . Ariadne." Who can tell! Cosima, whom many of her friends nicknamed Ariadne, received a note out of Nietzsche's mental darkness: "Ariadne, I love you. Dionysus." She held her peace.

Whatever the answer to the enigma may be, the ecstasy of Nietzsche's departure, this removal into madness, rounds out a circle of attraction and repulsion.

16

FINALE

⟨⟩⟩⟩⟩⟩⟩

The works and personalities of Wagner and Nietzsche cannot be separated from the ominous effect of their renown, from the dark destiny that evoked slogans which could so conveniently be culled from their oeuvres. Even the most faithful chronicle should not suppress such discordant notes.

For Wagner, the tie between this impact and his musical legacy is more obvious than in Nietzsche's philosophical and artistic writings. During the first half of our century, Nietzsche's image was largely stamped by *The Will to Power*, published posthumously in 1906 at the instigation of his sister. Peter Gast betrayed his idol by piecing together this alleged magnum opus out of *Nachlass* aphorisms. The Nazi ideologists made use of some of the formulations with devilish cunning. The Fascists, possessed of a totally different kind of hubris, were knocking at the wrong door. Nietzsche's bumptiousness between *Zarathustra* and his mental downfall has nothing in common with that.

Who was this man who could attract people like Richard and Cosima Wagner, as well as Jacob Burckhardt? Most certainly a frighteningly unconditional man who ultimately mythologized himself. Everyone drew back from the man whose thoughts reached out into the future, arousing distrust and incredulity.

Wagner's Germanism (which actually supplied persuasive musical accents for the national dictatorship of the thirties and forties), his chauvinistic side—these were things that Nietzsche could not accept. They struck him as petty German, not worldly German, a Germanism that was lesser and faded. In a world dismantling the walls of national aristocracy and self-observation, in a Europe now growing together spiritually and soon, let us hope, economically and politically as well, in a world that Nietzsche had foreseen, the worship of a Master in a provincial corner would be an anachronism.

The diametric opposite of what the National Socialists made of him, Nietzsche provoked a change in Germany's intellectual atmosphere, first making possible the psychologizing of German prose. This intellectual climate of his no longer admitted the traditional contrast of North and South, as manifested in the concepts of "classical" and "romantic." His neo-classical goal was really "the good European."

On the other hand, the actor Wagner donned a Dürer beret and played a pure-bred German Master for his credulous nation —he whose first admirers and helpers had been European artists and *décadents* like Baudelaire. Whereas Nietzsche's mind belongs to our, the twentieth, century, Wagner's oeuvre, in its format, its sense of a grand undertaking, its monumentality, its standard character, its giant composition, its demand for endless patience, declares itself as being of the century of the *Nibelungen Ring,* its own.

The friendship of these two men, which we have sought to delineate, was only a semblance. Nietzsche, a psychologist who anticipated the possible consequences of Wagnerian music, went through a calvary towards his independence. If, on the one hand, he had to admire without any illusion, he was frightened, on the other hand, by dangers concealed from most people. He was won by the magic of a musical inspiration, yet rebelled against bombast and empty noise. The dissolution of music with Wagner and its finality were seen by Nietzsche as fundamentally unavoidable and merely prototypical of the general predicament of music. In his eyes, Wagner was part of the downward development as a phenomenon of cultural history.

For Wagner's original argument against "grand opera" turned into a rejection of the Classical style per se of music. And yet everything about Wagner aroused emulation, not just his success. Nietzsche, hating the Wagnerites while suffering over Wagner, asserted that one could only make money with sick music. At the same time, he warned of the danger in the coming consumption of music. His disquiet about the future wardens of the Wagnerian art-legacy mingled with a concern about a general routine of musical practice. Logically, in the first *Untimely Reflection,* he recognized the cultivation of the classic composers as a possible alibi for cultural philistines; and he declared it dangerous to edify oneself on their works from time to time, that is to say, yield to those vapid and egotistical stirrings guaranteed to every ticket buyer in our concert halls and theaters.

More than anything, Nietzsche was pained that his aspiring discipleship to Wagner could not be fulfilled. His self-assured defiance did not let him be a follower any more than it allowed him to gather the pupils he so deeply longed for. He had to slough off an unhappy love for his "mystagogue," a love that wouldn't die.

Nietzsche was always distressed by the pictures of Makart,[1] the most fashionable and sought-after of painters. In his studio, Wagner and his architect Gottfried Semper would often drop by during the period of the Munich *Meistersinger* and find ideas for pomp and bogus Middle Ages. But this factory of sensual dreams with a claim to totality merely saddened the philosopher. He saw that the riches of the lush summer spreading over these paintings would be followed by winter. He refused to identify with the *Après nous le déluge* spirit that was patent here; on the contrary, he already saw the Flood coming. This very difference of perspectives clarifies the reasons why so many circuitous mental routes must be taken, so much aesthetics must be channeled to the present, so many stylistic enigmas must be puzzled out, when we listen to Wagner's music or contemplate Makart's pictures. Yet none of these things are necessary for reading the aphorisms of Nietzsche's *Re-Evaluation of All Values.*

Nietzsche's conflict with Wagner was and is a struggle of unequal means. Only gradually does the brilliance of the sensual orchestra sound, which Wagner could deploy as a powerful advocate, begin yielding to the knowledge of the ideological strata beyond it. More than Wagner himself, the consequences, in part resulting from misunderstandings, provoked criticism. But the fight against the principle of Wagnerism arose with Nietzsche. And the battle to free the music from the fetters of the ideology is still underway, in a process of purification.

No one should mistake this book for an attempt at taking sides between Wagner and Nietzsche, both of whom were so consistently necessary for their era. The strivings to determine their positions and clarify their relationship to one another and to posterity will not terminate. In this regard, psychological accents are inevitable. Wagner, in "explaining" Nietzsche's emotions, used psychological motives, especially self-righteousness. And Nietzsche even depicted himself as envious; he operated with a psychology of resentment by positing an immaculate sense of life, free of any scruples, as a pure value, and he saw this sense of life as imperiled by Wagner's personality and work. His urge for such a self-affirmation was all the stronger since he had ultimately rejected just about every other security of a societal nature: the community of professional scholars, the Protestant Christianity of his ancestors, and finally his homeland and State. Wagner returned to all these traditional values. As a moral and musical existence, as both an individual and a composer, he stood close to his *Zeitgeist*.

Nietzsche's "exceptional human being" signified an attempt at self-liberation from the misery of isolation. He failed in so far as his zealous scorn of Wagner betrays how crucial that man always was for him, that friend who had become his foe and from whom he thought he was so remote. The questions arising for him out of Wagner's music remained ultimately unanswered. Nietzsche lamented that music through Wagner had lost its affirmative character. Yet he experienced only the beginnings of that loss.

NOTES

1 · The Tristan Overture

1. Not to be confused with the art historian of the same name who lived from 1878 to 1947.
2. Gustav K., 1843–1902, N.'s school chum from Naumburg. In the house of his father, a personal friend of Mendelssohn-Bartholdy, Nietzsche had his first contact with music. Krug was later president of the Wagner Association in Cologne and also composed music himself.
3. Franz. B. (1811–1868), originally a philosopher, since 1843 a writer on music; 1844 the editor of Schumann's *Neue Zeitschrift für Musik* in the spirit of Liszt and Wagner, then a teacher at the Leipzig Conservatory; 1859, one of the founders of the *Allgemeiner Deutscher Musikverein* (General German Association for Music). Works: *Grundzüge der Geschichte der Musik* (1848), *Geschichte der Musik in Italian, Deutschland und Frankreich* (1852), *Die Musik der Gegenwart und die Gesamtkunst der Zukunft* (1854), *Die Organisation des Musikwesens durch den Staat* (1865), etc.
4. Paul D. 1845–1919, philosophy historian, scholar of East Indian culture, founder of the Schopenhauer Society, author of *Die Elemente der Metaphysik*
5. Carl Baron von G., 1844–1904, a Prussian gentleman-in-waiting and owner of an estate through primogeniture. Befriended with Nietzsche since Schulpforta. Died by suicide.
6. Max K., 1854–1941, German writer. *Meister Timpe* (1888) and other novels of social criticism.
7. Peter Gast, real name Heinrich Köselitz, 1854–1918 (cf. p. 202ff).
8. Baron Reinhard von Seydlitz-Kurzback, 1850–1931, writer and painter. Nietzsche had become friendly with him in Bayreuth and kept up a correspondence with him. He was later president of the Wagner Association.
9. Theognis of Megara, Greek poet, c. 500 B.C.
10. Clara Schumann, 1819–1896, studied with her father Friedrich Wieck. First public piano appearance at ten; concert tours at thirteen. She achieved the peak of her mastery with her husband Robert Schumann as his first and finest interpreter. After his death (1856), she lived in Berlin, then in Lichtenthal by Baden-Baden as of 1863. She taught at Frankfurt's Hochschen Konservatorium until 1892. An opponent of the "New Germans," and a

gifted composer. She edited the complete edition of Schumann.

11. *Manfred Meditation*, a four-handed piano composition of Nietzsche's (spring 1872), based on Byron's tragedy *Manfred* (1817). In *Ecce Homo*, Nietzsche says: "I must have a deep kinship with Byron's *Manfred:* I found all these abysses in myself—at thirteen I was ripe for this work." Hans von Bülow said he had never seen the like on composition paper, it was "the rape on the Euterpe."

12. Erwin Rohde, 1845–1898, like Nietzsche a Classical philologist, professor in Kiel, Tübingen, Heidelberg. Magnum opus: *Psyche, Seelenkult und Unsterblichkeitsglaube der Griechen* (1890–94). He became a Wagnerite—with qualifications. *Human, All Too Human* estranged him from Nietzsche, but he kept up with Nietzsche's works. In 1889, he received a page from Nietzsche in Turino: it was signed "Dionysos."

13. Wilhelmine Schröder-Devrient, 1804–1860, dramatic soprano at the Dresden opera, married from 1823 to 1828 to the actor Karl August Devrient.

14. Johanna W., 1828–1894, Wagner's niece, a pupil of Viardot-Garcia in Paris. The first Elisabeth in *Tannhäuser* (1844). Member of the Berlin Royal Opera 1850–1862. After the loss of her voice, a prominent actress in Berlin.

2 · *The Encounter*

1. Hans Guido Baron of B., 1830–1894, conductor and pianist, an epoch-making interpreter. His second wife Marie Schanzer, published his letters and writings posthumously (8 vol., 1895–1908).

2. Gottfried Semper, 1803–1879, architect and friend of Wagner. Built Dresden's Opera and *Gemäldegalerie* (Museum), the Vienna *Burgtheater*, etc.

3. Friedrich Z., 1825–1891, Classics professor in Leipzig. In 1850, founded and published *Das Literarische Centralblatt.*

4. Lou(ise) von Salomé, born 1861 in St. Petersburg, the youngest child and only daughter of a general of Russian-French descent; her mother came from an old Hamburg family. Prepared by Hendrik Gillot for studying in Zurich, particularly philosophy. In 1887, marriage to the orientalist Friedrich Carl Andreas. Died 1937. In 1894, published her book *Friedrich Nietzsche in seinen Werken (Friedrich Nietzsche in His Works).*

5. Heinrich R., 1845–1919, like Deussen and Rohde, a university friend of Nietzsche's, also friendly with Rée since the time they studied at the University of Leipzig. A follower of Kant's. As of 1872, he taught at Basel, but later gave it up.

6. Menippos of Gadara, Greek philosopher, c. 280 B.C. Developed the polemics of the Cynics into satire, in which he mocked the lives and teachings of the philosophers. A model for Varro's satires.

7. An illustrated periodical of political satire, founded in Berlin in 1848 and ended in 1944. Supported Bismarck.
8. Athenais, christened Eudocia after baptism, c. 400–460, daughter of the philosopher Leontios of Athens, married Theodosius II in 421. Was driven from court, and lived in Jerusalem until her death. Oeuvre: An epic on her husband's war against the Persians, an adaptation of the life of the martyr Cyprianos of Antioch (one of the sources of the Faust legend).
9. C. Theodor W., 1780–1842, cantor at St. Thomas in Leipzig as of 1823; cantor at the Holy Cross in Dresden from 1814 to 1817. An important theoretician and teacher. Wagner was his pupil for many years.
10. Georg H. 1817–1875, a revolutionary poet, invaded Baden in 1848 with a Franco-German column of workers, was beaten at Schopfheim, and had to flee. His *Poems of a Living Man*, written in Switzerland and Paris, had a rebellious impact. Heine praised him as the "iron lark of the revolution."
11. Bruno W., 1860–1928, writer (poetry, novels, memoirs), religious philosopher, Socialist.
12. Gottfried Keller, the greatest Swiss writer, devoted his life's work to the struggle against falsehood and hypocrisy.
13. Felix M.-B., 1809–1847, pianist, conductor, since 1835 the head of Leipzig's *Gewandhaus*. Concert overtures, symphonies, chamber music, oratorios, etc.
14. Heraclitus, 540 (544)–480 (483) B.C., Greek philosopher. Nicknamed "The Dark One" because of the prophetic language of his work *On Nature*. His doctrine: All existence is constantly being born and dying; human reason is part of cosmic reason (logos), it gives rise to order and law.
15. Empedocles, c. 500–c.430 B.C., pre-Socratic natural philosopher and physician, supposedly threw himself into Mount Etna, but probably died as an emigré outside of Greece. Almost deified by his people, he temporarily headed the Agrigentian democracy. His doctrine: There is no being born or dying, but only fusing and separating of the four elements fire, water, air, and earth; love and hate as primal forces are present in all processes.
16. Franz von Liszt, 1811–1886, Royal *Kapellmeister* at Weimar as of 1842, exerted a great influence on the representatives of the "New German School." Piano pieces, orchestral works, church music.
17. Giacomo Meyerbeer (real name: Jakob Liebmann Beer), German composer, visited Italy and Paris, General Musical Director of the Berlin Opera as of 1842. Chief advocate of French grand opéra. Operas: *The Huguenots, L'Africaine, The Prophet*.

3 · Schopenhauer

1. Arthur Schopenhauer 1788–1860, lived in Frankfurt as a private scholar as of 1831. Main work: *The World as Will and Idea* (2 volumes, 1818). Besides influencing Nietzsche and Wagner, he also made an impact on Burckhardt, Raabe, Freud, et al.
2. Franz von Lenbach, 1836–1904, Munich painter, celebrated portraitist of the aristocracy in old style. His small oil sketches of landscapes attest to his talent for color.
3. Plato, 427–347, B.C., Athenian philosopher, was a pupil of Socrates for eight years, fought in his works against the educational ideal of the Sophists, studied the sciences, founded the Academy in 387. Works: *Phaidon, Symposium, The Republic, Timaios,* etc. Established what later became known as metaphysics.
4. Aristotle, 384–322 B.C., Greek philosopher, disciple of Plato, tutor to Alexander the Great as of 343. Founded a philosophical school. Works: *Logic, Metaphysics, Physics, Politics, Rhetoric, Poetics* (with an aesthetics valid for a long time, especially in regard to tragedy), etc.
5. Ludwig Andreas Feuerbach, 1804–1872, philosopher, Hegelian disciple, influential thinker for the period before the German revolution of 1848. Critique of Christianity from an anthropological viewpoint: Christianity as an objectification of human emotions and as such an "estrangement" from its own essence. Works: *The Essence of Christianity* (1841), *Essence of Religion* (1845).

4 · Tribschen: "Isle of the Blessed"

1. Nietzsche published his philological works in the *Rheinisches Museum,* and, according to Ritschl's instructions, he compiled a register of the first 24 volumes (1842–1869).
2. Hermann Levi later became Chief Royal Conductor in Munich. After Nietzsche visited him at his invitation there, the philosopher wrote on September 2, 1886 to his sister: ". . . he was even more of a Bizet enthusiast than I."
3. Aeschylus, c. 525–456 B.C., the eldest of the great Greek tragedians. Works: *The Oresteia, Prometheus Bound, The Seven Against Thebes,* etc.
4. Pindar (Pindaros), 518 (520) to after 446 B.C., Greek choral poet in Thebes. Solemn, lofty style, complicated meters. Set his own odes to music (not extant).
5. Heinrich Porges, 1837–1900, Munich journalist and writer on music, in 1863 co-editor of the *Neue Zeitschrift für Musik,* championed the New Germans. Works: *On Performing the Ninth Symphony under Wagner* (1872), *The Stage Rehearsals for the 1876 Festspiele* (1877), *Tristan and Isolde* (1906).
6. Carl Tausig, 1841–1871, famous piano virtuoso, pupil of Liszt.

7. Felix Mottl, 1856–1911, one of the greatest of the Wagner conductors. 1881, Royal *Kapellmeister* in Karlsruhe, as of 1903 in Munich, also head of the Music Academy. In 1907, director of the Royal Opera. Composed operas, chamber music, and lieder.
8. Angelo Neumann, 1838–1910, originally a stage tenor, then a theater manager in Prague, Leipzig, and Vienna. In 1882, founded his traveling Wagner theater with the settings and costumes of Bayreuth. *Memories of Richard Wagner* (1907).
9. Peter Cornelius, 1824–1874, actor and composer, Liszt disciple of the New German direction, but not a mere imitator. Particularly original in his lieder, for which he often wrote his own lyrics. Operas: *The Barber of Bagdad* (1858), *The Cid* (1865).
10. Hans Richter, 1843–1916, one of the most outstanding conductors of his time, became choir director in the Munich opera at Wagner's recommendation. 1871–1875 in Budapest, afterwards *Kapellmeister* of the Vienna Opera, conducting the philharmonic concerts there. As of 1900, in Great Britain. Conductor of numerous Bayreuth Festivals since their beginning.
11. Ivan Sergeivich Turgenev, 1818–1883, Russian writer, banished to his estates because of his tribute to Gogol at the latter's death, lived abroad as of 1855: in Baden-Baden before the Franco-Prussian War, and, as of 1870, in Paris, where he died. Paul Rée often visited him there after sending him his *Psychological Reflections*. Voluminous oeuvre, lasting influence on the Western image of Russia and on Western Realism and Impressionism in literature.
12. Pauline Viardot-Garcia, 1821–1910, French singer, daughter of the older Manual Garcia, a famous voice teacher in Paris and later London. Sang in concerts and on the stage, performed for a while in London and Paris, but mostly on concert tours, also composed lieder and operettas.
13. Publisher of Richard Wagner's memoirs *Mein Leben* (1911).

5 · *Life with Friends*

1. Robert W. Gutman, *Richard Wagner.*
2. Socrates of Athens, c. 470–399 B.C. Sentenced to death by the Attic Court for allegedly "refusing to recognize the gods of the state religion, introducing new deities, and misleading the youth." Rejected natural philosophy. Fundamental paradox: Good and right is not what tradition regards as such. Among his disciples, the paradox turned into a re-evaluation of all values, which did not shy away from unseemly topics. The soul must be tested to see whether what it thinks it knows is a worthwhile knowledge or not. (In Plato, this became dialectics.)
3. Euripides, fifth century B.C., Greek tragedian. In his plays, the

chorus was no longer important. Only 18 dramas are left of his vast oeuvre, e.g. *Medea, Electra,* etc.

4. Karl Klindworth, 1830–1916, student of Liszt, pianist and composer.

5. Marie Countess von Schleinitz, (see p. 96).

6. Franz Wüller, 1832–1902, conductor and composer; *Kapellmeister* and head of the Music School in Munich.

7. Catulle Mendès, 1841–1909, French writer. Made Wagner known in France.

8. Théophile Gautier, 1811–1872, French writer, art critic, specialist in ballet criticism. His daughter Judith (well-known writer, 1850–1917), briefly married to Catulle Mendès, was friendly with Wagner.

9. Jean-Marie Count de Villier de l'Isle-Adam, 1838–1889, French writer, also influenced by Wagner. Although a devout Catholic, studied occultism, Free Masonry, theosophy. Forerunner of neo-Romanticism.

10. Camille Saint-Saëns, 1835–1921, French composer. Operas (*Samson and Delilah,* etc.), orchestral music, choral works, chamber music, etc. Heroic, bombastic style.

11. Henri Fouquès-Duparc, 1848–1933, French composer.

12. Maurice Joly, 1821–1878, French writer and lawyer.

13. Adolf Mosengel had been a voluntary orderly with Nietzsche during the Franco-Prussian War.

14. Malwida von Meysenbug, 1816–1903, was the daughter of the Hessian cabinet councillor Rivalier (of Huguenot ancestry), who was made a baron in 1825 by the Electoral Prince. In 1843, Malwida turned her back on the attitudes of her family and devoted herself to the emancipation of women. Through her fiancé, the writer Althaus, she joined the democratic movement that brought about the 1848 revolution. When her engagement was over, she joined Fröbel's College for Women in Hamburg, until it was closed because of reactionary pressure. She translated Alexander Herzen's memoirs into German. Nietzsche called her love for her foster-daughter Olga Herzen "one of the most splendid revelations of Caritas." (cf. also pp. 123ff.)

15. Marie Countess d'Agoult, née de Flavigny, 1805–1876, French writer (pseudonym Daniel Stern), the companion of Liszt, by whom she had three children, including Cosima.

16. Caroline Princess Sayn-Wittgenstein, 1819–1887, Liszt's companion as of 1848, moved with him to Altenburg, Weimar, which thus became the center of Europe's musical life.

17. Pierre (Abby P.) Perrin, 1620–1675, French writer, collaborated with the composer Cambert on the first opera in the French language.

18. Victor Hugo, 1802–1885, French writer of the Romantic school. Buried in the Pantheon.

19. Friedrich Hegar, 1841–1927, composed late Romantic orchestral and chamber music as well as male-voice chorales.
20. Jacob Burckhardt, 1818–1897, Swiss cultural and art historian in Basel. Works: *Historical Reflections* (posthum. 1905), *The Civilization of the Renaissance in Italy* (1860), *Cicerone* (1855), *The History of Greek Civilization* (1898–1902).
21. Franz Overbeck, 1837–1905, theology professor at Basel from early 1870. His pamphlet *On the Christianity of our Present-Day Theology* came out in 1873, at the same time as Nietzsche's *David Strauss*. Overbeck's intimate friendship with Nietzsche led to his assisting him when the friend collapsed in Turino.

6 · *Tragedy and Musical Drama*

1. Felix Draeseke, 1835–1935, composer and composition teacher.
2. Ulrich von Wilamowitz-Moellendorff, 1848–1931, professor of Classics at the universities of Greifswald, Göttingen, Berlin. Textual interpreter and critic.
3. Friedrich Feustel, banker, friendly with Wagner, entrusted with the business management of the Bayreuth enterprise.

7 · *Disrupting a Dream*

1. Hector Berlioz, 1803–1869, French composer. Symphonies (e.g. *Symphonie Fantastique*), operas (*Benvenuto Cellini*), *Requiem, Te Deum,* etc; a theory of instrumentation.
2. Alexander Herzen, 1812–1870, Russian writer, social politician, the leader of the Russian emigrés in Western Europe since 1847. Champion of Socialist ideas.
3. Johann Georg Albrechtsberger, 1736–1809, composer; royal organist and *Kapellmeister* at St. Stephen's Cathedral, Vienna.
4. Winifred Wagner, b.1897, wife of Siegfried Wagner. After his death in 1930, she took over the artistic management of the *Festspiele* until the end of World War II.
5. Otto and Mathilde Wesendonk. Mathilde was a close friend of Wagner's in Zurich during his work on *Tristan*. She also wrote the *Five Poems* ("Wesendonk Lieder") that Richard Wagner set to music in 1857–58.
6. Actually a "one-voiced song for two," here a reference to the name Monod. Gabriel Monod, 1844–1912, was a French historian at the Collège de France and at the Ecole Pratique des Hautes Etudes, both in Paris. A teacher and friend to Romain Rolland. He married Malwida's foster-daughter Olga Herzen in spring 1873.
7. Thales of Miletus, c. 600 B.C., Greek philosopher of nature, one of the Seven Sages. Especially important for his vast knowledge of astronomy.

8. David Friedrich Strauss, 1808–1874. In his *Life of Jesus,* he abandoned not the historicity of Jesus, but the validity of the Gospels, which he explained as an unconscious mythological formation in the first Christian communities. As a result, he lost his chair at Tübingen and was transfered to Ludwigsburg where he taught at a *Gymnasium* (secondary school).

9. Paul Rée, 1849–1901, son of a West Prussian seigneurial estate owner. At his father's behest, he at first studied law. At the outbreak of the Franco-Prussian War, he volunteered for the army and was wounded near Gravelotte. Studied philosophy next and got his doctorate at Leipzig in 1875. First meeting with Nietzsche in Basel, spring 1873. Together with Gersdorff, he attended Nietzsche's course on *The Pre-Platonic Philosophers.* In 1882, his friendship with Nietzsche was terminated.

8 · Worries and Doubts

1. Felix Dahn, 1834–1912, German writer, history professor in Munich. (*A Battle for Rome,* 1876, etc.)
2. The original of the letter no longer exists. There is only a copy that Wagner made and sent to King Ludwig of Bavaria. The verses are from Hölderlin's *Song of the German.*
3. Ernst Bertram: *Nietzsche.* Berlin, 1929.

9 · The First Festival

1. Edouard Schuré, 1841–1929, French critic, author of musicological and theosophic studies. Plays, novels, poems. A champion of Wagner; several meetings with the composer. Contributor to the *Revue Wagnérienne* (started in 1885).
2. Eduard Hanslick, 1825–1904, Austrian critic and writer on music, antagonistic to Wagner and Bruckner. Champion of Brahms.
3. Ludwig Speidel, 1830–1903, from an old musical family. After early writings, he became a theater critic. Classical representative of the great Viennese *feuilleton* during the late nineteenth century. A leading critic of the Viennese Burgtheater (*Neue Freie Presse,* 1877–1884), but not always free of biases.
4. Dr. Bernhard Förster, later husband of Elisabeth Nietzsche, taught secondary school in Berlin as of 1870. In 1882, because of conflicts over his anti-Semitic movement, he had to leave both this job and his position as teacher at the State Art Academy. In spring 1885, he returned from Paraguay, founding a colonial settlement society and recruiting immigrants for the La Plata territory. Married Elisabeth Nietzsche on May 22, 1885. Died in 1889 either of a stroke or through suicide.
5. Karl Jaspers: *Nietzsche and Christianity,* Hameln, Germany, 1947.

6. Marie Baumgartner-Koechlin, from Alsace, the mother of Nietzsche's student Adolf Baumgartner, who later became a professor of history at Basel. The mother translated *Schopenhauer as Educator* and *Richard Wagner in Bayreuth* into French.
7. Louise Ott, from Alsace, resided in Paris. Her correspondence with Nietzsche was published in the yearbook *Der Aquädukt* in 1938.

11 · The Apostasy

1. Paul Baron von Wolzogen, 1848–1938, writer on music, editor of the *Bayreuther Blätter*. Wrote on problems of Wagner's music.
2. Carl Fuchs was a professor at Danzig.
3. Gian Lorenzo Bernini, 1598–1680, architect and sculptor. His magnum opus is the colonnades on St. Peter's Square in Rome.
4. Robert Browning, 1812–1889, English Victorian poet. Married the poet Elizabeth Barrett in 1846.
5. Voltaire (actually François-Marie Arouet), 1694–1778, French writer and philosopher. Exponent of the Enlightenment. Buried in the Panthéon. Vast oeuvre: poems, epics, philosophy, plays, historical writings. Also novels and tales.
6. Mathilde Maier lived in Mainz.
7. Karl Eduard Heinrich Baron von Stein zu Nord-und Ostheim, 1857–1897, came from an officers' family in the Rhön mountains. Switched from theology to Schopenhauer and then to radical positivism. His first book was *The Ideals of Materialism.* Stein came to Bayreuth through Malwida von Meysenbug, at first for a year. He did not witness the first Festival. Acquired his *Habilitation* title in Halle, lectured on Schopenhauer and Wagner, published (in 1883) *Dramatic Scenes: Heroes and the World.* Lived in the certainty of an early death. Main work: *The Origin of the New Aesthetics* (1886).
8. Paul von Joukowsky (Zhukovsky), 1845–1912, painter, son of an important Russian poet. Participated in the stage sets for the first *Parsifal.* Advised his young compatriot Lou von Salomé about conforming her wardrobe to conditions in Bayreuth, which gave rise to gossip. The house he rented in Bayreuth was next door to Haus Wahnfried. During the Festival, Malwida and Heinrich von Stein lived with him.
9. Henry James, 1843–1916, American novelist and author of many tales and short stories. Studied at Harvard and various European universities, was friendly with Flaubert and Turgenev in Paris, finally settled in England in 1876. Considered one of the great writers in the history of the (psychological) novel; wrote about the robust, *nouveau riche* American middle class in contrast to the intellectual, often decadent European elite. Works include: *The American* (1877), *Washington Square* (1881), *The Golden Bowl* (1904).
10. Engelbert Humperdinck, 1854–1921, German composer, follower

of Richard Wagner. Fairytale operas, orchestral works, chamber music, etc.

11. Giovanni Palestrina (real name Giovanni Pierluigi da Palestrina), 1525 (?)–1594, composer, renovater of Catholic church music.

12. Prosper Mérimée, 1803–1870, French author of tales and short stories, and Romantic chamber dramas. His novella *Carmen* appeared in 1845.

13. Jacques Offenbach, 1819–1880, German composer, moved to Paris at fourteen, active as a cellist and conductor. A crucial developer of the operetta. He achieved a worldwide success with his opera *Tales of Hoffmann,* which wasn't premiered till after his death.

14. Sarah Bernhardt (real name: Henriette Rosina Bernard), 1844–1923, famous French tragedienne. A monument to her stands in Paris.

15. Joseph Rubinstein, assistant conductor to Wagner in Bayreuth.

16. In her book, Lou von Salomé uses the term "astral friendship" in regard to Rée, but it actually referred to Wagner.

17. Lou von Salomé gave Nietzsche the poem when departing from Tautenburg. She had written it down upon leaving her Russian homeland:

> *A friend must love his friend the way*
> *I love you, enigmatic life—*
> *Whether I crowed or wept in you,*
> *Whether you gave me joy or pain.*
>
> *I love you, life, with all your hurt;*
> *And if you must destroy me, then*
> *I must tear loose out of your arms,*
> *The way a friend leaves his friend's breast.*
>
> *I hold you tight with all my strength!*
> *Let all your flames ignite me now,*
> *Let me in the ardor of the struggle*
> *Probe your enigma ever deeper.*
>
> *To live and think millennia!*
> *Enclose me now in both your arms:*
> *If you have no more joy to give me—*
> *Then fine, there still remains your pain.*

Even in 1887, Nietzsche still felt bound to Lou in this poem and its music ("a profession of faith"). The *Hymn to Life,* expanded and revised by Gast, was published by Fritzsch in 1887 for chorus with orchestral accompaniment. In 1882, Gast wrote to Nietzsche: "I truly do not believe that with this Call, which today strikes me as very somber, you will 'seduce' even the people for whom your philosophy is the right nourishment. . . . The music sounds Christian. Indeed, if you had given me the music without the words, I would have mistaken it for a Crusaders' March, Christian-warlike; the not seldom shrill dissonances evoke clashing shields for me. . . . A hostile, foe-seeking, military feeling can be heard."

18. Gast re-composed the opera *The Secret Marriage* (originally written by Cimarosa and Paisiello in 1792) and entitled it *The Lion of Venice*, comic opera in five acts. It was twice produced in Danzig during 1891, with the piano version being published in 1901.

19. Karl Schlechta: *The Nietzsche Case*, Munich, 1959.

12 · Death in Venice

1. In regard to the letter of condolence to Cosima: The draft to Nietzsche's letter of February 14, composed one day after Wagner's death, is still extant: ". . . you served that which does not die with a man even though it is born in him. . . . Thus today I look upon you, and thus I looked upon you in the past, although from a great distance, only upon you, as the most honored woman who could ever be in my heart."

15 · The Summing-Up

1. Houston Stewart Chamberlain, 1855–1927, English philosophical writer. Wagner's son-in-law.

2. Malwida's reply prompted new and vicious attacks, but when Nietzsche died in 1900, Malwida sent laurel branches to him from Sorrento, where they had spent such happy times together. Three years later she herself died, at the age of eighty-six.

16 · Finale

1. Hans Makart, 1840–1884, a student of Piloty, painted historical and allegorical pictures, whose overladen decorativeness influenced the fashions and the interior design of the so-called *Gründerjahre*, the "period of promoterism" (1871–73).

INDEX